WOMEN AND CRIME

The per

Women and Crime

Edited by Satyanshu K. Mukherjee
and Jocelynne A. Scutt

aic **AUSTRALIAN INSTITUTE OF CRIMINOLOGY**
in association with
GEORGE ALLEN & UNWIN
Sydney   London   Boston

First published in 1981 by
George Allen & Unwin Australia Pty. Ltd.,
8 Napier Street,
North Sydney, N.S.W., 2060

This book is copyright under the Berne Convention. All rights are reserved. Apart from any fair dealing for the purpose of private study, research, criticism or review as permitted under the Copyright Act, 1956, no part of this publication may be reproduced, stored in a retrieval system, or transmitted in any form or by any means, electronic, electrical, chemical, mechanical, optical, photocopying, recording or otherwise without the prior permission of the Copyright owner. Inquiries should be addressed to the publishers.

© Australian Institute of Criminology 1981

National Library of Australia
Cataloguing-in-Publication entry:

Women and Crime.
   Includes index.
   ISBN 0 86861 059 3
   ISBN 0 86861 067 4 (pbk.).

    1. Female offenders — Australia. I. Mukherjee, Satyanshu Kumar.
II. Scutt, Jocelynne A.

364.3'74'0994

Library of Congress Catalog Card Number: 81-65766

Printed in Singapore by Koon Wah Printing Pte Ltd.

Contents

Acknowledgements	vii
Contributors	viii
Introduction	xii

1. Sexism in Criminal Law   1
   Jocelynne A. Scutt

2. Hidden from History: Women Victims of Crime   22
   Anne Summers

3. Women, Crime and Punishment   31
   Elizabeth Windschuttle

4. The Mythinterpretation of Female Crime   51
   Roslyn Omodei

5. Theorizing About Female Crime   70
   Ngaire Naffin

6. The Processing of Juveniles in Victoria   92
   Anne Edwards Hiller and Linda Hancock

7. The Myth of Rising Female Crime   127
   Satyanshu K. Mukherjee and R. William Fitzgerald

8. Women in Constraints 167
   Janette Hartz-Karp

9. Prisons, Prisoners and the Community 196
   Sandra A.K. Willson

   Index 205

Acknowledgements

Holding seminars and conferences is the function of the Training Division of the Institute and we are grateful that the proposal to hold the seminar on 'Women and Crime' was considered a valuable enterprise. We thank the contributors to this volume and the participants in the seminar whose comments have only improved the quality of the papers.

Several individuals within the Institute facilitated the publication of this volume. Peter Kay and Jack Sandry, the former and present heads of the Publications Section respectively, have accomplished the 'style' editing, and Christine Grant has done an excellent job on typesetting and layout. In the Research Division, Barbara Jubb and Evelyn Jacobsen have carried out the tedious task of typing and proofreading. We are indebted to them all.

Contributors

Jocelynne A. Scutt

After graduating LL.B. from the University of Western Australia, Jocelynne A. Scutt completed a Master of Laws and Diploma of Jurisprudence at the University of Sydney. Specialising in criminal law and constitutional law, she completed an LL.M. degree and S.J.D. at the University of Michigan, Ann Arbor, and a Diploma of Legal Studies at the University of Cambridge (Girton College). From 1975-1976 she was Research Scholar at the Max Planck Institute in Freiburg, West Germany. She has published extensively in the area of female crime and alternatives to imprisonment. Currently a research criminologist at the Australian Institute of Criminology, she is a member of the Women's Electoral Lobby, the Feminist Legal Action Group and the New South Wales' Women's Advisory Council to the Premier. Jocelynne Scutt is active in the feminist movement in Sydney and Canberra.

Anne Summers

Anne Summers has been active in the women's movement in Adelaide and Sydney. In Sydney she helped establish, *Refractory Girl,* a women's studies journal. In 1974 she helped found Elsie Women's Refuge. One book, *Damned Whores and God's Police,* was published in 1975 and another *Her Story: Australian Women in Print 1788-1975,* with Margaret Bettison, in 1980. She is currently the political correspondent and Head of Bureau, Canberra, for the *Australian Financial Review.*

Elizabeth Windschuttle

Elizabeth Windschuttle has been active in the women's movement since 1972 and was a founding member of Women's Electoral Lobby. In 1975 she was a member of the first Australian Women's Delegation to Post-War Vietnam. She graduated from Sydney University in 1970, and is currently at the University of New South Wales writing a doctoral thesis on 'Ruling Class Women in Early Nineteenth-Century Australia'. She is editor of *Women, Class and History: Feminist Perspective on Australia 1788-1978*, (Fontana, 1980).

Roslyn Omodei

Roslyn Omodei is a post graduate student in Sociology at the University of New South Wales. Her thesis work focuses on the political activity of Australian women in the 1920s. She is an active member of the Sydney-based Feminist Legal Action Group, and was recently involved with Wendy Bacon and Robyn Lansdowne on the F.L.A.G. study of female homicide offenders in New South Wales. Most of her work on female delinquency was completed while a student at Flinders University in South Australia.

Ngaire Naffin

A law graduate from the University of Adelaide, in 1977 Ngaire Naffin joined the South Australian Police Department. She was employed for three years as the Police Department's Research Officer in Criminology. She is currently tutoring in Criminal Law at the University of Adelaide, and is completing a Master of Laws Degree on 'The Self Image of the Female Offender'.

Anne Edwards Hiller

Born in England, Anne Edwards Hiller obtained her Ph.D. degree in Sociology from the University of London. She worked as a lecturer in Newcastle, then as a Research Fellow at Durham University until in 1968 she joined the Anthropology and Sociology Department at Monash University, Melbourne. Her main teaching and research interests lie in the field now called the sociology of deviance and social control. She has published on a variety of topics — juvenile delinquency, child maltreatment, prisons, deviance in the press, women and deviance, sex roles and mental illness, and in 1975 coedited the book *Social Deviance in Australia,* published by Cheshire. She has also been involved in groups and activities relating to policy development and reform in areas such as mental health, child maltreatment, women and madness, and women and the law.

Linda Hancock

Linda Hancock obtained her Ph.D. in Sociology from Monash University. She has been teaching Sociology at Swinburne College of Technology since 1973. Her doctorate dissertation was on 'Selective Law Enforcement: Police and Court Discretion in the Processing of Juvenile Offenders'. Her research interests and publications are in the areas of feminist studies, social welfare and criminal justice issues, especially those concerning juveniles.

Satyanshu K. Mukherjee

Satyanshu Mukherjee was educated in India and the United States. He is currently a researcher at the Australian Institute of Criminology.

R. William Fitzgerald

Bill Fitzgerald holds a B.A. (Hons) Sociology from the University of New South Wales. He was a member of the Research Division of the Australian Institute of Criminology for two years from October 1977. Before joining the Institute he worked as a consultant for various bodies and participated in research activities.

Janette Hartz-Karp

Janette Hartz-Karp graduated from the University of California, Los Angeles (U.C.L.A.), completing the degrees of M.A. African Studies, and M.A. Sociology. She is completing a doctoral thesis on never-married women over the age of thirty in Western Australia — role adaptations to a negatively evaluated status. Since 1976, she has been a part-time lecturer in universities in California, U.S.A. and later Western Australia, teaching in social psychology, social problems, the sociology of deviant behaviour, the family and women's issues. She is currently employed as the Senior Planning and Research Officer, W.A. Department of Corrections.

Sandra A.K. Willson

Since her release from prison in 1977, Sandra Willson has been actively involved in prison issues. She is a member of two committees with the Department of Corrective Services, giving them the benefit of her vast experience. In 1979 she founded the first half-way house for women released from prison in New South Wales, as well as becoming involved in drug rehabilitation. She is on the executive of the Network for Drug and Alcohol Agencies in New South Wales, and has been nominated by other workers in this field for Woman of the Year. She is also currently active on behalf of women appearing before the Magistrate's Courts in Sydney.

Introduction

During the 1970s, interest in the study of crimes by women gathered momentum in several countries, a significant result of which was the publication of a number of books and articles on the subject. One of the main reasons for this interest was the re-emergence of the various women's movements in the late 1960s. While their fundamental impact was welcome in that a grossly and unjustifiably ignored area received the deserved attention, there were some unwelcome results as well; that is, several researchers used the opportunity to present a misconstrued relationship between various women's movements and crimes by women.

In Australia, while the interest in the area has been growing, empirical research was lacking. In late 1978, as part of a large project on crime trends, the Australian Institute of Criminology produced a historical and statistical study of crimes by males and females in twentieth century Australia. The results of this study seem to dispel some of the myths surrounding criminality of women and hence the Institute considered it appropriate to share this knowledge with Australian scholars, researchers and practitioners.

In June 1979, the Institute convened a seminar on 'Women and Crime', the purpose of which was to effect a sharing of knowledge and exchange of views on women as participants and 'consumers' within the Australian criminal justice system. People with practical experience of the issues involved, others involved in academic research, and those engaged in the administration of criminal justice were invited for this seminar.

The present volume consists of a number of original papers written especially for the seminar and these formed the core of the conference. The organisers, the two editors of this book, felt that the publication of these original papers would inform the general community about the facts of women and crime and enhance its knowledge as well as serve as an impetus to more research in the area. The papers in this volume dispute with cold hard facts the substance of the claim that 'women's liberation' is turning more women to crime. The volume is also intended to serve as an Australian contribution to the growing literature on women and crime.

1 Sexism in Criminal Law

JOCELYNNE A. SCUTT

> This humanity is male and man defines woman not in herself but as relative to him; she is not regarded as an autonomous being . . . She is defined and differentiated with reference to man and not he with reference to her; she is the incidental, the inessential as opposed to the essential. He is the Subject, he is the Absolute — she is the Other. . .[1]

Women — as inhabitants of the criminal or non-criminal world — have been granted the right to adopt one, albeit schizophrenic, role: that of wife/mother and sex-object. The framing of Australian criminal laws, those designed to 'protect' women from 'deviant' acts and those designed to penalise us for our own deviance, serve to reinforce the stereotype.

Criminal laws have been drafted to perpetuate the dependency of women. Sometimes laws are framed to 'personalise' outlawed acts, seeing a psychological imbalance on the part of the woman as excusing or mitigating the offence. Some laws are designed in ignorance of basic inequalities existing between the sexes. Laws are thus unsatisfactory to women. The dependency approach refuses to acknowledge us as people, entitled to have control over our own activities and person. The psychological approach fails to confront social and economic factors vital to any explanation of 'why' women commit particular crimes. Laws framed without reference to basic inequalities effectively remove from women legal defences applicable to men.

Yet the law does an apparent *volte face* where women become victims of crime. Practices and procedures assume a responsibility in the woman that is denied her in other spheres. Her role as sex-object comes to the fore, the mythical male picture of woman as eternal temptress operating to deny women criminal law protection. However the liability deemed to exist in the woman-victim does not derive from any uprighteous dependability; rather, her guilt is predicated upon her irresponsibility: she invited the crime/flaunted herself/accepted a lift/accepted an invitation from the assailant. Thus, even where she is 'responsible' according to the law, that same law maintains for woman her well-played part of 'foolish little girl' or 'wicked, wicked woman'. Her acts are not seen in their social context. She continues, by law and by aggressor, to be denied her autonomy.

The Law of Coverture

At common law it was originally held that by marriage:

> ... the husband and wife are one person in law, that is, *the very being or legal existence of the wife is suspended during marriage,* or at least is incorporated or consolidated into that of her husband; under whose wing, protection and care she performs everything...[2]

Under this doctrine it was considered at law that where a wife committed a crime in the presence of her husband, she was presumed to have committed it under coercion. The wife would therefore be entitled to an acquittal, if there was no evidence that she was principally instrumental in the commission of the crime; there was no requirement that the woman act under threats, pressure, or instructions from her husband.[3] The presumption excluded the commission of treason or murder, and was limited to crimes amounting to felonies and indictable misdemeanours, but not extending to summary offences.[4]

Although this rule might be seen as favouring women over men, it is dangerous to accept such a simplistic interpretation. First, the presumption endorsed the idea that no married woman could be possessed of a will: her will was enveloped in that of her husband, and she was presumed not to be capable of acting independently of him. Thus in law a woman remained in a position akin to a child. At common law, a child under the age of eight years could not be held responsible for criminal acts: an irrebuttable presumption that he or she had no capacity to commit such acts precluded guilt; under fourteen years a rebuttable presumption existed to preclude guilt, unless it could be shown that the child in fact possessed sufficient intellect to know that it had committed the act in question and that the act in question was wrong.[5]

Second, the presumption operated only where she was in the strict physical presence of her husband: thus the implication was that all husbands should control (or should be capable of controlling) their wives. Furthermore, if this notion did not survive, then a wife committing a crime jointly with her husband would be subjected to a more severe penalty: where capital punishment existed in relation to felonies, the husband was entitled to benefit of clergy.[6] This would operate to render him liable to a light punishment only. The wife, however, was not entitled to benefit of clergy and could have been put to death.[7]

Thus in law, by reason of coverture, a woman had no power of self-determination as to whether she wished to act within the law or outside it. Just as she had no right to sign a contract in her own name, nor to own real property, nor to decide where she should make her home[8], a married woman was presumed to be incapable of determining independently that she would act in committing a crime.

Today in most jurisdictions the defence of marital coercion has been dispensed with or is subject to moves for repeal.[9] Yet it is instructive to look at the rationale surrounding its abolition. The passage of legislation in Canada, New Zealand, the United Kingdom and each of the Australian States has eliminated the presumption.[10] Generally it is now provided that:

> Any presumption of law that an offence committed by a wife in the presence of her husband is hereby abolished, but on a charge against a wife for any offence, other than treason or murder, it shall be a good defence to prove that the offence was committed in the presence of, and under the coercion of, the husband.[11]

Adopted in support of this amendment is the statement of Frankfurter J. in the United States case of *U.S.* v. *Dege:*[12]

> For this court now to act on Hawkins' [*Pleas of the Crown*] formulation of the medieval view that husband and wife 'are esteemed but as one Person in Law, and are presumed to have but one Will' would indeed be 'blind imitation of the past'. It would require us to disregard the various changes in the status of woman — the extension of her rights and correlative duties — whereby a wife's legal submission to her husband has been wholly wiped out, not only in the English-speaking world generally, but emphatically so in this country.[13]

Thus a woman is today rendered at law capable of directing her own criminal acts. However in true perversity, although the law recognises 'a wife's legal submission to her husband' as being 'wholly wiped out' in relation to marital coercion, on another level marital coercion is presumed to continue to exist: in domestic rape. Where a man rapes his wife, most criminal lawyers adhere to the view that he cannot be prosecuted for the crime. The view more ancient than that of Hawkins holds sway — that 'by her matrimonial consent the wife hath given up herself in this kind unto the husband'.[14] Although the law is prepared to find responsibility in a wife for forming an evil intention, it refuses to recognise her simple ability to consent or refuse to consent to sexual intercourse, adopting the 17th century view of Sir Matthew Hale.[15]

Prostitution and the Law

The law of prostitution also plays a double game with women. On one level, women are held responsible: thus most laws are framed to deal only with women prostitutes, precluding the idea that men may trade their bodies. Further, the laws regard only as criminal the woman who solicits to engage in sexual intercourse for money — those men who solicit to engage in sexual intercourse for which they pay are not normally included.[16] On a second level, women-as-prostitutes are irresponsible. They are taken to be incapable of managing their ill-got incomes: they are effectively precluded by law from deploying their funds in keeping a househusband or other companion.

In New South Wales in 1977, 2,075 prosecutions for the offence of loitering/soliciting for the purpose of prostitution were launched. Of these, the majority (1,871, or 90.2 per cent) resulted in a fine; two (0.1 per cent) in findings of not guilty; three (0.1 per cent) in imprisonment.[17] The law under which women were prosecuted was the *Summary Offences Act* (N.S.W.) 1970, which provided that it is an offence for a woman to solicit or loiter in, near, or within view from a public place, for the purposes of prostitution. This type of law is allegedly founded upon principles stated in the *Report of the Wolfenden Committee,* commencing with the idea that the criminal law is '. . . not concerned with private morals or with ethical sanctions'. The law in this area is concerned:

> . . . not with prostitution itself but with the manner in which the activity of prostitutes and those associated with them offend against public order and decency, expose the ordinary citizen to what is offensive or involve the exploitation of others. . .[18]

Futhermore, the Committee said:

> In this field, [the] function [of the law] is to preserve public order and decency, to protect the citizen from what is offensive and injurious, and to provide sufficient safeguards against exploitation and corruption of others, particularly those who are especially vulnerable because they are young, weak in mind or body, inexperienced or in a state of special physical, official or economic dependence.[19]

Yet is the law designed to fulfil the stated need? In each Australian jurisdiction in 1978, no man was arrested and prosecuted for approaching a woman and suggesting that she engage in sexual intercourse with him for payment of a fee. Some jurisdictions[20] hold customers liable, but this is not so in Australia. Under the similar United Kingdom law[21], a man who was prosecuted for soliciting where he had been 'kerb crawling' and suggesting to various known prostitutes that they join him, was held not to come within the terms of the provision; he was not engaged in an 'immoral purpose' in terms of the section. The court said that although the words 'immoral purpose' in their ordinary meaning connote 'a wide and general sense' and involve '. . . all purposes involving conduct which has the property of being wrong rather than right in the judgment of the ordinary contemporary citizen' within the context of the statute, the words could not be taken at their ordinary meaning but must '. . . be limited, at least, to a sexual purpose'.[22] Thus the court concluded that a man who kerb-crawls to select a prostitute is not engaged in a 'sexual purpose'; a woman who solicits to select a customer is engaged in a 'sexual purpose'. However, clearly, the customer could be classified as 'offending against the public order' and exposing 'the ordinary (female) citizen to what is offensive'. The law thus promotes a double standard in classing the woman-leaning-up-against-the-wall in Kings Cross or Piccadilly as 'offensive', but failing to similarly categorise the man leering from a kerbside, whistling from a car, hooting from a building site, or jostling the woman in the street and offering a price.[23]

Why this double standard? Because the prostitute is ostensibly seen as playing exclusively her role as sex-object/harlot (as distinct from the part of wife/mother, although in reality she may fulfil this portion of her role, as well)[24], the law is free to penalise her. As has been said, the argument for not penalising the buyer is that the imposition of social sanctions for such behaviour '. . . on those who may be married and respectable are out of proportion to the gravity of their offences. . .'.[25] Yet, underlying this rationalisation, is a more telling reality. The law penalises the woman for selling her tools of trade in a transaction that might enable her to control her own income (and her own sexuality). It draws a distinction between the woman plying her trade in what could result in an independent means of living, and the woman selling herself in one mammoth transaction — marriage — which is legitimate, for it cannot result in one's independence. The law does not take into account the lack of equal opportunity for women in legitimate and lucrative careers open to men, for the law is not concerned to endorse any right of a woman to receive finances enabling her to become an independent individual.[26]

That this is the rationale of prostitution laws becomes clear in studying advertising provisions and provisions precluding persons from living off the proceeds of prostitution of another person. The 'new' legislation recently passed through the New South Wales Parliament illustrates this well. Section 8 of the *Prostitution Act* (N.S.W.) 1979 provides that:

> A person shall not, in any manner, publish or cause to be published, an advertisement, or erect or cause to be erected any sign, indicating that any premises are used, or are available for use or that any person is available, for the purposes of prostitution.

The legislation renders it impossible for any prostitute effectively to sell her services, on an independent basis, without coming into conflict with the criminal law. The prostitute is precluded from advertising, yet certainly prostitution will continue. The situation inevitably remains that organised crime and police corruption will underlie the explicit sale of sex in New South Wales — and women will remain under the guardianship of those forces, rather than being able to set up business independently.[27]

Similarly, section 5 precludes a woman from emulating the male breadwinner. A person, not being a child or young person who lives with, or is habitually in the company of, a reputed prostitute and has no visible lawful means of support 'shall be deemed knowingly to live wholly or in part on the earnings of prostitution of another person unless he satisfies the court. . . that he has sufficient lawful means of support'. As existing laws of extortion and theft protect the prostitute's earnings — just as they protect monies earned in any other trade or profession — it is questionable whether such a provision is necessary. The answer is that prostitutes are not to be permitted to deploy their earnings as they wish — at least where it comes to supporting a partner — lover, friend, or husband; or even a dependent mother, father, brother, or sister. And it is startling to note that it was only by reason of an amendment inserting the words 'not being a child or young person' (Message of 24.4.79) that prostitutes were not effectively precluded from supporting their own children.

It is wrong to suppose that every prostitute-friend relationship is coercive (and if it were, as previously stated, rules generally applicable to coercion would cover the case). As Dr Jennifer James of the University of Washington concluded after studying, for a three year period, 140 prostitutes:

> There's no more force involved in prostitution than, I think, in the average husband-wife relationship. There are some cases of pimps beating prostitutes; there has been a rare case of a pimp shooting a prostitute, but there have been just as many cases of husbands beating wives and husbands shooting wives.[28]

What should be recognised is that the prostitute is the wage-earner. The analogy to be drawn is that of the man whose earnings support his wife and children — but whose earnings are, nevertheless, his. The wages of the prostitute should be hers, however she chooses to budget, whomever she chooses to include in her household. Yet what appears to offend the criminal law and criminal law-makers is the independent role that the woman may play, filling the part, not of 'independent spouse', but of 'head of household'. Again, the law precludes the woman from a responsible role.

The Law Relating to Infanticide

The law of infanticide illustrates clearly the 'band-aid' attitude of the criminal law towards socio-political problems created by role stereotyping. It illustrates too well the refusal of society to recognise the sexism inherent in our culture and endemic in the family unit as it exists under patriarchy.

Under section 22A of the *Crimes Act* (N.S.W.) 1900, it is provided that where a woman, by any wilful act or omission, causes the death of her child, when the child is under the age of twelve months, she will be guilty of infanticide if:

> . . . at the time of the act or omission the balance of her mind was disturbed by reason of her not having fully recovered from the effect of giving birth to the child or by reason of the effect of lactation consequent upon the birth of the child. . .

Where a woman is prosecuted for murder, the jury is entitled, if it considers that the conditions are fulfilled, to bring in a verdict of infanticide. In the case of infanticide, the punishment for the woman will be that which she would have received had she been found guilty of the offence of manslaughter.

In cases of child-killing, sometimes this provision is used, although on occasion discretion is exercised by the police and/or prosecutors not to prosecute where it seems apparent that the woman was not in control when she undertook the act.

On its face, the provision may appear to be an 'easy out' for women, or simply a recognition of medically accepted fact. Neither of these approaches is acceptable, for both ignore the reality of woman's situation. If it is a 'medically accepted fact' that following the birth of a child some women suffer 'post-natal depression', it remains to be asked why this is so, and further, why support services are so lacking that 'depression' or 'lactation' lead women to kill their own children.

People completing 'great tasks' — for example, the writing of the Great Australian Novel, completion of a Ph.D., final exams, the 'first night' of a dramatic production — often experience 'lows' when the job is done. In such cases there will be adulation to offset the low: such jobs are well rewarded within our current system. Furthermore, the individual's mode of living usually presents some means of escape offsetting the depression. However where a person produces a child, social attitudes have led her to believe that this is a production of worth, that praise will be long and continuing. . . yet the woman is left alone, with total responsibility for taking care of the infant's every need. She has no means of escaping depression, yet is required to feel perpetually pleased with her offspring.

John Bowlby and his cohorts[29] continue to hold sway with a sizable portion of the community, and governments continue to program resources with his theories as justification. Governments are currently unconcerned to finance good childcare centres;

governments continue to regulate the economy with the view that the wife/mother should play a lone role, in the home, of child-minder. Community attitudes continue to deplore 'working mothers' (meaning those in paid employment, failing to recognise the work involved in being an unpaid child-carer for the greater part — if not the whole — day). The community still enthuses about the 'maternal instinct' (now fashionably titled 'bonding') and agonises over the latch-key child. Locked into a situation where she is responsible for full-time care of the child, it is little wonder that, for some women, the responsibility is too much, the effort impossible, and the result is child-killing.

However the creation of a special offence is again a token response, a band-aid measure on the part of the criminal law, to extreme cases where the woman visibly (in criminal law terms) fails to cope. Political and social changes are necessary to deal with the issue at the beginning, not at what is an inevitable result of socio-political neglect.

If the patriarchal family was eliminated from our society and non-sexist, non-classist living arrangements adopted, there would be no necessity for introducing legislation in the form of infanticide provisions. Infanticide provisions, by dealing on the personal psychological level with what is a problem of social structure and political impotence, based in the myth of motherhood[30], absolve society from the responsibility of having regard to the reality of woman's needs. Additionally, the non-prosecution route serves only to reinforce the idea of the woman-as-mother — ever coping and supremely happy in her lot. If those women who visibly cannot cope and reveal too clearly their failure to be supremely happy in the wife-mother role are classified 'mentally unstable', 'psychologically unbalanced', 'mentally aberrant', there is no need to look beyond that individual explanation for the roots of a greater malaise.[31]

Domestic Violence, Self-Defence and Provocation

The dependency status of woman is reflected in past laws as to murder and spouse assault, and today legal practices and principles may effectively deny women recourse to the law. In the past, husband and wife in legal language were termed 'baron' and 'feme'. The twelfth editor of *Blackstone's Commentaries* in 1793 commented upon the inclination to consider these terms 'unmeaning' and 'technical':

> ... we [must] recollect that if the feme kills her baron, it is regarded by the laws as a much more atrocious crime; as she not only breaks through the restraints of humanity and conjugal affection, but throws off all subjection to the authority of her husband. And therefore the law denominated her crime a species of treason, and condemns her to the same punishment as if she had killed the king. And for every species of treason (though in petit treason the punishment of men was only to be drawn and hanged)... the sentence of women was to be drawn and burnt alive.[32]

Today, the United States in particular has in some jurisdictions taken a biased approach to the murder of a wife. Some States have explicitly written into the law that the killing of a wife by her husband, where he has discovered her in an act of adultery, will not be unlawful.[33] In Australia, adultery is relevant to Australian law in relation to provocation. Provocation is a mitigating plea that may result in a verdict of manslaughter on a prosecution for murder. Provocation in law consists of three main elements:

> The act of provocation, the loss of self-control, both actual and reasonable, and the retaliation proportionate to the provocation. The defence cannot require the issue to be left to the jury unless there has been produced a credible narrative of events suggesting the presence of these three elements.... Provocation in law means something more than a provocative incident. That is only one of the constituent elements.[34]

In *Attorney-General for Ceylon* v. *Perera*[35] the Privy Council held that the defence of provocation could arise where a person intends to kill or inflict grievous bodily harm (which in the normal course would render the killing murder), but the intention to do so 'arises from sudden passion involving loss of self-control by reason of provocation'. The court lighted upon the paradigm situation:

> An illustration is to be found in the case of a man finding his wife in the act of adultery who kills her... and the law has always regarded that, although an intentional act, as amounting only to manslaughter by reason of provocation received, although no doubt the accused intended to cause death or grievous bodily harm.[36]

The House of Lords in 1946 went so far as to hold that provocation in the instance of the forming of intention to kill was limited, as a defence, to the case of spouse murder where an act of adultery was the triggering factor.[37] Howard, in his *Australian Criminal Law* surmises that the provocation-mitigation would be applicable to the case of a wife finding her husband in adultery and killing him in passion, for '. . . there is no reason to suggest itself why a wife should not be just as annoyed by adultery as her husband' — however, he points out that there has never been a case of that type.[38]

This illustrates an interesting point. Perhaps no case of a wife killing her husband in the flame of passion while he is in an adulterous situation has ever arisen. Perhaps no wife has ever found her husband in the act of adultery; perhaps wives do not kill under those circumstances. Another explanation might be that a wife discovering her husband in the act of adultery reacts differently from what, for husbands, must be a somewhat usual pattern (for otherwise the mitigation rule obviously would not have developed). Perhaps women brood about the situation and use other methods than instant knifing or shooting. From the viewpoint of expertise, access to weapons such as guns, and social conditioning to react in a fighting manner, the woman would be clearly less able to react spontaneously with effect than the man. Her method might, for example, be poisoning. Yet if this is the case, premeditation is clear, and the woman would not be able to escape with a lighter punishment; she would be found guilty of murder.[39] Thus the man's social conditioning and physique enable him to lash-back and to come within the bounds of a mitigating defence. The woman's social conditioning and physique preclude her from reacting in the same way, and thus tend to preclude her from gaining the benefit of that rule of mitigation.

Laws relating to domestic assaults reflect a like policy. The dependency status of women is illustrated by laws relating to spouse assault. Defences relating to spouse assault are effectively denied to women. Thus originally at common law it was held that a man had a right to beat his wife; there was no right in a woman to beat her husband. In *In re Cochrane*[40] the court stated that a husband has, '. . . by law power and dominion over his wife.' This entitled him to keep her by force 'within the bounds of duty', in addition to giving him the right to beat her — '. . . but not in a cruel or violent manner.'[41] In *Cloborn's Case*[42] the wife complained that her husband had spat in her face, whirled her about, called her a 'damned whore' and given her a box on the ear. The court noted that spitting in the face was an actionable wrong where the victim was not a wife, as was assault, however a husband should not be penalised. Court rulings later modified the position, so that a husband had no right to beat his wife, but only to admonish her and confine her to his house. Today it is considered that a husband has no right to assault his wife — and may in law be prosecuted for such an act. It is further held that he may no longer kidnap nor imprison his wife.[43] Nonetheless, it continues to be contended that no man may be prosecuted for the rape of his wife, where he is the protagonist. The woman is thus confirmed in her wife/sex-object role.

Where a person is subjected to an attack such as assault, the law has developed rules relating to self-defence. However self-defence is available only where a person is being criminally attacked. Thus originally at common law — where the husband had a right to beat his wife — the existence of rules relating to self-defence were of no avail to her. Her husband had a right to beat her; she had no right to beat him. If she retaliated or attempted to defend herself, she had no defence in law because he was not undertaking an unlawful act. If it is accepted today that a woman may be raped, with impunity, by her husband, then the woman has no right to defend herself against acts of intercourse where she does not consent. If, for example, the husband is in the midst of non-consensual sexual intercourse with his wife, and she takes up a knife that the two have put under the pillow to protect themselves against burglars, and plunges it into his body, killing him, she will have no defence in law, for her husband was not engaged in a criminal act.[44]

With spouse assault, however, self-defence may be relevant in that a husband or wife may retaliate against force. In such a case, the retaliation could come within the terms of self-defence, so that the retaliatory assault would not be classified as criminal. Where self-defence is in issue, the factors that must be shown to exist in order for the defence to be made out are:

- The person who has been attacked (in alleged self-defence) acted in such a manner that a reasonable person in the shoes of the person who retaliated would have been put in apprehension of an immediate, unprivileged, harmful or offensive touching;

- the person attacking in self-defence should in fact have been in *bona fide* apprehension of such touching; and the person attacking in self-defence should have used only a reasonable degree of force and reasonable means of retaliation to prevent the harmful or offensive touching.[45]

In discussing self-defence it has been said that when attacked an individual '. . . may repel force by force, and within limits differing with the facts of cases, give back blow for blow'. Yet again it is clear that the defence has been constructed with persons of equal physical stature in mind. Cases can be found where it has been held that too great a force was used, when one individual retaliated against fists with a knife or gun. Although the rule takes into account, on its face, the facts of individual cases, it can clearly be seen that women (being, generally, due to social conditioning and physical stature, less aggressively able than men) have not been taken into account directly within the terms of the defence. It is appropriate to ask whether the court would consider self-defence made out and exonerate the woman from guilt where her husband attacked her with fists and she retaliated with a knife. As numerous marital murders take place in the kitchen by way of a carving or kitchen knife, and women are convicted of offences in just this way, it is obvious that the structures of self-defence rules are not designed to cater for women.

Second, if the woman takes the beating without retaliating, or retaliating only by way of fists, biting, kicking and the like, she will not be exonerated from guilt by way of any self-defence rule if she chooses to take a knife while her husband sleeps and kills him. It is here that lawyers, judges, sociologists and the community will say that her way out is not to kill the husband and seek to have some spurious rule developed to govern the case so that she will be held not guilty, but to leave him and seek a divorce. Although this is the rational way out, when a person is in a dependent situation, has no access to finances of her own, has children to support, is constantly subjected to a barrage from the public and the media as to the 'unfairness' of her taking on paid employment[46], it is less than feasible to talk of divorce as the 'solution'.

Rape and the Law

Just as in other crimes the law refuses to see a woman in her social and cultural context, so too in rape law. In law, rape is defined as sexual penetration by a man, of a woman, without her consent. It could therefore be contended that the law recognises in women a rationality, a responsibility, in terms of their own lives, of which sexual activity is a part. The term 'consent' signifies, according to *The Dictionary of English Law:*

> [A]n act of reason accompanied with deliberation, the mind weighing, as in a balance, the good or evil on either side. Consent supposes three things — a physical power, a mental power, and a free and serious use of them.

Yet no 'act of reason' seems to be required for it to be considered that 'consent' to sexual intercourse has been given, so that an act is not rape. Smith and Hogan in *Criminal Law* contend that:

> It is probable that only threats of immediate personal violence... will negative consent for the purposes of rape...[47]

Under Scots law, rape:

> ... like robbery, may be committed by threats of imminent harm... it may not be rape to wear down a woman's resistance by persuasion, or even perhaps by ill-treatment, such as kidnapping and imprisoning her, if in the end she consents to intercourse, provided that that consent was obtained 'without any use of threats or violence at the time or recently before'.[48]

Kidnapping, ill-treatment, imprisonment in any language would appear to rule out 'a physical power, a mental power, and a free and serious use of them'... but apparently not, at least where one is a woman.

Futhermore, the dicta of judges reveals a distorted view of female responsibility in the instance of rape. This takes the well-worn path of dismissing the victim as 'foolish', 'provocative', 'leading the offender on'. Yet, at the same time as the courts consider her to have failed to exercise mature responsibility, they place responsibility for the offence on her shoulders. Thus in *Ives*[49] the offender first saw the victim in a hamburger shop where a conversation took place in which 'strip jack naked' was mentioned. The party then went to a remote area where liquor was consumed and the girl was raped. Her 'complicity' in the affair was seen as a reason for reducing the penalty. In *Walker*[50] the victim was a companion of the rapist. As she 'had been prepared to share the culprit's company in the privacy of his own room', where she went with him after a dance, it was held the penalty should be lightened.

Not only drinking is seen as an act, on the part of the woman, that can render her 'responsible' for the crime:

> Judges [have] warned women 'time and time again' against hitchhiking or accepting lifts with strangers. . . such behaviour all too often [leads] to sex attacks. . .[51]

Thus in *Toohey*[52] the victim '. . . accepted a lift from lads who called at her home some two weeks after they had raped her'. Earlier she had accepted an invitation that was followed by an act of rape. The jury considered the first act to be 'rape with mitigating circumstances' (presumably, her 'foolishness'); the second act was considered to be no crime at all. One academic lawyer comments:

> Perhaps the clearest examples of rape with mitigating circumstances occur when a foolish girl accepts a lift from young lads whom she knows vaguely or not at all. . .[53]

Perhaps the most concise statement of woman's 'irresponsible responsibility' is to be found in the words of a Western Australian judge:

> . . . imprudent behaviour of many young women. . . lessen[s] the moral culpability of the offender. . . There [are] too many young women hitching lifts and accepting rides with cars full of young men they [do] not know, in bars, and [do] their best to bring disaster on themselves. These foolish young women should behave with more dignity and show some elementary prudence. . .[54]

The implication is that where a woman exercises her right to move, she will be taken to have caused factors external to herself to operate. That is, no responsibility (or little responsibility), is seen to lie in the persons undertaking a criminal act of rape. On the contrary, the victim's actions are considered to have led almost inevitably to a criminal outcome. The woman takes on a double responsibility where she is victim of a sexual offence: that of her own choice of a lift, and that of the male person who acts contrary to her wishes.

Rather than exercising responsibility? foolishness? — by accepting a ride in another person's car, perhaps all girls and women should simply obtain a car licence and a vehicle. Yet even this would not suffice to absolve women from responsibility for rape, as succinctly stated in a recent letter to the editor of the *Sydney Morning Herald*:

I would like to register a strong dissent from the implication of your item appearing today in the Granny Column and titled 'How essential? Spotted at a northern suburban "essential users only" petrol station during emergency petrol rationing. . . a uniformed schoolgirl filling up her Ford Cortina'. The suggestion in the story appears to be that schoolgirls should not have access to petrol in times of emergency — and perhaps that a car is a luxury where schoolgirls are concerned.

It should be pointed out that if, for example, schoolgirls (or any girls/women) hitch-hike — and are raped by the party giving the lift — judges constantly reiterate the idea that they are responsible for the crime, because they hitch-hiked. Furthermore, in Canada it is well documented that during a strike of oilpersons some years ago, the number of rapes and other sexual offences against women rose. The direct link seemed to be with the strike, for women were forced to hitch-hike in greater numbers than was previously the case.

It should also be observed that women generally have less access to cars: this is no doubt related to lack of truly equal pay, lack of access to equally well-paid jobs; the social attitude that men should drive cars, without such an emphasis upon this talent for women, etc. In view of the above remarks as to hitch-hiking and rape, it is perhaps just as well that schoolgirls are now becoming car owners and drivers, and are able to choose this mode of transport.

The girl of whom you wrote, had she chosen not to drive to school, may well have become a victim of rape while hitch-hiking — and have been blamed for the attack. Had she taken public transport, she may well have had to endure sexual harassment in the way of frotteurism and the like.

Of course, had her car broken down during the journey or run out of petrol en route, the schoolgirl might yet have been subjected to a sexual attack, which is frequently the case where women seek help from passing motorists on the occasion of motor breakdown. . .[55]

For despite the emphasis in judicial pronouncements being upon the **acceptance** of lifts, it is clear that 'accepting a lift' is not the most important factor in the commission of rape; rather, the important issue is the gender of the person undertaking the act of accepting a lift. Thus a young woman — or any woman — accepting a lift is 'foolish' if she becomes the victim of a crime committed by the driver of the car. In complementary fashion, a young woman — any woman — who picks up a male hitch-hiker, herself being the car-driver, is labelled 'foolish' where she becomes the victim of a crime committed by the party accepting the lift. In rape, foolishness and responsibility lie together in the one individual — the woman victim.

It can be shown that in whatever manner a woman acts, she can become the victim of a sexual offence. Rapes do not only take place in cars, they occur in the homes of victims; they occur in the homes of attackers; they occur in alleys, in deserted bushland, in offices, in hostels, in hotels and boarding-houses. Rapes are carried out by family members of the victim — so there is little hope of escape.[56] A high percentage of rapes are planned. . . so that whatever the victim chose to do could not interfere with the commission of the crime.[57] Just as men are obliged to walk about the streets at night — or during the day — so too are women. . . who may thus become victims of rape. Just as men sleep in their own homes at night, so too do women. . . who may thus become victims of rape.[58] The irony of rape is that in the very crime wherein women are deemed to have power to prevent commission of the act, women have the least power to do so.

Conclusion

Any assessment of where women stand in relation to the criminal law must take into account the manner in which that law has been designed. The law that is in force in Australia has been built up over many years by judges — all male, until recently[59] — and by legislators — predominantly male.[60] Men and women have been socialised differently and different demands have been made upon their talents and capacities. Thus it is clear that a law designed by males will not necessarily be suited to the needs of females.

As with many of our other institutions of power, the law has functioned to maintain the status quo. Where women are concerned, the law has been drawn with reference to the way in which men define women — as dependent wives with no ability to make their own decisions; or as wretched whores responsible for their 'ability' to lead men into committing offences against them. If the law is to reinstate itself as in any way relevant to the true needs, abilities and responsibilities of women, it must be redrawn from the perspective of woman as person. The blindly accepted litany of the Acts Interpretation Acts that 'male' includes 'female' and 'he' includes 'she' must become a reality rather than a statement empty of meaning.

---

1. Simone de Beauvoir, *The Second Sex,* Penguin Books, London, 1948.

2. *Blackstone's Commentaries* (1770, 4th Ed.), Bk. 1, c.15, at p. 442; Bk. II, c.29, at p. 433.

3. Archbold, *Criminal Pleading* (1848, 11th Ed.) at p. 17; Glanville Williams, *The Criminal Law — The General Part* (1961), at section 249; *Manuels* v *Crafter* (1940) S.A.S.R. 7; *Williams* v *Shippey* (1844) 3 L.T.O.S. 342; *R.* v *Whelan* (1937) S.A.S.R. 237.

4. *Williams* v *Shippey* (1844) 3 L.T.O.S. 342; see generally Law Reform Commissioner, *Report No. 2, Criminal Liability of Married Persons (Special Rules)*, Govt. Printer, Melbourne, 1976.

5. Benefit of clergy was a procedure developed to mitigate the worst consequences of harsh penalties existing in the law during the early period of English history after the Conquest. Although applicable, in theory, only to individuals who belonged to the clergy, the test was passed by numerous persons who did not. (The test was that of reading a particular piece of prose.) Women, not being entitled to join the clergy because of their sex, were not able to use the benefit of clergy escape. (It is interesting to note that the rules could be waived to include males who were not clergy but who could read, yet could not be waived to render women 'honorary men'.)

6. See Glanville Williams, *op. cit.*, at section 249; *Seventh Report of the Criminal Law Commissioner of 1833*, at p. 21.

7. See generally Charles L. Newman, *Sourcebook on Probation, Parole and Pardons*, 3rd Ed., Charles C. Thomas, Springfield, Ill., 1968.

8. See generally J. Eekelaar, *Family Security and Family Breakdown*, Penguin, London, 1971.

9. Canada — *Criminal Code* 1892, section 13; *Crimes Act* 1893 (New Zealand), section 24; *Criminal Code Act* 1899 (Queensland), section 32; *Criminal Code Act* 1902 (Western Australia); *Criminal Code Act* 1924 (Tasmania), section 20; *Crimes Act (Amendment) Act* 1924 (N.S.W.), section 17; *Criminal Justice Act* 1925 (England), section 47; *Criminal Law Consolidation Amendment Act* 1940 (South Australia), section 12; *Crimes (Married Persons Liability) Act* 1977 (Victoria), section 2.

10. See section 47 *Criminal Justice Act* 1925 (England); for the various State provisions see Victorian Law Reform Commissioner, *op. cit.* and P.J. Pace, 'Marital Coercion — Anachronism of Modernism?' (1979) *Criminal Law Review* 82.

11. See Victorian Law Reform Commissioner, *op. cit.*

12. 364 U.S. 51 (1960).

13. *U.S.* v *Dege* 364 U.S. 51, 53.

14. *Hale's Pleas of the Crown*, Vol. 1, at p. 629.

15. For a refutation of the Hale position, see Jocelynne A. Scutt, 'Consent in Rape: The Problem of the Marriage Contract' (1977), 3 *Monash University Law Review* 255.

16. Some jurisdictions in the U.S. — for example, Washington, D.C. and New York, have such provisions. See fn. 20 *post* and also comments fn. 23 *post*.

17. Department of the Attorney General and of Justice N.S.W. Bureau of Crime Statistics and Research, *Statistical Report No. 9, Series 2, Court Statistics 1977*, (1978), at p. 82.

18. *Wolfenden Report* (England).
19. *Ibid.*
20. For example, New York, Washington D.C. Note that these laws can hardly be called effective. When the 1968 law in New York came into effect, convictions of prostitutes for the first year numbered 3,500; only two convictions of the 112 patrons actually arrested came about. It would be foolish to suggest that two men engaged in 3,500 acts of prostitution during the period in question. On this and the operation of the law in Washington D.C. see N. Dorsen, 'Women the Criminal Code and the Correction System' in *Women's Role in Contempory Society*, (Report of the New York Commission on Human Rights, Avon Books, New York, 1972), 505 at p. 507. See also comments Jocelynne A. Scutt, 'Debunking the Theory of the Female "Masked Criminal"' (1978) 11 *A.N.Z.J. Criminology* 23, at p. 26 *et. seq.*
21. *Sexual Offences Act* 1956 (U.K.); see *Crook* v *Edmonson* [1966] 1 All E.R. 833, 66 Cr. 90. Note that this case was subjected to criticism in *R.* v *Dodd* 66 Cr. App. Rep. 87, however the latter case involved soliciting, on the part of the man, two girls of 14 years. It was held relevant that soliciting sexual intercourse from 14 year old girls was not only immoral, but criminal within terms of the *Sexual Offences Act* 1956 (U.K.) section 6.
22. *Crook* v *Edmonson* [1966] 1 All E.R. 833.
23. It should be noted that since the repeal of the *Summary Offences Act* 1970 (N.S.W.), a new provision has been drafted that would be applicable to situations offending sensibilities of the public: 'A person shall not, without reasonable excuse, in, near, or within view or hearing from a public place or school behave in such a manner as would be likely to cause reasonable persons justifiably in all the circumstances to be seriously alarmed or seriously affronted'. (*Offences in Public Places Act* 1979 N.S.W.). Although the word 'soliciting' is no longer used, clearly those who solicit may be brought within the ambit of the offence. That the arresting officer is required to cast his mind to all the surrounding circumstances hardly leads to a belief that prostitutes will not come within the provision. Although the provision might be applied (at least on its face) to the customer and a leering, whistling male, there is no cause for believing it will be applied in this manner.
24. See Gail Sheehy, *Hustling*, NY, 1976, on housewives and prostitution.
25. John Kaplan, 'The Edward G. Donley Memorial Lecture: Non-Victim Crime and the Regulation of Prostitution' (1979) 79 *West Virginia Law Review*, 593 at p. 598.
26. See Margaret Power, 'The Wages of Sex' (1974) 46 *The Australian Quarterly* 2.
27. This has indeed been the case. See Jan Aitkin, 'Prostitution in New South Wales' (unpublished paper presented at the Pan-Pacific Conference on Drugs and Alcohol, Canberra, A.C.T., March 1980).
28. Cited Karen de Crow, *Sexist Justice — How Legal Sexism Affects You*, Random House, New York, 1974.
29. John Bowlby, *44 Juvenile Thieves*, W.H.O. Geneval, 1946. On this issue, see, for example, Jocelynne A. Scutt, 'The Politics of the "Broken Home" in the Determination of Female Criminality' (1977) *The Australian Quarterly* 37.

30. See Lee Comer, 'The Myth of Motherhood' in *The Otherhalf*, Jan Mercer, editor, Penguin, 1975.
31. On the use of the mental health diversionary system as reinforcing social problems suffered by women, due to patriarchy/sexism, by way of an individualistic analysis, see P. Chessler, *Women and Madness*, Doubleday, 1973; also B. Freidan, *The Feminine Mystique*, 1969.
32. *Blackstone's Commentaries* 12th Ed., 1793.
33. For example, Texas. See Karen de Crow, *op. cit.*
34. Colin Howard, *Australian Criminal Law*, Law Book Company, Sydney, 1972.
35. [1953] A.C. 200.
36. *Attorney General for Ceylon* v *Perera* [1953] A.C. 200, 205-206.
37. This ruling was later revised.
38. Howard, *op. cit.*, at p. 88, fn. 74.
39. On general principles of provocation dealing with this issue, see for example R.P. Roulston, *Introduction to Criminal Law in New South Wales* Butterworths, Sydney, 1975, at p. 92 *et. seq.*
40. (1840) 8 Dowl. 630.
41. *In re Cochrane* (1840) 8 Dowl. 630. See further sources cited Scutt, 'Spouse Assault: Closing the Door on Criminal Acts', (1980) 54, A.L.J., 720.
42. (1629) Hetl. 149.
43. *R.* v *Reid* (1973) 1 Q.B. 299, and see *R.* v *Jackson* (1891) 1 Q.B. 671.
44. On rape in marriage see fn. 15 *ante*.
45. See generally R.P. Roulston, *op. cit.*, at pp. 67 and 100 *et. seq.*
46. Further on this issue, see D. Cox, *Working Married Women and Youth Unemployment*, South Australian Premier's Department, Women's Advisory Unit, Adelaide, 1978; N.S.W. Women's Advisory Council, *A Woman's Place is Everywhere — a working woman's guide to employment facts*, Department of the Premier of New South Wales, Women's Advisory Council, Sydney, 1979.
47. J. Smith and B. Hogan, *Criminal Law* 3rd Ed., 1974, at p. 29.
48. G. Gordon, *The Criminal Law of Scotland*, Edinburgh, 1967, at p. 830. Further on the issue of consent in rape, see Jocelynne A. Scutt, 'Consent Versus Submission: Threats and The Element of Fear in Rape' (1977) 13 *University of Western Australia Law Review* 52.
49. [1973] Qd.R. 128.
50. 1.12.1966, 2707/66; cited John E. Newton, *Factors Affecting Sentencing in Rape Cases*, Australian Institute of Criminology, Canberra, 1976.
51. Begg, J. in Central Criminal Court, Sydney, New South Wales; cited Ellen Goodman, 'The Victim of Rape: **What** Progress?' (1979) 14 (1) *Australian Journal of Social Issues* 21.
52. 19 June, 1979; cited F. Rinaldi, 'Case and Comment — Kenny' (1980) 4 *Criminal Law Journal* 57, at 58.
53. *Ibid.*
54. Mr Justice Jones, cited 'Australian Women Against Rape', 1979 pamphlet.
55. J. Terry, Member W.E.L., Sydney, published in *WEL Informed*, WEL, Sydney, 1978.
56. See for example, *Battered Women: Issues of Public Policy — A consult-*

ation sponsored by the United States Commission on Civil Rights, Washington, D.C., January 30-31, 1978.

57. M. Amir, *Patterns in Forcible Rape,* University of Chicago Press, Chicago, 1971.

58. See for example, M. Amir, *op. cit.;* Duncan Chappell, Robley Geis and Gilbert Geis eds., *Forcible Rape — The Crime, the Victim and the Offender,* Columbia University Press, N.Y., 1977; Susan Brownmiller, *Against Our Will — Men, Women and Rape,* Simon and Schuster, N.Y., 1975.

59. Australia has no women on the High Court bench; there is only one woman judge at Supreme Court level; a woman heads the Family Court of Australia and there are several women judges on that court; a woman was appointed in 1980 to the District Court in New South Wales — to sit with no less than forty male judges.

60. Today in 1980 there are only six women in the Senate and no women in the House of Representatives. On the issue of women in politics, see 'Women in Party Politics — papers from the Women's Electoral Lobby Seminar held in Sydney, July 1977' (1977) 49 (3) *The Australian Quarterly* 3.

2 Hidden from History: Women Victims of Crime

ANNE SUMMERS

We have been sold numerous myths about our past. Only in recent years have researchers begun to challenge them: the romanticism of the myths has been shown to shroud exploitation, conquest and degradation. It is now recognised, for example, that when the British colonisers landed in eastern Australia in 1788 they were not given the friendly welcome by Aborigines that school-day history books had us believe. Instead, the arrival of whites was in most places bitterly resisted and often Aborigines resorted to tactics of guerilla warfare, attempting to outwit the invaders.

While it is true that where previously only the doings of men were considered to be important, women are beginning to be restored to history, but much of this restoration process is indiscriminate and lacks insight. It is no more than tokenism, such as where firms often employ women 'up front' in conspicuous jobs but make no attempt to introduce the flexibility in working hours or arrangements which are necessary for women with responsibilities for children.

To see what women have done in Australia's past involves asking modern questions of ancient records; if we simply take documents at their face value we merely ingest the contemporary attitudes to women and neglect the wider social and economic conditions determining them.

Thus, if we take at face value a commonplace belief that the first white women settlers of this country were all convicts, and thus criminals, refusing to look further, we miss an important element of their situation.

Offenders vs. Victims

In Australia, women criminals have occupied a special, romantic part in our history, yet women victims of crime — by far the larger group — have been almost totally overlooked. It is obviously more fun, and perhaps even titillating, to dredge up exploits of criminals of either sex and women criminals have always had an extra attraction, especially if they have committed spectacular crimes of violence or fraud. Many Australians have a particular sympathy with outlaws — hence the potency of the Ned Kelly mythology. A more modern example would be the help given by the public, especially by women, to the prison escapees Newcombe and Simmons while they were on the run.[1]

Women criminals have an extra magnetism, and are increasingly the subject of feature films. At a Sydney Film Festival, Chabrol's *Violette Noziere* was screened. It is an account of a teenage French girl who, during the 1930s, murdered her mother and stepfather. The film makes the main point I wish to make — that women criminals are very often themselves victims of crime. In the case of Violette Noziere, she was the victim of rape by her stepfather and, while this was not the sole motive for her crime — she also wished to free herself from the stultifying life her parents imposed upon her — it undoubtedly fired her intent.

I will not argue that all women criminals are acting from revenge; often, in fact, the reverse is the case. Women react to crimes perpetrated upon them in the way they react to almost everything else — passively, uncomplainingly, with little expectation of redress. It is only occasionally that a woman will be inspired to counter-violence.

Australian Women Convicts

While the female convicts have traditionally been usually dismissed as mere criminals — Sydney's notorious current criminality is often seen as a direct product of its convict origins — a closer look at the women who were sent here as convicts shows that upon arrival their roles were reversed and from being criminals, albeit guilty of petty crimes, they became victims.[2]

The British authorities were always explicit that the purpose for sending women convicts to Australia was to curb rebellions among the men. Women were sent as whores, a vocation they had no option but to accept, but were then castigated for doing so. The stereotype which developed to encompass these women and their situations is summed up in *Damned Whores and God's Police*, because the women were forced to be whores and then damned for being so.

The facts are:

- In order to raise numbers, women were sentenced to transportation for less serious crimes than men: whereas only hardened male offenders under sentence of transportation were actually transported to the colonies, all women under sentence, provided they were healthy and under 45, were transported.

- Despite this discriminatory treatment, the proportion of women convicts was always markedly lower than the men. When transportation was abolished to New South Wales in 1841, a total of just over 78,000 men had been sent out, compared with 9,500 women. As a distinct minority in a barbaric environment the women had little option but to accede to being assigned to male settlers, guards and other convicts. Reports at the time show this practice was not regarded as reprehensible and while there was, from time to time, token protest from England, the authorities did nothing to stop it. In 1803, 40 women were listed, baldly, in the account books, as 'women allowed to the New South Wales Corps'. The best a women could do was to find a man and live with him, thus gaining herself some kind of protection from uninvited sexual abuse.

- Despite conditions which forced women into whoredom, there was little sympathy for their situation; rather they were continually berated for shameful conduct and even given additional sentences for such crimes as being found in bed with a man.

- Because of the general low repute in which women convicts were held, it was difficult for them to gain respectability by marriage. Even as free settlers began to arrive and the seeds of a civilised society were sown, women convicts remained as pariahs, spurned by everyone — often including the children they had borne as the result of their enforced whoredom.

These women were not paragons of virtue; often they committed further crimes upon arrival, though generally these would barely merit the label today — swearing, drunkenness and so on (while crimes such as wife-beating or even wife-selling were not treated very seriously). But the overriding reality was that most convict women had to put up with abduction, rape, and beatings, not just as isolated incidents which could be brushed away as aberrations, but as part of their everyday lives. All of these things were crimes then and are crimes today.

My analysis, in 1975, of their position was based almost entirely on secondary sources, published material, including government reports, contemporary accounts and analyses by historians of the 20th century.[3] As such it has been attacked and a number of people have argued that my basic proposition is wrong. One researcher has used computers to prove that most of the convict women were prostitutes in England and thus my conclusions were unwarranted. I do not take this criticism seriously since, even if it were true, and I do not believe that it is, the mere fact of prior prostitution would in no way justify the treatment the women received upon arrival in Australia. It need hardly be said that being a whore in Sydney was very different from being a prostitute in England — the major differences being choice and remuneration, both of which were absent in Sydney.

The researches of Robert Hughes, whose work has been entirely with primary sources, totally confirms my analysis.[4] I am not here just trying to prove that I am right; I am hoping that, as more people accept the analysis, it will filter through into our perceptions of our history and into school text-books, to eventually dissolve one of the great myths of our past.

Australian Women Victims

Another myth requiring attention as being neglected concerns Aboriginal women. We still know very little about what happened to them as white civilisation disrupted their lives but we do know that the story is similar to that of the female convicts — a saga of abduction and rape. They are a group who are perceived nowadays as being victims of the huge crime of white colonisation but little attention has been paid to the specific ways in which they were victimised as women.[5]

Men and women can equally be victims of any crime but women are subject to victimisation because of their sex. Sexual crimes against women constitute probably the greatest area of victimisation. Although we know this to be true in our society today, we seldom confront this perception as we wade back into our history. A famous incident in Sydney's past exemplifies this point.

In 1886, an event occurred which was labelled by the respectable press, then as now, the *Sydney Morning Herald*, as 'The Mount Rennie Outrage'. The case is important for a number of reasons. In September 1886, an unemployed servant-girl Mary Jane Hicks, was picked up by a cab driver in Sussex Street, Sydney, and driven to a place called Mount Rennie in Moore Park, where he attempted to rape her. She protested and was rescued by a gang of lads, known then as 'larrikins' — they were young, unemployed, street-wise, snappily dressed, very much like the gangs hanging round any shopping centre in Sydney's Western suburbs today. These boys took her to a deserted part of Moore Park and a pack-rape took place. Two police arrived on the scene while the girl, injured and in great distress, was still there (some workmen had witnessed the event and run for help) but the boys had gone.

The next day a number of larrikins from Redfern and Waterloo were rounded up, and over the succeeding weeks arrests continued until eventually 16 men faced charges of rape. After the preliminary hearing, 12 defendants were committed for trial. Justice proceeded rather more quickly then than it does now and on 22 November — just over two months after the crime — the trial began and with it one of the most celebrated events in New South Wales legal and social history.

The trial lasted six days and established what must have been a record in trial proceedings. The trial judge, Justice Windeyer, had an overseas holiday awaiting him at the end of the week and he stretched the proceedings on some days from 9 am to 3 am the following morning. Often the jury was asleep, the court was gaslit and dim and identification of the defendants nigh impossible. The final address by the judge, after listening to addresses by the seven defence counsel and the crown, lasted for 10 hours. An exhausted jury retired for two and a quarter hours, returning with convictions for nine of the 12. At midnight on 27 November, the mandatory sentence of death was delivered. Then began a most extraordinary series of public and political events as groups debated and lobbied for or against execution of the penalty.

The principal witness in the trial had of course been Mary Jane Hicks, the victim. In the furore that followed, she was never heard from. It seems she disappeared from history, to leave behind only her name in court and police records as the victim of one of the multitude of pack-rapes that has characterised our history. Yet the ensuing debate about whether or not to hang the men — all of whom incidentally were aged around 17 — was conducted almost entirely in terms of keeping 'the streets safe for women' (from the pro-hangers) and 'maintaining civilisation' (the anti-hangers) — the latter proposition surely having to include the right of women to be free from rape.

I will not recount the immense detail of the public protests and the political machinations which followed — except to say that after much political intervention, the sentences of six of the boys were commuted to life imprisonment, the first three years of which to be spent in irons, and four were ultimately hanged in what was, to my knowledge, the last execution for rape in New South Wales.[6]

The major point about this case, from a feminist analysis, is the invisibility of the central figure — the young woman who was the victim.

On the night before his death, one of the boys swore a confession in which he declared his innocence and, claiming much divine assistance, retailed the events of the day at Mount Rennie, claiming that no rape had taken place. On his account, an innocent man had died. While I believe that the police used the crime to round up a number of larrikins they did not like, and it seems that several of those convicted were probably not involved, the crime is beyond doubt.

Confidential papers of Lord Carrington, the New South Wales Governor at the time, contain an eye-witness account from one of the workmen who ultimately rescued the girl. It leaves little doubt that a violent rape took place and that the girl frequently tried to escape her attackers, on one occasion trying to drown herself in a creek.

Having independent corroboration leaves little doubt about what happened (and that in itself is unusual for most crimes, but especially so for rape where some States still require it for a conviction), but this is not really the point. This case typifies one of the central problems of women as victims of crime. First, the crime is not acknowledged, and second, the woman is blamed for it.

As with the female convicts 150 years earlier, the Mount Rennie case provided a microcosm of the arguments about woman's role in society, and more importantly about the limits of that role. Mary Jane Hicks, the Mount Rennie victim, was suspect because of her age, the fact that she was unemployed and, when in work, was a servant-girl. Like the convicts, she had no class protection and again like the convicts she had no opportunity to influence the debate which her attack precipitated.

Woman as Invisible Victim

Mary Jane Hicks' invisibility is important because it is the constant factor in crimes against women.

Recently, I was at Parramatta Jail speaking with Resurgents[7] about a number of aspects of male/female relations including rape. Before the formal part of the discussion began, one prisoner told me of interviews with convicted rapists, which had taken place in the jail as part of a research project. He told me he had heard a number of these interviews and while he was horrified by most of them, one of them had left him convinced that an injustice had taken place. The prisoner briefly described the circumstances, whereby the man convicted had driven a woman to a party, had stayed in the car and fallen asleep, while his mates took the woman inside and raped her. Later he awoke and drove her home. For this act, admittedly as an accessory, he had received 20 years imprisonment. On the face of it, it seemed rough (leaving aside the question of the length of sentence) and perhaps under other circumstances I might, especially in that environment where one's sympathies always tend to be with the prisoners, have thought that here was a case of unjust accusation.

It is important to note, in passing, that in the description of the rape, the woman was again the invisible central character: the cause of this man's long sentence, as told to me, but not existing as a person in any way.

As it was, a number of details of the story 'clicked' with me and I asked when and where it had happened, learning that it was a rape in which I had, through the Sydney Rape Crisis Centre, become deeply involved.

It took place in 1974, and was in a number of ways very similar to the Mount Rennie Case, involving the same number of men, mostly unemployed, though they were a little older than the Redfern larrikins. The trial in this case was very long, being delayed over nearly two and a half years. But the key issue was that, like Mary Jane Hicks, the victim of this rape had disappeared too. I had come to know her quite well, being involved in taking her to hospital, hours of talking with her, eventually going with her to the police, and waiting around for the first week of the trial to be called as a witness. I was never called again, so did not know when the trial resumed and could only infer from a later newspaper report that the men sentenced in a case that sounded similar were those involved in this case.

Similarly, the social fall-out was large. The event had begun at a hotel in Balmain where the victim worked as a part-time barmaid. Once the word went around Balmain, people stopped patronising the pub. It went out of business. And although the aftermath was not so great as that which followed Mount Rennie — the education system was changed, laws were changed, and attempts were made to find entertainment for youth — nevertheless it brought home to me that a crime is seldom without a consequence.

But again the central character was missing.

As coincidence would have it, the night before I visited Parramatta Jail, I had run into a woman whose face seemed familiar but whom I could not immediately place. I spoke to her, tentatively giving her a name. She replied that she had changed her name, left Australia for three years and had just arrived back to start again. She was the victim of the Balmain rape. And the man who is in Parramatta protesting his innocence in fact broke this woman's nose, held her down while he sent his mate to 'bring back the pub' and generally supervised an attack which lasted for over six hours.

Conclusion

It is some kind of tribute to the women's movement that a rape victim is able to reappear, but we have not yet achieved enough for her not to have felt it imperative to disappear for a while. She wanted to forget, rather than escape ostracism, though there inevitably was some. And while I can understand her motives, I hope that we can soon change our society sufficiently so that women victims do not feel they must run away and hide, but feel it is their right and even their duty to stand up to loudly accuse and condemn their attackers.

At present this process is ritualised, distorted and made barbaric in the case of rape by court procedures. This must be changed. For while women victims of crime feel ashamed or oppressed, and feel their minority status prevents them from being able to make a legitimate complaint, their status as victims gets scant recognition. Just as the myths of the female convicts are still with us, but slowly disappearing, so the stigma of current female victims remains. I believe that in dealing with one, we can ultimately improve the lot of the other.

---

1. See Les Newcombe, *Inside Out*, Angus and Robertson, Sydney, 1979; Jan Simmonds, *For Simmo*, Cassell Australia, Sydney, 1979.
2. This argument is developed further in Anne Summers, *Damned Whores and God's Police*, Penguin Books, Ringwood, Vic., 1975.
3. *Ibid.*
4. Robert Hughes, forthcoming.
5. Sue Jane Hunt, 'Aboriginal Women and Colonial Authority' in *In Pursuit of Justice — Australian Women and the Law 1788-1979*, Mackinolty and Radi, (eds.), Hale and Iremonger, Sydney, 1979, p. 32-40.
6. Anne Summers, work in progress.
7. Parramatta Recidivists Group, Parramatta Gaol, New South Wales.

3 Women, Crime and Punishment

ELIZABETH WINDSCHUTTLE

Historical and sociological studies of crime have paid comparatively little attention to women. This is partly due to the common belief that, because female criminals have been statistically fewer in number, female criminality is a less significant social issue. Female crimes have also been seen as more trivial. Women's offences, such as shoplifting, have involved comparatively smaller amounts of property loss, and less harmful crimes against the person. A large proportion of female criminals have been guilty only of offences involving prostitution. Additionally there is a general assumption enshrined in the social sciences, especially history, that women's actions themselves are less significant and less worthy of study.[1]

Yet historical study offers considerable insight into the question. Theories of crime and punishment, both in the past and today, have reflected the ideas and social conflicts of the period and the society they have served. Theories currently dominating the criminology of women are based on biological and psychological accounts of causality. Women are assumed to be subject to unique drives and urges. It is still argued that women become criminals because of the menstrual cycle, through menopausal symptoms or, in the case of prostitutes, because of unresolved oedipal conflicts or maternal deprivation. However, men who use prostitutes are not regarded as socially deviant. Rather, recourse to prostitutes is seen as an expression of a 'normal' sex drive.[2] Theories of causality such as these have been incorporated into legal definitions of female crime and lead to uncritical acceptance of official crime statistics. Thus, officially, it is prostitutes and not their clients who are seen as the offenders.

Liberalism and the 'Double Standard'

The development of capitalist economic relations in the eighteenth century greatly increased opportunities for crime. Extension of commerce and trade and expansion of money transactions were matched by growth of the criminal law to protect property and maintain the new system. Criminal law emerged as the main agent of social control in a society lacking a police force or standing army. However, this 'fat and swelling sheaf of laws which threatened thieves with death'[3] derived from an earlier era. Late in the eighteenth century, legal reform more appropriate to capitalism was advocated. After the English middle class gained political power through the 1832 Reform Bill, these reforms were put into practice in the prison system.

Liberalism, the ideology of the rising middle class, provided the basis for new theories about the causes of crime and offered its own versions about the solution. Most influential was Beccaria, whose criminological work was published in English in 1765.[4] Beccaria's liberal views saw the potential offender as an independent, reasoning individual, weighing up the consequences of crime and deciding the balance of advantage. Criminals were assumed to have like powers of resistance as other individuals and to deserve the same punishment for the same crime. Punishment, moreover, should fit the crime. Beccaria advocated the termination of the gross and capricious terror of the old criminal law and the abolition of capital punishment as the principal deterrent. He urged a fixed and graduated scale of more lenient but more certain punishments with prison sentences as the main tool of the law.

English liberals such as John Howard and Jeremy Bentham took up these ideas. Bentham advocated the construction of the *penal panopticon* in which prisoners would be kept in solitary confinement so they could reflect upon their sins and guilt. The only human contact they should have was the authority figures who would sermonise and admonish them. Liberal criminology thus held that, as people chose of their own free will to commit crime, the appropriate punishment was to do everything to persuade them to regret their crime.

However, this liberal theory and practice was **not** regarded as applicable to crime committed by women. The rise of the middle class saw the development of a special body of thought about the place of women in society. While middle class men immersed themselves each day in the competitive, avaricious world of commerce where the only morals or values were those of the 'cash nexus'; their women were to be kept out of the market place. Women's roles were those of the moral and spiritual guardians both of society and of the family upon which society was assumed to be built. The family relations preserved by women were to be generous and genteel.

This contradiction between the middle class' public and private value systems produced a double standard in relation to women. If women deserted their roles, this threatened the family and thus the fabric of society, it was believed.[5] The female deviant, whether she be a prostitute, alcoholic, vagrant, murderess or thief, **doubly** threatened the social order, first by sinning and second by removing the moral constraints she held on the rest of society. Also, if a woman sinned, then, through her influence as wife and mother, she spawned other sinners. Thus women were judged more harshly than men and a greater social stigma was attached to their misdemeanours.

The most revealing instance of this dual attitude towards male and female behaviour related to their sexual conduct.[6] Adultery and promiscuity were approved for men but were considered to destroy the value of women as the property of husbands or fathers[7], to corrupt family stability and to endanger the welfare of the community. Translated to criminality, the double standard prescribed different attitudes toward male and female criminals. Men could commit crime, but be reformed. If women committed crime, they were destroyed utterly. They were irreclaimable.

Women Penal Reformers

When liberal criminologists and penologists came to dominate the penal system in the nineteenth century, they displaced a competing movement that arose at the same time. In the late eighteenth century, evangelicalism became a force in the Anglican and some of the dissenting churches. It was a crusade in which the Tory ruling class saw a drastic need to define a role for the large mass of unemployed and destitute who had been driven off the land and into the cities by commercial agriculture. Evangelicals were concerned to stop the spread of Jacobin ideas and the development of a revolutionary situation such as occurred in

France. Their main weapon of prevention was philanthropy which aimed to alleviate the destitution of the poor, spread moral propaganda and Christianity among them and turn them into dutiful, industrious citizens. Women philanthropists played a major role in the evangelical movement as they believed the caring and nurturing roles to be their special province.[8] Evangelicalism was more conservative than the rising liberal ideology, depending more on older paternalist ideas than on the concept of individualism and 'free choice'.

Penal reform was an important part of the evangelical armoury. Crime was seen by evangelicals to be but one part of the syndrome afflicting the urban poor. Crime was largely the product of the adverse influences of the industrial and urban environment with its poverty, ignorance, sickness and unemployment. The evangelicals thus originated a theory of criminality that later was termed 'social determinism'. Evangelical Elizabeth Fry linked these social conditions: 'All reflecting persons will surely unite in the sentiment that the female placed in prison for her crimes, in the hospital for her sickness, in the asylum for her insanity, or in the workhouse for her poverty' needed succour from more fortunate women.[9]

Fry believed women were capable of rehabilitation. The success of an early experiment conducted by Fry at Newgate Gaol was described in 1818. Visiting ladies' committees had organised improvements in clothing and hygiene and instructed women prisoners in religion. In a few months, it was said, there had been a marked improvement in their behaviour. 'Without exaggeration . . . a transformation' had occurred:

> Riot, licentiousness, and filth, exchanged for order, sobriety, and comparative neatness in the chamber, the apparel, and the persons of the prisoners. . . The prison no more resounded with obscenity and imprecations, and licentious songs; and to use the coarse, but the just, expression of one who knew the prison well, 'this hell upon earth' exhibited the appearance of an industrious manufactory, or a well regulated family.[10]

Fry proposed that female criminals could be reformed only under the superintendence of female prison officers. Female wardens would prevent sexual abuse of prisoners by male guards; they would set examples of true womanhood; they would be more sympathetic to female prisoners. Male and female prisoners, she believed, should be separately housed.[11] Fry's convictions ran counter to mainstream liberal views. She opposed solitary or separate confinement within prisons because she believed it deterred rehabilitation. She advocated that prisoners be engaged in useful, productive work within prison to prepare themselves for an outside job and to give themselves a feeling of worth. Enforced idleness, meaningless or tedious tasks, she was convinced, degraded prisoners and contributed to further deterioration. Above all, she was committed to the belief that 'fallen' women were as redeemable as male criminals. Fry's work with prisoners was emulated by female compatriots in the colonies of New South Wales in the 1820s and Van Diemen's Land in the 1840s. In Sydney, a committee system was set up at the Female Factory at Parramatta, New South Wales, by Eliza Darling, the wife of Governor Darling, at the instigation of Fry in 1829. It was claimed to have had some success in reforming prisoners in the factory.[12] The Sydney Ladies Committee established a system of rewards whereby ex-prisoners of the Factory who went into service were to receive a small sum of money for good behaviour. The Ladies Committee decided to reward 'those who continue in one service', who were able to receive 'a certificate of good behaviour from their Master and Mistress'. Money for this fund came from the proceeds of a sewing scheme instituted in the factory. Inmates used material donated to the Factory to make clothes which were then sold to the public. Further proceeds came from a used clothing stall established in Parramatta. The Ladies Committee also conducted an evening school which provided moral and religious instruction in accordance with the type outlined by Elizabeth Fry in her manual on ladies' visiting committees.[13]

Although a Prison Act of 1823 under Peel had incorporated many of Fry's ideas, such as separate women's buildings in prisons and female officers supervising female prisoners, very few of her concepts were brought into force. After 1832, a liberal organisation, the Society for Improving Prison Discipline, became the most influential lobby. Its policies of hard labour, solitary confinement and use of the treadmill were implemented. For several decades, these became features of the prison system for both male and female prisoners. Fry and her followers in the colonies were eclipsed. 'Mrs Fry is an amiable and excellent woman' commented the liberal reformer Sydney Smith, 'but hers are not the methods to stop crimes'. What was needed was 'coarse food, a dress of shame, hard, incessant, irksome and eternal labour, a planned and unrelenting exclusion of happiness and comforts'.[14]

The efforts of the Society for the Improvement of Prison Discipline were mainly responsible for bringing about state control and bureaucratisation of the penal system. In the eighteenth century, prisons had been local establishments run by private individuals under contract and working for profit. Steps were made after 1835 to centralise the prison administration. An Act in 1839 gave power to the Secretary of State to completely supervise construction of prisons and conduct inside them. The bureaucracy which evolved from this pushed for development of 'model prisons' and the first of these was established in Pentonville in 1842. Over 50 were built in England in 1850. The model prison at Port Arthur, Tasmania, was on these lines. These institutions enshrined in their regulatory codes the system of punishment which Fry opposed.

Some women involved in prison reform went along with these new developments. The wife of Governor John Franklin of Van Diemen's Land, Jane Franklin, had been charged by Fry with the responsibility of supervising the conditions of female convicts and establishing a ladies' visiting committee to the Female Factory in Hobart. But it soon appeared that Franklin was not a supporter of Fry's ideas. She complained in 1842 that there had been moves to institute new measures similar to those in England for male convicts but not for the women. Measures such as hard labour, solitary confinement and shaving of women's hair, she believed, would contribute to 'corrective discipline'. Franklin's position demonstrated all the features of the shift to state control of prisons. She opposed the concept of women convicts serving their sentences with individual homes under the system of assignment and favoured their incarceration in a proper penitentiary constructed of separate cells.[15]

Towards the end of her life, Fry's ideas had become very unfashionable. When she died in 1845 solitary confinement was becoming increasingly popular. However, her convictions about female criminality and penology were kept alive by other women evangelicals. 'Our experience. . . has shown us conclusively', claimed reformers in Matilda Wrench's edition of *Visits to Female Prisons at Home and Abroad* in 1852, that female criminals were not innately evil but the product of their environment. 'In nine cases out of ten, no choice was ever made, for none was offered'.[16]

Another of Fry's later followers was the journalist Harriet Martineau who, in 1865, deplored the general impression given by a report on female prisoners in the previous year that 'women, once bad, are utterly hopeless, and that the only alternative for them is being shut up in prisons like wild beasts in cages'.[17] She accepted the idea that women were harder to reclaim[18], but argued that this was because less attention had been paid to female rehabilitation because it was considered a useless exercise.[19] She asked readers to consider why women became criminals. They had been forced into anti-social behaviour by the ravages of their environment: 'Most miserable they are: for the most part, prostitutes, or ruined by betrayal and poverty.'[20] She recorded:

> In the report of last year's prisoners we are told that women when criminal are worse than men; for that, while female convicts are little more than a third of the whole number, 42 per cent of the women in gaol had been convicted before, to 32 per cent of the men; and that of the convicts who had been in prison above ten times before, there were 2,773 women to 1,173 men. Nobody could be surprised at this who had learned anything of the life led in our female prisons.[21]

Social Determinism

In the mid and late nineteenth century, the idea that social environment led people into crime was expressed forcefully from several new directions. Those taking this view wanted to change society for various reasons. They saw crime as one of the main manifestations of the problem. This view was taken by socialists wanting a complete social transformation, by social reformers wanting to clean up pockets of poverty, and feminists wanting legal rights and opportunities expanded for women. The socialist Frederick Engels in 1844 described in graphic detail the extent of prostitution in the slums of the great industrial centres of London, Manchester and Birmingham. He attributed this partly to middle-class sexploitation:

> . . . the middle classes are themselves in no small degree responsible for the extent to which prostitution exists — how many of the 40,000 prostitutes who fill the streets of London every evening are dependent for their livelihood on the virtuous bourgeois? How many of them were first seduced by a member of the middle classes, so that they now have to sell their persons to passers-by in order to live?. . . who can blame them for this?[22]

Primarily, however, Engels saw that poverty and insecurity bred the sort of cultural responses working people made to their environment:

> A class which can only buy a very few — and those the most sensual — pleasures in return for the hardest labour, can hardly be criticised for blindly indulging in those pleasures to wild excess. The workers form a class whose education has been grossly neglected and whose welfare is threatened by all sorts of mishaps. They know nothing of security. Why on earth should they be provident in any way? Why should they lead 'respectable' lives and think of some future happiness instead of indulging in some immediate pleasure which happens to come their way? For **them** of all people, future happiness is something of a hypothetical nature, because of the perpetually shifting and uncertain conditions under which they are forced to exist.[23]

Engels portrayed the scenario in which young women were introduced to prostitution and then to crime:

> In Sheffield on Sundays young people hang about the streets all day gambling by tossing coins or by organising dog fights. They frequent gin shops assiduously... Nearly all of them were under 17 years of age... Known prostitutes were among the company. In the circumstances it is not surprising to hear from many witnesses that in Sheffield it is very common for irregular sexual intercourse...[for]... girls as young as 14 or 15 years [to] have already become prostitutes. Crimes of savage violence are of common occurrence.[24]

The social reforming journalist, Henry Mayhew, documented the life of criminals in his monumental study of London slums. Mayhew sought and classified trades pursued by prostitutes arrested in the decade 1850s–1860s. Milliners, servants, laundresses, shoemakers, tailors, hatters and trimmers were the principal occupations.[25] Servants, he believed, formed one-third of prostitutes.[26] In Mayhew's opinion, starvation wages and economic fluctuations were mainly responsible for the widespread incidence of prostitution. Recognising that females became prostitutes as a result of adverse parental influence, poverty and lack of education, he nevertheless regarded an innate weakness in the prostitute's character as important reason. In second and third place he put among the probable causes of a girl's 'fall', 'natural levity and the example around them... love of dress and display coupled with the desire for a sweetheart'.[27] Mayhew wanted better regulation of seasonal fluctuations in trade and labour market planning through surveys of labour supply and demand to reduce temporary impoverishment, unemployment and thus crime.

Mayhew argued that although at law prostitution was not a crime, the law enforcement system treated prostitutes as criminals. Prostitutes were continually harassed by police. In 1857, following a burst of protest, the police attempted to clear them from the major streets of London.[28] However, this did not restrain demand for prostitutes and in the 1860s the state intervened to regulate, rather than abolish, the trade through the Contagious Diseases Acts.

These Acts (1864, 1866 and 1869) were introduced to guarantee a supply of 'clean' prostitutes for unmarried soldiers and sailors garrisoned in various towns in Ireland and Southern England. Women 'known' to be prostitutes were subjected to periodical examination and if found to have venereal disease were incarcerated in a certified 'lock' hospital (hospitals with venereal disease wards) for a period not to exceed nine months. The police had very arbitrary powers to arrest women who were suspected of being prostitutes, who were to submit voluntarily to an examination or go before a local magistrate. The onus was on the woman to prove she was innocent, thus reversing the tradition of English law of being innocent until proved guilty. Wide enabling powers granted to police meant they could arrest women whom they believed indulged in promiscuous behaviour, whether they received money for it or not.

A small group of women responded to the Acts by campaigning for their repeal on the grounds that they denied British justice and that State recognition of prostitution was un-Christian. The principal campaigner, Josephine Butler, followed the tradition of social determinist penal reformers. The connection between destitution and prostitution seemed to her obvious. Destitution was the result of lack of employment for women and the starvation wages paid to seamstresses and other women workers. These evils, in their turn, were related to the lack of educational and training facilities for girls, so that women workers comprised mainly unskilled and low-grade labour.[29]

The idea that by changing the environment one could prevent female crime and rehabilitate female prisoners persisted throughout the nineteenth century. In 1898 Eliza Orme restated many of the views Harriet Martineau had expressed 33 years earlier.[30] Indeed, Orme's statistics were uncannily similar to those recorded by

Martineau. Female prisoners comprised one-third of the prison population and recidivism among women remained at the same level.

However, by 1898 the aims of Elizabeth Fry and her colleagues earlier in the century had come to fruition. Female prison quarters were segregated and staffed by female warders. This had not, however, aided the rehabilitation of women. Orme responded to this fact by criticising the type of women employed in the job. They were appointed 'with absolute disregard to any industrial training. They were overworked and the type of person in the job is often unsuitable.'[31]

The modern feminist historian, Estelle Freedman, has argued that the matriarchal penal institution, which replaced the patriarchal one, subsequently incorporated most of the attitudes of the old system towards female prisoners.[32] The main difference was that women were given tasks such as laundry and needlework rather than solitary confinement or hard labour. For the most part, the only employment these tasks prepared female prisoners for on release was domestic service. This was the traditional role also decreed by orphanages, 'schools of industry' and other institutions for poor girls in the nineteenth century.[33] While domestic service training was justified by reformers for its rehabilitative value, these middle class women had a vested interest in creating a class of servants to work in their own households and in those of women like themselves. Women penal reformers, many of whom also became involved in the late nineteenth century feminist movement, were thus seeking their own emancipation by generating a labour force to do their domestic work.

Atavism and Social Darwinism

Though social determinism was a theory held through the nineteenth century, it remained the view of the minority of those who thought about female criminality. The dominant view in the second half of the nineteenth century came to be that of biological determinism which was articulated most forcefully after the publication of Darwin's *Origin of the Species* in 1859.

An article titled 'Criminal Women' in the *Cornhill Magazine* in 1866 provided the classic example of the different standards of morality applied to male and female criminals:

It is notorious that a bad man — we mean one whose... training has led him into crime — is not so vile as a bad woman. If we take a man and woman guilty of a similar offence in the eye of the law, we shall invariably find that there is more hope of influencing the former than the latter. Equally criminal in one sense, in another sense there is a difference. The man's nature may be said to be hardened, the woman's destroyed. Women of this stamp are generally so bold and unblushing in crime, so indifferent to right and wrong, so lost to all sense of shame, so destitute of the instincts of womanhood, that they may be justly compared to wild beasts than to women. To say the least, the honour of womanhood requires that a new appelation be invented for them.[33a]

Female criminals were, the writer argued, less highly evolved human beings. They were:

... more uncivilised than the savage, more degraded than the slave, less true to all natural and womanly instincts than the untutored squaw of a North American tribe... they [were] so ignorant, so obtuse, that instruction — oral instruction — might as well be even in an unknown tongue, so little do they understand it.[33b]

This reference to female criminals' atavistic characteristics showed the influence of Darwin's theories. Three writers on female criminality later in the nineteenth century, Pauline Tarnowsky, Caesar Lombroso and W. Ferrerro used these theories rigorously. The latter two wrote a seminal work called *La donna delinquenta* or *The Female Offender*. The work of these three was originally based on the concept of atavism. This was the belief that all anti-social or criminal elements in society were in fact biological throwbacks from an earlier evolutionary stage in human development. In his early works, Lombroso firmly maintained that deviants were less highly evolved than 'normal' law abiding citizens.[34] Social Darwinism, on the other hand, referred to the belief that individuals or groups developed necessary psychological or physiological characteristics to enable them to function more efficiently in their predetermined roles. Thus, Lombroso later argued that prostitutes evolved in a way that made them unusually attractive when young. Murderesses or violent women on the other hand evolved an unusual strength.[35]

Pauline Tarnowsky, Lombroso and Ferrerro hoped to discover clearly identifiable characteristics which would build up into a recognisable criminal type. Tarnowsky found signs of 'degeneracy' among many of the prostitutes she studied — abnormalities of skin and teeth.[36] Lombroso studied pictures of female criminals, measured their skulls and counted the moles and tatoos in order to find consistent signs of degeneration or atavism.[37]

All were forced finally to admit that their studies were inconclusive.[38] Lombroso and Ferrerro however, instead of abandoning their theory, used the concept of biological determinism to explain why 'true criminals' were rarely found among the female population.[39] The lifestyle of women was biologically predetermined according to these theories. Women were basically immobile because they were child-rearers. As a result, they were more conservative and law abiding[40] and were congenitally less inclined to crime, so the true criminal type, and even the occasional criminal, were rare among women. However, the 'born' female criminal was excessively evil and cruel in her crime. 'Rarely is a woman wicked, but when she is she surpasses the man'.[41]

The concept of a woman's 'natural role' or her 'true nature' was axiomatic to their work. This view of womanhood was based on the mores and lifestyle of the Victorian middle class woman, a woman far distant from those who constituted the majority of women of the criminal class. Lombroso and Ferrerro separated criminality from the social context in which it took place, and disregarded the impact of the adverse influences of social and economic disorder in the period of industrialisation and urbanisation. As Leon Radzinowicz said, their theory:

> ... served the interests and relieved the conscience of those at the top to look upon the dangerous classes as an independent category, detached from the prevailing social conditions. They were portrayed as a race apart, morally depraved and vicious, living by violating the fundamental law of orderly society, which was that a man should maintain himself by honest, steady work.[42]

Although he exposes the ideological nature of these 19th century theorists, Radzinowicz does not offer an alternative concept of the cause of female criminality in the nineteenth century. He reserves his causal theories for criminals in general both male and female, and confines them to the twentieth century.[43] His discussion of women is limited mainly to two areas. First, in considering women and capital punishment[44], he shows that eighteenth century capital laws applied equally to men and women.[45] Then by 1857, a proposal to abolish the death penalty for women was rejected by the government. It was considered important to avoid any impression that women could escape solely by virtue of their sex.[46] Second, on the issue of women and prostitution, he discusses the numbers of prostitutes and their legal status but does not address himself to the cause of prostitution.[47]

Australian Convict Women

In the 1960s, Australian historians made a contribution to the question of English female criminals in discussions about the nature of the convicts. They had two aims: first, to determine whether convicts should be regarded as 'political prisoners' or 'genuine' criminals; second, to see if the Australian experience hardened or rehabilitated them. The two main researchers in this period were Lloyd Robson and H.S. Payne. It was unfortunate so little attention had been paid to female convicts, Payne remarked. 'All too frequently she has been impugned in a few brief generalisations, such as: "The women and boys were generally speaking of a lower grade even than the men, and the boys were reckoned almost as irreclaimable as the women".'[48] He criticised the attitude of previous historians of condemning female convicts on the basis of too little evidence, much of which was subjective.[49]

Payne and Robson were an advance on earlier writings. By using statistical evidence they hoped to uncover more specific and less subjective characteristics about female offenders. Their findings about female convicts' backgrounds were similar, but their interpretations varied considerably. Both stressed the urban background of these women[50] and particularly the fact that many of them had moved from their birthplace to towns or cities to live, inferring disorientation and therefore more possibility of turning to crime. The average age of the convicts was 27[51] and two-thirds were of single status.[52] Up to one in four women was a prostitute[53] and most prostitutes came from an urban area.[54] Their former occupations ranged over a wide variety of types of servants.[55] Both Payne and Robson agreed on the rate of convictions. Two-thirds had been convicted of an offence before the one for which they were transported.[56]

Payne concluded that of the female convicts, half did not deserve the label of 'utterly irreclaimable and worthless'.[57] He found in a sample of 150 convicts sent to Van Diemen's Land between 1843-1853, 44.9 per cent either had no conviction or very few subsequently in the colony; more than one-third had no recorded conviction apart from the one for which they were transported; 43 per cent were married in the colony; many of the offences that did occur indicated that the penal and probation system was inadequately administered, especially with a view to rehabilitation; frequent colonial newspaper reports ignored the fact that one out of every three female convicts was rehabilitated in the colony.[58] He concluded there was a 'nucleus' which was not habitually criminal. Indeed, the fact that they married soon in the colony, and gave very little trouble to the authorities, underlined their eligibility as colonial wives and the general efficacy of marriage.[59]

Robson, on the other hand, argued that female convicts were generally of a 'bad' character, 'an indifferent batch of settlers'. He based his argument on their past records in the United Kingdom and Ireland showing that over half (52 per cent) of the women were transported for a category called 'other larcenies' and a smaller proportion (18 per cent) for theft of wearing apparel.[60] Robson's study was disappointing also for the fact that it contained unhistorical moralistic assertions such as: the women 'convicted by the Glasgow Court of Justiciary were the worst of a bad lot'.[61]

Statistical Evidence

Despite this moralistic tendency, Robson's work, together with Payne's, marked a considerable breakthrough in the study of female crime. For the first time, an attempt was made to argue a case through social statistics, to use evidence of a far less ideological nature than that of previous studies.

Then came the work of J.M. Beattie in 1975 which to date is the most scholarly investigation based on statistics available.[62]

Beattie aimed to show the pattern of offences committed by women and to suggest what they revealed about the place of women in society and the nature of crime in seventeenth and eighteenth century England. He examined judicial records of two south-eastern counties, Surrey (including the city of London) and Sussex. He found that:

. Eighty per cent of those charged with felonies over all these years were men; that is, in the categories of property offences and personal violence men outnumbered women 3 to 1.

• Women committed the same crimes as men, and as with men, about half of the charges laid were related to property offences, while crimes against the person totalled one third.

Women's crime was greater in the urban areas than rural areas. Women's crime also accounted for a much higher proportion of the total crime in the city than in the countryside.

Although the differences Beattie found between urban and rural areas derive in part from the greater opportunity for theft in urban areas, and to some extent from age and sex structure of the urban population, they also, more fundamentally, can be seen to reflect differing social and economic situations of women in London, on the one hand, and in rural Surrey and Sussex on the other. Differences in patterns of crime in urban and rural areas derived from, and are evidence of, differences in the nature of women's lives and work in these different settings, in the range of their social contacts and their economic opportunities and difficulties. They thus provide clues to the effects of changes in women's social and economic position as well as to the nature of women's crime.

The rural setting was deeply deferential. Social authority of a landed gentleman, combined with legal powers of a magistrate, plus intimate local knowledge resulted in a degree of control over peoples' lives, especially of the young, that could never be achieved in a large urban parish. Rural life was especially restrictive for women. Young girls were bound into service during adolescence as house servants and farmworkers. In a smaller and tighter rural community, their behaviour could be more closely scrutinised and courtship customs made more binding than in the more impersonal world of a large urban parish.[63]

In urban areas, checks imposed on women both by the community and the authorities could only operate less effectively. This relative freedom lay behind dismay at the evil effects of city life, expressed by so many commentators in the eighteenth century. By working more outside the home and through a social situation that made possible frequent and wider ranging human contacts, women's lives changed relatively more sharply than men's in transition from the countryside to the city.[64] In the city, Beattie argues that the influence of parents was weakened, control of masters over the personal lives of their servants less binding and authority of magistrates less compelling. The enlarged freedom of the city, and enlarged context of women's lives there, explains why women accounted for a much larger proportion of prosecutions for personal violence in the urban parishes of Surrey than in the rest of the county or in Sussex.[65]

The principal feature of female crime against property was not its consistently high level, but its frequent and sizable fluctuation. This suggests that most theft was the work of people who chose to steal or not, according to their circumstances and their ability to support themselves. Fluctuation in crimes seemed clearly to be tied to economic conditions, and to two factors in particular: prices of consumer goods, especially food; and availability of work.[66]

There was a striking relationship in London between the numbers of prosecutions and years of war and peace. During war, numbers of prosecutions declined. Conversely, the greatest increases were immediately after the war. Beattie argues that there is a clear connection between the amount of theft in the city and availability of work, for during the war, large pools of casual labour were absorbed. After war and the forces were demobilised, a glut of unemployed existed.[67] Theft by single women and widows fluctuated most violently in periods of economic change.[68] Fluctuations in women's property crimes, however, were less severe than men's and in some periods changes in crime did not parallel men's at all. This reflected the degree to which women in need could turn to men for support, or would turn to prostitution.[69] Patterns of women's crime against property in rural parishes of Surrey and in Sussex showed levels were much lower and fluctuations less extreme. Women were only infrequently prosecuted for theft in the countryside. Women did not seem to turn to theft as men apparently did in the deepening economic crisis in the countryside in the last two decades of the century.[70] Overall, Beattie concludes, patterns and levels of women's crime in the city were much closer to those of men than in the rural parishes of Surrey and Sussex.[71]

Conclusion

This discussion of women's crime has been confined within the definition of crime given by the state and recorded in the legal code. It has not questioned whether the activities of women that have been labelled as crimes deserve to be. From the point of view of working-class women, of course, many of the 'crimes' associated with prostitution (soliciting, disorderly conduct and the like) are manifestly discriminatory from the perspectives of both sex and class. The fact that women are arrested and gaoled for these activities may itself be regarded as a crime if one takes the interests of the victims of such laws. This is not to argue that all women's crime is simply a definition by the state — a proportion of it is crime directed at other women or other working-class people.

Within the parameters of state-defined criminality, a number of conclusions about women follow. The dominant liberal philosophy on which nineteenth century law reform was based — that of the criminal as an independent, reasoning individual, consciously committing crime for calculated gain — did not include women within its ambit. There were two main theories of female criminality. Both were deterministic. The first, deriving initially from evangelical penal reformers and later complemented by radicals such as Engels and Mayhew, held that women turned to crime following social or economic misfortune. Their environment determined their actions. The second, deriving from the Victorian double standard in social and sexual activities, and receiving a fillip from the concept of Social Darwinism, held that female crime arose when aberrations to women's biology and psychology occurred. Flaws in the 'true' nature of their womanhood determined their criminality.

Modern historical studies have tended to confirm the social deterministic position. Although female criminality has remained considerably less common than that of men, it does increase in response to certain conditions. Women who live in less restrictive, more anonymous urban environments, who are more independent of male protectors but more dependent on the labour market and thus more subject to the vagaries of the industrial economy, are more likely to turn to crime. In other words, female crime has increased the more that women's lives have resembled those of men.

The history of female criminality demonstrates how theories

of the causes of crime have determined the nature of the penal system that society has established. The response people have made to crime has depended upon their ideas of what has caused it. This has important implications for the way we ought to respond to crime today. If the social determinist position is correct, the appropriate response to be made to crime by women is to change the social environment causing it. This means eliminating poverty, inequality, unemployment and sexism. Crime is produced by our society. Only social transformation can put an end to it.

---

1. J.M. Beattie, 'The Criminality of Women in Eighteenth Century England', *Journal of Social History*, 8, Summer, 1975; Carol Smart, *Women, Crime and Criminology*, Routledge and Kegan Paul, London, 1976; Mary Hartman, 'Crime and the Respectable Woman: Towards a Pattern of Middle Class Female Criminality in Nineteenth Century France and England', *Feminist Studies*, 2, No. 1, 1974; Mary Hartman, *Victorian Murderesses: A True History of Thirteen Respectable French and English Women Accused of Unspeakable Crimes*, Schocken Books, 1977; H.S. Payne, 'A Statistical Study of Female Convicts in Tasmania, 1843-1853', *Tasmanian Historical Research Association Papers and Proceedings*, 9, 1961; L.L. Robson, *Convict Settlers in Australia*, Melbourne, 1965 (chapter on female convicts based on article 'The Origins of Women Convicts Sent to Australia', *Historical Studies*, No. 11, November 1963); Leon Radzinowicz, *History of English Criminal Law*, 4 vols., 1948-68; Ann Smith, *Women in Prison: A Study of Prison Methods*, London, 1962; J.J. Tobias, *Crime and Industrial Society in the Nineteenth Century*, New York, 1966; J.R. and D.J. Walkowitz, 'We are not Beasts of the Field: Prostitution and the Poor in Plymouth and Southampton under the Contagious Diseases Act', in M.S. Hartman and Lois Banners (eds.), *Clio's Consciousness Raised*, New York, 1974; Estelle Freedman, 'Their Sisters Keepers: Historical Perspective of Female Correctional Institutions in the United States, 1870-1900', *Feminist Studies*, 2, No. 1, 1974, pp. 77-95.

2. Greenwald (1958) and Davis (1971) cited by C. Smart, *op. cit.*, p. 18.

3. Douglas Hay, 'Property, Authority and the Criminal Law', in Douglas Hay, Peter Linebaugh, E.P. Thompson (eds.), *Albion's Fatal Tree*, Allen Lane, London, 1975, p. 18.

4. Cesare Beccaria, *On Crimes and Punishments*, trans. Henry Paolucci, New York, 1963.

5. K. Thomas, 'The Double Standard', *Journal of the History of Ideas*, 1959, pp. 195-216; Brian Harrison, 'Underneath the Victorians', *Victorian Studies*, 3, March 1967, pp. 239-262; F.B. Smith, 'Sexuality in Britain 1800-1900', *University of Newcastle Historical Journal*, 2, No. 3, February 1974; Francoise Basch, *Relative Creatures*, London, 1974.

6. For another instance of the double standard related to female intem-

perance, see Elizabeth Windschuttle, 'Women, Class and Temperance: Moral Reform in Eastern Australia, 1832-1857', *The Push from the Bush*, No. 3, May 1979, Journal of Social History of the 1838 collective of the Australian Bicentennial History Project, University of Western Australia.

7. For example, abduction of heiresses, L. Radzinowicz, *op. cit.*, Vol. 1, pp. 436-437.

8. F.K. Prochaska, 'Women in English Philanthropy 1790-1830', *International Review of Social History*, Vol. 19, part 3, 1974.

9. Elizabeth Fry, *Observations in Visiting, Superintendence and Government of Female Prisoners*, London, 1827, p. 8.

10. E. Jeffrey, 'Prison Discipline', *Edinburgh Review*, Vol. 30, 1818, p. 484.

11. E. Fry, *op. cit.*

12. Darling to Murray, *Historical Records of Australia*, Vol. 14, 18 February 1829, pp. 656-657.

13. *Sydney Gazette*, 3 January 1829, p. 4; 8 January 1829; Darling to Murray, *Historical Records of Australia*, Vol. 14, 18 February 1829, pp. 656-657.

14. A.G.L. Shaw, *Convicts and the Colonies*, London, 1966, p. 135.

15. Journal of Lady Jane Franklin, 1841-1843, Tasmanian Archives.

16. Matilda Wrench (ed.), *Visits to Female Prisons at Home and Abroad*, London, 1852, pp. 304-307.

17. Harriet Martineau, 'Life in the Criminal Class', *Edinburgh Review*, 1865, p. 363.

18. *Ibid.*, pp. 366-367.

19. *Ibid.*, p. 364.

20. *Ibid.*

21. *Ibid.*, pp. 363-364.

22. Frederick Engels, *The Condition of the Working Class in England*, Oxford, 1958, pp. 144-145.

23. *Ibid.*, p. 145.

24. *Ibid.*, p. 232.

25. Peter Quennell (ed.), *London's Underworld*, Middlesex, 1950, p. 127.

26. Francoise Basch, *op. cit.*, p. 199.

27. *Ibid.*

28. E.M. Sigsworth and T.J. Wyke, 'A Study of Victorian Prostitution and Venereal Disease', in M. Vicinus (ed.), *Suffer and Be Still*, Ontario, 1972, p. 219.

29. Constance Rover, *Love, Morals and the Feminists*, London, 1960, p. 77.

30. Eliza Orme, 'Our Female Criminals', *Fortnightly Review*, Vol. 69, 1898, pp. 790-796.

31. *Ibid.*, p. 795.

32. E. Freedman, *op. cit.*, pp. 90-91.

33. Elizabeth Windschuttle, 'The Female School of Industry, Sydney, 1826-1847', History IV Honours thesis, University of Sydney, 1977.

33a. Anon, 'Criminal Women', *Cornhill Magazine*, 1866.

33b. *Ibid.*, p. 153.

50 Women and Crime

34. Carol Smart, *op. cit.*, p. 31.
35. *Ibid.*
36. Ann Smith, *op. cit.*, p. 4.
37. Carol Smart, *op. cit.*, pp. 31-32.
38. Ann Smith, *op. cit.*, p. 4.
39. Carol Smart, *op. cit.*, p. 32.
40. *Ibid.*
41. *Ibid.*, p. 192.
42. Leon Radzinowicz, *Ideology and Crime*, London, 1968, pp. 38-39.
43. *Ibid.*, chapters 3 and 4.
44. Leon Radzinowicz, *History of English Criminal Law*, Vol. I, *op. cit.*, pp. 11, 12, 209, 211-213, 239.
45. *Ibid.*, p. 11.
46. *Ibid.*, Vol. III, p. 337.
47. *Ibid.*, Vol. III, pp. 19-21, 243-245, 276-281, 287-291.
48. H.S. Payne, *op. cit.*, p. 56.
49. *Ibid.*
50. *Ibid.*, p. 57; L. Robson, *op. cit.*, p. 75.
51. Payne, *ibid.*, p. 66; Robson, *ibid.*, p. 75.
52. Robson, *ibid.*, p. 75.
53. Payne, *op. cit.*, p. 59; Robson, *ibid.*, p. 78.
54. Payne, *ibid.*, p. 59.
55. Robson, *op. cit.*, p. 76.
56. Robson, *ibid.*, p. 76; Payne, *op. cit.*, p. 59.
57. Robson, *ibid.*, p. 74.
58. Payne, *op. cit.*, pp. 65-66.
59. *Ibid.*, p. 59.
60. Robson, *op. cit.*, pp. 78-81.
61. *Ibid.*, p. 76.
62. J.M. Beattie, *op. cit.*
63. *Ibid.*, p. 99.
64. *Ibid.*, p. 102.
65. *Ibid.*
66. *Ibid.*, p. 103.
67. *Ibid.*
68. *Ibid.*, p. 107.
69. *Ibid.*, p. 108.
70. *Ibid.*, pp. 107-108.
71. *Ibid.*, p. 109.

4 The Mythinterpretation of Female Crime

ROSLYN OMODEI

Today it would probably be considered that there is no room for myth in a society such as ours which is oriented to the development of science and technology. Myths are usually connected, in the minds of the western world, with traditional or perhaps medieval societies. However, women's studies have recently unearthed a multitude of popular beliefs, stereotypes and myths, ranging from 'women can't do mathematics' through to the universality of the maternal instinct, which have had a profound effect on the socialisation of females in our society and on the opportunities that have been made available for women in the social sphere. Myths about women and their innate capacities have pervaded every aspect of society; they have effected and been perpetrated by many specific elements of our social organisation. This is as true of the legal order as it is of the education system. This paper aims to examine in detail the perpetration and maintenance of one of the most pervasive of myths relating to female crime — that female delinquency is predominantly sexual delinquency.

The Significance of Myth

> Myth fulfils in primitive culture an indispensable function: it expresses, enhances and codifies beliefs; it safeguards and enforces morality; it vouches for the efficiency of ritual and contains practical rules for the guidance of man. Myth is thus a vital ingredient of human civilization; it is not an idle tale, but a hard-worked active force; it is not an intellectual explanation or an artistic imagery, but a pragmatic charter of primitive faith and moral wisdom.
>
> (Malinowski, 1926: 19)

Myths become part of a society's system of values and beliefs. Myths can therefore have profound effects on social organisation and may play a significant role in the education of the young into the ways of the society. An interpretation of human behaviour in the context of myth is not then, simply a misinterpretation of that behaviour. An interpretation through myth can be far more sinister than that because, as Malinowski argues, a myth orders and validates a particular world-view, it is a 'pragmatic charter', it redefines experience in terms of a set of moral beliefs which are vital for the social organisation of society. In validating a particular world view myth plays an important role in defining types of behaviour as either acceptable or unacceptable. The more pervading and longstanding the myth, the more behaviour consistent with the myth, or prescribed by the myth will be taken as 'natural'.

Malinowski's discussion of myth was explicitly in terms of the role of myth in traditional societies. However the phenomenon of myth is not so far removed from our so-called modern society. It is not difficult to locate concepts in our society which express, enhance and codify beliefs, which safeguard and enforce morality and which become practical guides for behaviour in our society. Many of the stereotypes which exist in our society serve this function. They act as models, either positive or negative models, and are used to reinforce, to challenge, to teach, to negate behaviour patterns in such a way as to preserve the dominant moral codes and belief systems of our society.

There is a difference of course, between myth and stereotypes, even though both myth and stereotypes do perform many similar functions. To put the relationship in a simplistic way, we may say that a stereotype which does not have a basis in the observable behaviour of individuals is a myth. Not all myths involve stereotypes, not all stereotypes are myths. However, some myths may develop from stereotypes that do have a basis in human experience, that is, some myths exist which support stereotypes by emphasising the undesirability of behaviour which does not conform to the stereotype. It is this relation which exists between the stereotype of femininity and the myths surrounding female crime and delinquency. Certainly the efficacy of stereotype in our society is never so clear as in the case of the stereotypes of masculinity and femininity. The stereotypes of masculinity and femininity provide us with reference points for assessing the behaviour of adult males and females in general, and help shape the expectations and behaviour of our adolescent males and females in particular.

The typical adult woman in our society — noting that typical does not necessarily mean statistically most common — is oriented to the domestic sphere; her major concerns are held to be the physical and emotional wellbeing of other family members. The woman has the major responsibility for child raising. She is the moral guardian of the family and of society. The adult woman's role as wife and mother is defined through her sexuality and reproductive capacities; it is the adult woman in the family situation who is defined as the one responsible for the moral development of her children and for the moral atmosphere of the home. As an extension of this stereotype, the adolescent girl soon learns to orient her behaviour towards the adult role of wife and mother, and so, a major occupation of adolescent girls is generally assumed to be that of finding a suitable boyfriend. Hand in hand with this, though, the adolescent girl is also given to understand that it is her responsibility to control the development of that relationship, both physically and emotionally. In the process of developing heterosexual relationships, the adolescent girl is also expected to be able to exercise constraint over the direction of that development. Maintaining society's standards as to what is right and wrong in a heterosexual relationship is more clearly thought to be the responsibility of the girl than of the boy.

Whether or not this is a fair representation of the actual activity of adolescent girls is not the issue here. The point is rather, that this is certainly a commonly held conceptualisation of the adolescent female's central concerns, and one which, as we shall see later has had a significant effect on explanations of female delinquency. For the sake of brevity this conceptualisation of the role of women in our society will be referred to subsequently as the 'femininity stereotype'.

Before investigating the role of stereotypes of womanhood in relation to female offenders, it would be useful to have a quick look at the stereotypes of male behaviour in our society.

In contrast to the adult woman, the adult male is expected to be oriented to the public sphere — to the sphere of work, economics and politics. The man has responsibility for provision of the means of existence, he is the breadwinner, the major wage earner in the family. The man's role as breadwinner is defined through his work role in the social workforce. The man is expected to take responsibility to provide the material needs of his family; his main goals are thereby portrayed to be occupational and financial goals. The adolescent boy, then, in an extention of this stereotype, is concerned with establishing himself in the workforce and in acquiring the material possessions necessary for gaining status in the competitive world outside the domestic sphere. Once again, for the sake of brevity, this conceptualisation will be referred to as the 'masculinity stereotype'.

The Female Offender

Unfortunately, what are presented here as the stereotypes of the adult male and female roles in our society and the consequent expected behaviours of male and female adolescents have actually been used as **explanations** for the differential rates of male and female delinquency in the past. The interpretation of female delinquency in the context of the femininity stereotype assumes that the main goals of adolescent girls are what is termed relational goals, that is, they are aimed towards the development of stable heterosexual relationships. Any criminal activity on the part of the adolescent girl has then been seen in terms of the inability to achieve these goals; and criminal activity on the part of an adult woman is seen to contravene her responsibility as moral guardian of family and society. Similarly the delinquent activities of boys are explained in terms of the inability to gain status in society through achievement of occupational and financial goals.

The use of the femininity stereotype to explain the delinquent activity of girls has resulted in several myths developing regarding female delinquency. The most pervasive of these myths is that **female delinquency is predominantly sexual delinquency**. A close examination of this assertion not only supports the contention that it is myth, but also highlights many of the consequences that the acceptance of this myth has had on both the criminal justice system and the treatment of young offenders.

The creation of the belief that female delinquency is predominantly sexual delinquency lies in the historical development of both criminology theory and of the juvenile justice system. The analysis of female criminality *per se* has its theoretical basis in the work of Lombroso and his associates of the 1890s. Lombroso argued that the significantly lower rate of female offending than male offending can be explained by the social processes of law enforcement. In support of this claim though, he argued that if the prostitutive activities of women and girls were included in criminal statistics, they would appear as criminal as their male counterparts (1968: 192). Here we find two important assertions — first, that prostitutive activities constitute an area of female deviance that has no male counterpart, and second, that a large part of female deviance is sexual in nature. Lombroso also located the cause of criminality in the biological makeup of the individuals concerned. Thus, by the very physical nature of women, they were more likely to be sexual deviants than criminals.

It is clear that Lombroso's explanation of female criminality has the popular conception, or rather misconception, of the role of women in society as its main reference point. The social organisation of work which denied lower class women any access to wage labour other than factory work or outwork (when the women worked up to 16 hours a day in their own homes for a pittance) was not considered to be relevant to the deviant activity of these women. Rather, Lombroso, and many who followed him, concentrated on the position of women as defined by their sexuality rather than as individuals who were often relegated to the most inequitable positions in society.

In some ways Lombroso's explanation can be interpreted as a product of the era in which he lived. And it is true that the work of Lombroso and his associates is generally considered to be a sad episode in criminology theory. Unfortunately, though, where female criminality is concerned Lombroso's work has remained the touchstone of criminology theory until very recently.

The year 1950 saw the publication of Otto Pollak's *The Criminality of Women*. The spirit of Pollak's work is consistent with that of Lombroso. Pollak maintains that the level of crime committed by women is substantially lower than is reflected in statistics available. The lower official figures on female crime is, however, explained by the fact that the victims, police and courts are less prepared to act against a woman than a man. The interesting part of Pollak's work lies in the explanation of this discrimination in favour of women that exists in the criminal justice system.

Women are less likely to be charged and convicted, Pollak argues, because they are better able to conceal their crime, they are also more likely to be the instigators of crime than the perpetrators of crime. Their ability to conceal their criminal activity is due to the cunning and deceit which are natural to women. Pollak locates this ability for dishonesty in the passive role women play in sexual intercourse where, unlike the man, women are able to conceal sexual arousal or to make a good pretence of sexual arousal. Pollak argues that the woman's ability to conceal or manufacture response gives women a basis on which to deceive men in all respects. Women, Pollak contends, by their sexual nature have an ambiguous attitude to honesty and deceit. The basis of female criminality then is sexual in nature.

There are many interesting shifts in Pollak's arguments. The significance of his argument lies in explaining the relationship of the criminal justice system to women in terms of innate personality characteristics of women, which are due to women's sexuality. All female criminality then, has its basis ultimately in women's sexuality. All female criminality is some expression of sexual dishonesty. In focusing on women's sexuality as the main cause of female criminality, Pollak not only ignored the dynamics of sexual politics where a woman may be expected to engage in sexual activity without her acquiesence but, more importantly, he, like Lombroso, ignored the social constraints and pressures placed on women. Pollak fails to consider that women are not guided solely by sexual instincts; he fails to recognise that women act in the social sector of our society and are subjected to many of the social demands to which men are subjected. The need to maintain a reasonable standard of living while being denied financial support and experiencing unequal opportunities to participate in the social workforce is not considered by Pollak to be a significant cause of female criminality. I would argue that it is these sorts of structural constraints, inherent to the social organisation of our society which need to be the starting point in an explanation of female criminality, rather than the assumed sexual instincts of women.

The large 1950s increase in sociological interest in delinquency did little to dispel the characterisation of female deviance initiated by Lombroso and elaborated by Pollak. In fact much of the work done in the 1950s and since, tends to support the interpretation of female delinquency as primarily sexual in nature, and certainly many of the assumptions about the inherent nature of woman and the role of women in society were accepted as valid.

The developments of the 1950s did aim to explain delinquency in terms of the inherent inequalities of the social structure of

Western industrialised societies. In this sense the work of the structuralists of the 1950s was a considerable advance on previous theories which focused on some aspect of physiology or psychology as determinant. Talcott Parsons' studies of American family life have played an important part in the development of delinquency theory. Parsons identified the social goals for adolescent boys and girls.

> Boys must make their own way, achieving status and income in a competitive occupational system. Most girls can look forward to support by a husband, but they must choose a husband on their own responsibility. . . A girl must 'catch' an acceptable man by exercise of her own feminine attraction in sharp competition with other girls and without adult support.
>
> (Parsons, 1954: 344)

Based on the acceptance of Parsons' identification of the social goals of adolescents, Cohen and other delinquency theorists, developed the concept of role frustration in an attempt to explain delinquency in terms of social factors rather than biological or psychological factors. Cohen and other subculture theorists suggest that certain groups in society, in particular the working-class and ethnic minorities, experience difficulty in achieving what are essentially middle-class goals.

However, Cohen does not discuss delinquency of girls as a subcultural phenomenon, rather he uses the premises of his argument to exclude female delinquency from his theoretical framework. Subcultures, he argues, develop to provide a means of goal gratification to working-class boys who are unable to achieve middle-class occupational/financial goals by socially legitimate means. Cohen does argue that some girls will also experience inability to achieve societal goals; however, following Parsons, Cohen identifies 'the female's situation in society, the admiration, respect and property she commands, [to] depend to a much greater degree on the kinds of relationships she establishes with members of the opposite sex' (1955: 141).

> The most conspicuous difference [between male and female delinquency] is that male delinquency. . . is versatile, whereas female delinquency is relatively specialized. It consists overwhelmingly of sexual delinquency. . .
>
> We have said that a female's status, security, response and the acceptability of her self-image as a woman or girl depend upon the establishment of satisfactory relationships with the other sex. To this end sexu-

ality, variously employed, is the most versatile and single sovereign means.
(Cohen, 1955: 144)

Since female delinquency is primarily involved in sexuality, the concept of subculture, which implies group delinquency, is inappropriate. The choices informing a girl's delinquent activity will be between socially structured alternatives — for 'quick dividends' or 'the long-run goal'. Cohen suggests that it is unlikely that a subculture of values and beliefs would operate in relation to this type of adolescent behaviour. The problem is posed as being more largely one for the individual girl herself.

Clearly Cohen's work perpetuates the 'female delinquency is predominantly sexual delinquency' interpretation. In emphasising the problem as 'one for the individual girl herself' Cohen denies the social basis of female delinquency. Female delinquent behaviour is thus portrayed as the behaviour of an individual who has made the wrong choices, as individual failure, rather than as the outcome of the social pressures and constraints which the girl experiences. Cohen emphasised the social nature of male delinquency, and yet was either unable or unwilling to extend this social analysis to female delinquency. In so doing Cohen allowed the interpretation of female delinquency as indicative of individual troubles to continue. The social causes of female delinquency were consequently denied.

The literature on delinquency which followed Cohen often based the discussion of female delinquency on a premise similar to Cohen's, namely, that female delinquency is primarily sexual delinquency. This formulation of delinquency in girls is still largely accepted today, for example in his book *Social Deviance,* Robert Bell asks:

> If one put aside all female delinquency directly and indirectly related to sexual activity what would be left? It might be. . . that generally female delinquency is really sexual delinquency.
> (Bell, 1976: 358)

At this point, we should look at the behaviour of female offenders to see how close the fit is between theory and fact.

We can see from Tables 1 and 2 that Queensland's official statistics on female delinquency do not support the statement that Robert Bell makes, since about half the female appearances before the children's courts are on account of offences committed. On

Table 1: Court appearances for females 8 years of age and over Queensland, 1973-74

	Number	Percentage
Appearance for offences (as distinct from number of charges)	339	48.6
Care and control and related appearances	358	51.4
	697	100.0

Table 2: Breakdown of offences committed by female juveniles Queensland, 1973-74

Offences	Number	Percentage
Stealing	173	45.8
Traffic offences	31	8.2
Liquor offences	21	5.6
Receiving	21	5.6
Illegal use of motor vehicle	21	5.6
Break, enter and steal	16	4.2
All other offences	95	25.0
	378	100.0

Source: J. Fielding, 1977.

the other hand the fact that half of the appearances are for care and control and related orders tends to give some credence to the argument that a significant proportion of female delinquency is sexual delinquency. Indeed, many writers have equated care and control appearances with sexual delinquency. Work done in America (Chesney-Lind, 1973) explores the use and interpretation of care and control applications focusing on this element of the organisation of the juvenile justice as the main source of the 'female delinquency is predominantly sexual delinquency' myth. Charges such as 'in need of care and control' or 'exposed to moral danger' implicitly allow interpretation of sexual misbehaviour. These charges may often be used to modify another charge or used in addition to a charge, such as larceny if the girl is thought to have been sexually active. It is also argued that this modification of charges or substitution of care and control and related charges occurs more frequently where girls are concerned than where boys are concerned. This could reflect qualitatively different types of behaviour by boys and girls, but it is more likely that this situation reflects substantially different attitudes of law enforcement officials to male and female delinquents. Girls are more likely to receive care and control orders than are boys, however there has never been any suggestion that the sexual activity of girls is not heterosexual in nature. Rather it is more likely that the sex difference in care and control and related charges is indicative of a double standard of morality than a fair reflection of the actual behaviour of girls and boys. In this way the juvenile justice system is reflecting the concerns of the wider community, the concerns which are consistent with the femininity stereotype. Consequently if we are trying to find evidence which questions the assertion that a significant proportion of female delinquency is sexual delinquency it may be difficult to do so using official statistics if these necessarily reflect the dominant assumptions of the wider society.

Fortunately, though, juvenile justice is not necessarily organised in this way. The situation in South Australia is quite different from that of Queensland, and of any other Australian state. In South Australia the *Juvenile Courts Act,* 1971 allows that children under the age of 16 years will not be charged with the commission of an offence, but will be alleged to be in need of care and control, and to have committed an offence. In this way all children under 16 years of age, male or female, are considered to be in need of care and control if they have committed an offence. This charge cannot, then, be made arbitrarily, or at the discretion of law enforcement officers, nor can it be made more frequently against girls than boys. In the statistics compiled by the Department for Community Welfare in South Australia the alleged need of care and control is taken as given, and the offence only is recorded — the procedure is the same for boys and for girls. This is a very important feature of the data from South Australia, since the criticism of sexualisation of offences does not hold.

The data I will look at refers to the year 1975-76. For the year under consideration there were a total of 8,345 cases before either the Juvenile Aid Panels or the Juvenile Court in South Australia. Girls accounted for 21 per cent of these appearances, and boys for 79 per cent of appearances. As a proportion of the relevant age group, this represents 1 per cent of girls and 3.5 per cent of boys. The offending male to female ratio of nearly 1:4 indicates a higher female participation rate than the figures for Queensland presented by Fielding (1977). However, this finding is consistent with the work of other investigators in Australia (Fielding, 1977), and for America and England (Giallombardo, 1976). Table 3 shows the offences committed by juveniles in South Australia, in the year 1975-76, by sex and category of offence. From the table it is clear that the largest group of offences for both girls and boys is larceny offences. The category of sex related offences has often included neglect, truancy and care and control charges. I have kept these categories of offences separate here, because as has already been mentioned, all children, male and female, under the age of 16 years are alleged to be in need of care and control and this charge will only appear where no offence has been committed — usually for children under school age. Even if sex related offences were combined with offences under the *Juvenile Courts Act,* only 65 girls, less than 4 per cent, from a total of 1,717 girls can be accounted for.

Table 3: Offences committed by juveniles
South Australia, 1975-76

	Offence Category	Girls Number	Girls Percentage	Boys Number	Boys Percentage
I	Against Person	50	2.9	321	4.8
II	Larceny	1,176	68.5	1,661	25.1
III	Other Property	152	8.9	1,625	24.5
IV	Road and Motor	93	5.4	1,415	21.3
V	Sex Related*	2	0.1	108	1.6
VI	Juvenile Courts Act**	63	3.7	79	1.2
VII	Good Order	84	4.9	618	9.3
VIII	Other	97	5.6	801	12.2
		1,717	100.0	6,628	100.0

* For the purpose of this study, this category includes rape, carnal knowledge, indecent interference, indecent exposure, gross indecency, indecent assault, attempted rape, buggery, solicit for prostitution and live on the earnings of prostitution.

** For the purpose of this study, this category includes the charges in need of care and control, neglected child, uncontrollable (*Juvenile Courts Act*) and truancy (*Education Act*).

It should be noted, however, that there are only two cases where girls were charged with sex related offences as such, and neither of these involved prostitution or soliciting. Clearly then, this data cannot support the proposition that female delinquency is primarily sexual delinquency, but rather indicates that **female delinquency primarily consists of petty property offences, and not of sexual delinquency**; and furthermore that sexual delinquency is the smallest category of offence committed by female juveniles. In addition, contrary to the masculinity/femininity stereotypes, boys are more likely to commit sex offences.

This pattern of offence obviously requires a different explanation from that based on the femininity stereotype. The differences shown here between Queensland and South Australia require us to seriously question the assumptions inherent in the organisation of the juvenile justice system. The role of the juvenile justice in defining the 'nature' of female delinquency is of course not the only incident of this phenomena. The social organisation of juvenile justice has been an area of academic inquiry since the mid 1960s when Cicourel's (1968) examination of the juvenile justice system highlighted the effect that the organisation of the system has on what is officially considered the nature and extent of juvenile delinquency. In other words the organisation of juvenile justice plays a not insignificant part in the definition of the 'problem' of juvenile delinquency. The Australian situation strongly suggests that the organisation of the juvenile justice system has a large effect on the official nature of female delinquency, in particular whether a significant proportion of female delinquency is sexual delinquency.

More support for the conclusion that the organisation of the juvenile justice system is a significant factor in the nature of female delinquency comes from England and Scotland. Carol Smart summarises the situation in England and Wales:

> [There] are special categories of 'offences' which are applicable only to adolescents which require special attention. These 'offences', **which are defined as non-criminal** in the UK, usually relate to truancy from school, being beyond the control of parents or being in moral danger... The statistics indicate that, of these 'offences', those most frequently involving girls are, in the UK, being in moral danger... This is significant because... [these] offences have connotations of sexual promiscuity. Consequently the statistics present a picture in which female juvenile delinquency appears to be mainly sexual while male juvenile delinquency is apparently

non-sexual but more aggressive and assertive.

(Smart, 1976: 11, my emphasis)

This situation seems to have been exacerbated by the *Children and Young Persons Act,* 1969, where the distinction between offenders and non-offenders in the 10-17 year age group was abolished for the purposes of treatment.[1] The effect of this is that the non-criminal care and control and related charges are treated by the juvenile justice system in the same way that criminal offences are treated. Consequently while these charges are formally non-criminal, for the young persons involved there is effectively no difference; being exposed to moral danger is just as delinquent as theft or assault.

In Scotland, on the other hand, the situation is quite different. Table 4 gives the breakdown of reasons for appearance in Scotland in 1968.

Table 4: Pattern of female juvenile offending
Scotland, 1968

Offence	Number	Percentage
Theft	203	68.8
Breaking and Entering	12	4.1
Vandalism	5	1.7
Breach of Peace	28	9.5
Juvenile Status Offences*	27	9.2
Sexual Offences*	4	1.3
Other Offences	16	5.4
	295	100.0

* These categories are similar to those given for South Australia in Table 3.
Source: D. May, 1977.

As with the South Australian data, nearly 70 per cent of offences are larceny offences and a relatively small number of offences are juvenile status offences or sexual offences. David May, in his Scottish study, observes:

> Far from being characterized by sex-related offences, only a minute 1.3 per cent of all offences recorded against the girls in the Aberdeen sample fell into the category of sexual offences *per se.* Even if we were to add on to this the juvenile status and breach of the peace offences — and

this would cover a very mixed bag of delinquent behaviour — this would still only include 20 per cent of the girls' offences that might loosely be regarded as indicative of 'incorrigibility' or 'waywardness'.

(May, 1977: 204)

The differences between female juvenile offending patterns in Scotland and England which have been demonstrated here are similar to the differences which were established earlier for South Australia and Queensland. There are two possible explanations for the differences we find here. The first explanation is based on the theoretical analyses of female delinquency which we examined earlier. According to these theories female delinquency is predominantly sexual delinquency and is a result of the adolescent girl being unable to achieve the appropriate societal goals, namely, those of establishing warm, stable, heterosexual relationships. Extending this analysis we would expect that where female delinquency was not sexual delinquency, but rather predominantly petty property offences, that the societal goals of girls would be substantially different from those existing where female delinquency does seem to be predominantly sexual delinquency. Accordingly we would expect marked differences in the social goals of girls in South Australia and Queensland and marked differences for England and Scotland; similar social goals of girls in Queensland and England and similarities in South Australia and Scotland. While not denying that some similarities and differences may exist, I would suggest that they would not be of the order necessary to explain the direction and, especially, the strength of the differences in female delinquent behaviour which we have noted here. Indeed with the uniform influence of the mass media industries one would expect a very close fit between the social goals of girls in all four places.

We would then have to reject the explanation that the differences in female offending in different places reflects the different social goals of girls. At the same time however it may well be that the wider social interpretations of the behaviour of girls differ. Societal expectations of girls behaviour as oriented to relational goals could lead to the interpretation of female offending according to this stereotype. More precisely one would expect that female delinquency was officially considered sexual delinquency in those places where female adolescent behaviour was interpreted in terms of the femininity stereotype. Consequently the second explanation, that the nature and extent of female delinquency varies from place to place according to the social organisation of juvenile justice in operation, must then be accepted. In the absence of argument supporting the particular cultural differences necessary to explain the patterns of female juvenile offending which we have seen, we need instead to look at the ways in which the behaviour of girls is interpreted and processed by law enforcement officials. In this way the extent to which the juvenile justice system elaborates the masculinity and femininity stereotypes can be more clearly seen. If the actual behaviour of girls is not so different in South Australia and Queensland, then whether or not this behaviour is interpreted in the context of the femininity stereotype becomes critical.

The comparison of the official statistics relating to female delinquency, where different systems of juvenile justice exist, requires us to look at the organisation of these systems as the initial step in the attempt to explain female delinquency. In order to retain a sociological perspective, we then need to investigate the deviant activity of girls, whether sexual or criminal, in terms of the social pressures, constraints and limitations they experience. We need to see the delinquent girl as a social product to the same extent as delinquent boys have been considered 'social products'.

Implications

Where the organisation of juvenile justice perpetrates the interpretation of female delinquency as predominantly sexual delinquency, one would also expect to find implications for the treatment of young female offenders. The most conspicuous implication is that girls incarcerated on care and control and related charges experience the same conditions of control as girls incarcerated for criminal offences. Although care and control charges are nominally non-criminal there is no distinction made between these non-criminal offences and criminal offences where treatment is concerned. Several studies have shown that in places where there is a large official proportion of sexual delinquency among female delinquents there is a correspondingly large proportion of young females incarcerated for this type of delinquency. For example, in England in 1960, the Ingleby Committee (Smart, 1976) reported substantial discrepencies in the proportion of girls and boys institutionalised for non-criminal offences. In this case there were 64 per cent of girls in institutions compared with only 5 per cent of boys institutionalised on account of non-criminal offences. This undoubtedly reflects the far higher percentage of girls than boys charged with non-criminal offences.

The practice of incarcerating young females on account of these non-criminal charges, which contravene moral principles, reflects the wider society's concern for the moral fibre of the future wives and mothers of society. Incarceration of female sexual deviants is often rationalised on the basis that this action is for the girls' own sake rather than to protect society. We should recall here that the criminal justice system is not empowered to incarcerate an adult female only on the basis that it will provide some protection for her; rather the rationalisation is principally in terms of protecting the community. Of course, what is 'neglected in such an explanation is that girls and boys who have committed "criminal" offences are sent to the same or similar institutions creating a situation in which sexual delinquency appears, in terms of treatment, to be equated with criminal behaviour' (Smart, 1976: 134).

The fact that young females may be incarcerated for behaviour which contravenes society's moral code is further compounded by the type of services available within these institutions. Indeed it can be easily demonstrated that the services offered to female offenders, adult or juvenile will not serve to enable the female offender to improve her social position on release from the institution. Carol Smart goes so far as to say that usually:

> . . . regimes employed in penal institutions for female offenders are typically those which reinforce the stereotypical traditional sex role of women in our culture. Inmates are usually given the opportunity to learn to sew, cook or do other domestic tasks, and in more liberal regimes they may be able to learn to type or take educational courses. . . Women have little opportunity therefore of learning how to escape from their doubly socially inferior position while in prison. On the contrary their dependent position in society is confirmed with the result that on release their ability to be self-determining and independent will not be improved.
> (Smart, 1976: 140-1)

The orientation of work in the prison setting is typically to the traditionally feminine tasks of cooking and sewing. This is the case even where women and girls are involved in some type of industrial work — which is likely to be industrial laundry service.

Retraining programs are generally not employed for women and girls, this being officially explained by the low numbers and relatively short sentences females receive. Work-release programs are usually not operating for women in prison, once again, because of the small numbers of women who could theoretically make use of these programs.

This situation reinforces the woman's very limited structural position. The female offender is likely to leave jail without any increase in the number of options open to her for financial or emotional support. In fact the female offender's stay in corrective institutions is more likely to result in fewer legitimate and stable opportunities being open to her because of the stigma attached to a person who has been incarcerated. This certainly places the young female offender who has been institutionalised for non-criminal offences in a very difficult position. Firstly her sexual behaviour is treated as criminal and secondly her low status and dependent position is likely to be reinforced. Her ability to become a self-determining member of the community has been structurally limited by the very process which is aiming to 'protect' her.

Conclusion

Myths are not easy to dispose, because myths are more than stories, they pervade many aspects of social organisation. In many cases they can become self-fulfilling prophecies as in the interpretation of female delinquency as sexual delinquency. The assumption that female delinquency is sexual delinquency can be seen to be deeply ingrained in sociological accounts of delinquency. This assumption can be seen to be operating in the organisation of juvenile justice wherever care and control, being exposed to moral danger and related charges exist, and, these are used more often in relation to juvenile females than juvenile males. The assumption that female delinquency is sexual delinquency can be seen to have effects in the treatment of young females where non-offenders are controlled in the same way as offenders, and where girls are not offered services which would help them escape the structural limitations of the femininity stereotype. Indeed, this myth, as with other myths relating to women which exist in our society, is perpetrated by the related social organisation. Just as the education system has been shown to perpetrate myths regarding the scientific ability of girls, so too has the legal system been actively supporting the interpretation of female delinquency as sexual delinquency. Clearly, it is not only academic interest which is required to correct this mythinterpretation, for academic interest is now widespread as is shown by this seminar and several other conferences on women and the law that have been held recently or are in the planning stages. No, what is required is legal action by people trained in legal processes to question such interpretations, to agitate for change. Nor is female delinquency the only area of female involvement in crime that is affected; explanations of female shoplifting ('I do it for the sake of the kids'), the cause and effect relationship between menstruation and female crime ('Biological determinism — they couldn't help themselves'), the class nature of female crime ('The poor and the disadvantaged' — as with males), and also the rape victim ('She must've asked for it' or 'What every woman always wanted, but was afraid to ask for') are all areas requiring careful critical concern.

Acknowledgement

The author wishes to thank Stuart Rees for reading and commenting on the first draft of this paper.

---

1. In discussion following this paper, Anne Edwards-Hiller noted that in 1968, and therefore prior to the *Children and Young Persons Act, 1969*, the pattern of female delinquency was different from that described by Smart. At this time criminal offences accounted for approximately 75 per cent, and care and control and related charges for approximately 25 per cent of female delinquency.

References

Bell, R. (1976). *Social Deviance*, (revised ed.). The Dorsey Press, Illinois.
Chesney-Lind, M. (1973). 'Judicial Enforcement of the Female Sex Role: The Family Court and the Female Delinquent'. *Issues in Criminology*, 8 (Fall).
Cicourel, A.V. (1968). *The Social Organization of Juvenile Justice*. Wiley, New York.
Cohen, A.K. (1955). *Delinquent Boys*. The Free Press, New York.
Fielding, J. (1977). 'Delinquency in Girls — Past Neglect, Future Con-

cern'. In P. Wilson (ed.) *Delinquency in Australia*. University of Queensland Press, St Lucia.

Giallombardo, R. (1976). *Juvenile Delinquency*, (third ed.). John Wiley & Sons, New York.

Lombroso, C. (1968). *Crime: Its Causes and Remedies*. Patterson Smith, New Jersey.

Malinowski, B. (1926). *Myth in Primitive Psychology*. Negro Universities Press, Connecticut.

May, D. (1977). 'Delinquent Girls before the Courts'. *Medicine, Science and Law*, 17, 3, pp. 203-12.

Parsons, T. (1954). *Essays in Sociological Theory*, (revised ed.). Free Press of Glencoe, New York.

Pollak, O. (1950). *The Criminality of Women*. University of Pennsylvania Press, Philadelphia.

Scutt, J.A. (1978). 'Debunking the Theory of the Female "Masked Criminal"'. *The Australian and New Zealand Journal of Criminology*, 11, pp. 23-42.

Scutt, J.A. (1979). 'The Myth of the "Chivalry Factor" in Female Crime'. *Australian Journal of Social Issues*, 14, pp. 3-20.

Smart, C. (1976). *Women, Crime and Criminology: A Feminist Critique*. Routledge and Kegan Paul, London.

5 Theorizing About Female Crime

NGAIRE NAFFIN

Numerous theories of male criminality speculate on its physiological origins. More liberal minded criminologists may turn to explanations of male offending founded on the individual's deprived socio-economic background. A third option remains: Marxist-derived analyses of male criminality focusing attention away from the individual offender and locating causes of criminality in the inherent structure of capitalist society. Researchers interested in the female offender are rewarded with no such gamut of theories. Criminology texts purporting to deal exhaustively with theories of criminality merely refer to the female offender (as an obvious afterthought) in a footnote or appendix.

Those texts expressing a particular interest in the female delinquent address themselves almost entirely to physiological or psychological causes. Unlike her male counterpart, the female offender is rarely considered in her social context, her criminality regarded as a rational and logical response to her social experience. Whereas Lombrosian notions of born criminals are no longer considered significant in explaining male criminality (except, perhaps, for their historical interest), theories of female criminality have stagnated at the biological determinist stage of development; our concept of the female offender still rests firmly in the biological mould.

A search of causes of this theoretical stagnation in the study of the female offender inevitably leads to fairly tentative speculation. A number of explanations have been offered: the low official rate of female crime and delinquency; the preponderance of male criminologists; the fact that women have been ignored throughout the field of sociology — the dearth of criminological material on women being symptomatic of this more general neglect.

As Thelma McCormack opines:

From the grand and global theorists of social change down to the current group constructing indicators and cybernetic models, little attention has been paid to women... women are found on the sidelines in roles, situations and contexts that are marginal, dependent, or deteriorating in their authority.[1]

A Review of Role Theories of Female Crime

Frances Heidensohn, in 1968, was the first criminologist to clearly voice the need for a theory of female criminality which was sensitive to the impact of the female sex role on the behaviour of women.

> [Such a theory] would take female deviance as an aspect of the female sex role and its relationship with the social structure, rather than trying to make it conform to patterns apparently observed in the male role and its particular articulation with social structure. It would analyse components of the role, alternative role sets, opportunities for role playing in society, supportive agencies available for aid in role playing, and would view the deviance of women as related to and within this perspective.[2]

Heidensohn thus paved the way for a radical revision of theory on the female offender. Moreover, the author provided the basic ingredients for this new approach in her admonition that it should take '... descriptions of the structure of modern societies and analyse how these provide a framework within which certain roles are acted out, such as those of the adolescent girl or the adult woman and how deviance occurs'.[3]

Heidensohn's call for a more sophisticated 'role theory' of female criminality was not the first comment on the significance of women's socialisation (into sex roles) for their criminal — or conformist — behaviour. Heidensohn is a pioneer, however, to the extent that she voiced her opinion at a time when the women's movement — which had been in virtual hibernation since the post-war years — was gathering momentum. Her identification of a need for a criminology sensitive to the effects of women's every day experience on their criminality therefore sparked off the new (sexual) political consciousness of women which had begun to cast doubts on the (to date assumed) functionality of a male-dominated society which limited its female members to the domestic sphere.

Indeed it is important to distinguish between (the development of) role theory — which predated Heidensohn — and the impact of the women's movement on criminological thought. Although there is considerable overlap between the two, role theory emerged at a time when both sociology and criminology were still primarily concerned with the individual's adjustment to society's needs, while the women's movement — from which role theory was later to take its direction — developed with the understanding that social roles, rather than individuals, should be fluid. Such discussion on the social impact of women's emergence into the public sphere stimulated by the new feminist ideology was to virtually assume the significance of theory on female criminality in its own right.

Early Theorists: The Emergence of Role Theory

As early as 1949, Talcott Parsons[4] posited the theory that the relatively low incidence of female crime in American society was due to the ready availability of a female adult (mother stayed at home) upon which the female child modelled her behaviour. The male child, however, frustrated by the lack of role model (father at work), and as a protest against the femininity of the mother, engaged in delinquent behaviour.

Three years later, Grosser[5] presented a more detailed exposition on role theory. Grosser's thesis is that while juvenile delinquency is role 'expressive' (of masculinity) or 'supportive' for males, it is *ipso facto* inconsistent with stereotyped notions of femininity. Accordingly it is this inability of females to 'express' themselves through their criminality that accounts for the sex ratio in crime statistics.

Cohen[6], building on Grosser's theory, contended in 1955 that the sub-culture of delinquency which presented a solution to the status problems of adolescents was uniquely male in character. Females were unable to 'prove' themselves by acts such as theft or vandalism as they represented the very antithesis of their sex role expectations: a successful relationship with a member of the opposite sex.

Role theorists of the 1950s laid the foundation for a more sophisticated treatment of the female offender in terms of her social situation. Theories offered by these criminologists are in themselves, however, limited in perspective: they are largely dependent on a simplistic dichotomy of sex differences which consistently ignores the causes of that sex differential (for example conditioning and lack of opportunity structures) and focuses uncritically on women's lifestyle in the 'here and now' — devoid of any historical analysis.

During the 1960s, the influence of role theory on explanations of female criminality began to wane. In sociology, however, role theory continued to develop — resulting in a proliferation of papers on women's attitudes towards, and behaviour within their sex role. In 1960, for example, Ruth Hartley conducted a survey into the attitude of working women on their jobs and found that they perceived their work '. . . as an extension of the nurturant, mothering role' and that '. . . they were working to improve the welfare of their families, and this was seen as in concert with, rather than in conflict with, the wife-mother role'.[7]

In 1965 Davis and Olsen surveyed a group of college girls to ascertain their attitude to the female sex role. Results clearly indicated that the subjects took the conventional view:

> They considered the woman's primary role as being in the home, over 87 per cent of the girls in the study ranking 'home and family' as top priority.[8]

Similarly, Douvan and Adelson found in their attitudinal study of adolescents conducted in 1966 that girls listed marriage, home and family as their major long term aims.[9] Indeed studies of the 1960s produced a consistent picture of women's perceptions of their sex role: the traditional view that their life should revolve around home-making and the pursuance of successful family relationships. These studies were, however, equally consistent in their failure to comment on the nature of the social conditioning necessary to produce such an homogeneous display of attitude.

The Women's Movement: Its Impact on Role Theory

'The contemporary women's movement was born in the latter part of the decade that saw the rise of a civil rights movement'[10] writes Rita James Simon: that is, the end of the 1960s. Predictably, the first detailed statement on the implications of the female sex role for understanding the female offender also coincided with the (re)emergence of the women's movement. Thus it was in 1969 that Marie-Andree Bertrand revived role theory, in its application to the study of female crime, placing it squarely within its social context. For the first time female criminality was depicted as a rational response to social experience. Bertrand said:

> The role theory is, in the end, the most complete explanation for the differential sex rate. While our culture condones and even expects a certain amount of acting out and aggressive behaviour in young boys, it is less tolerant of the foibles of young girls. Physical strength, shrewdness in business matters, for instance, are very compatible with our 'ideal types' of the 'normal' adult male, while such attributes — often at times necessary for the performance of recurrent crimes — are not usually associated with femininity because society does not want women trained or practiced in such matters.[11]

According to Bertrand, then, sex typed behaviour does not come 'naturally'. Rather, culture manipulates its members to produce sex typed behaviour. Moreover, Bertrand implies that society has a vested interest in precipitating and maintaining such sex differentiated behaviour. To reiterate, '. . . society does not want women trained or practiced in such matters.'[12] Thus Bertrand's version of role theory hinges strongly on the argument that it is to society's advantage to condition its sexes differently. Herein lies the beginning of a critical analysis of the relationship between sex roles and the behaviour of women.

Bertrand continues her analysis by re-emphasising the point that those socialised personality traits leading to 'femininity' in the possessor are, conveniently, also consistent with conformity to the criminal law.

> Hence, to a certain degree, it would be fair to say that the normal, conforming male is permitted, and will be prone to engage in a certain amount of antisocial and illegal behaviour. The opposite is true of females: the more conforming and the more 'normal', the less delinquent and misbehaving.[13]

Despite Bertrand's attempt to provide the embryo of an analytical sex role interpretation of female criminality such theory has not been forthcoming. The politicisation of the study of female crime in the 1970s has not meant the radical revision of existing explanations of female offending — nor development of new ones. Awareness of the powerful impact of the female sex role on women (both attitudinally and on their behaviour) has instead focused debate on the women's movement itself: will the movement encourage women to engage in more criminal activities? Is the female criminal a 'liberated' woman? Bertrand's aim to construct a dynamic role theory of female delinquency has been subsumed under the 'women's movement discussion'. Polemics have replaced theory making — Bertrand continuing to provide one of the few exceptions by her persistent attempt to place analysis of female criminality in a sturdy theoretical framework.

Simon provides a prime example of the 'women's lib' debate. Her thesis is that female offenders are not 'liberated' women. She supports her contention by tracing the development of 'the movement' and pinpointing the chief exponents of the movement's feminist ideology. Simon is then able to conclude:

> ... the demographic characteristics of (the Movement's) membership are extraordinarily homogeneous. In the main, the movement is led by, appeals to, and has as the large majority of its members young white women who are college educated and whose families are middle and upper-middle class... None of the groups within the movement has made any noticeable dent in the blue-collar female workers, on black women, or on high-school-educated housewives.[14]

Although unwilling to deny the possibility 'that the women's movement will (ultimately) significantly alter the behaviour, the perceptions, the beliefs and the lifestyles of women already involved in criminal careers'[15] Simon feels confident in her assertion:

> ... given the characteristics of the members of the women's movement, it is unlikely that it has (to date) had a significant impact, or that indeed it has made much of an impression on women already involved in crime. Indeed, most of these women have yet to hear of consciousness raising, and of sisterhood in a political sense; and those who have may well ridicule these sentiments or attack them as the empty mouthings of women whose lives have always been characterised by material comfort, stability and security.[16]

Adler, however, implies, to the contrary, that there is a rather direct link between the emancipation of women and their increased criminality. Adler opposes Simon's thesis by contending that:

> Like her legitimate-based sister, the female criminal knows too much to pretend or return to her former role as a second rate criminal confined to 'feminine' crimes such as shoplifting and prostitution. She has had a taste of financial victory. In some cases she has had a taste of blood. Her appetite, however, appears to be only whetted.[17]

Thus Adler argues, in melodramatic terms, that the female offender is in fact a product of a 'raised consciousness' founded on feminist ideology.

A number of writers have since returned to Simon's argument that the women's movement has not contributed to the increase in female crime, but for different reasons. Giordano, (initially like Simon) asserts:

> ... it is a mistake and an oversimplification to suggest such a direct link between the 'liberation' of females and increased involvement in crimes. This implies a degree of politicization and commitment on the part of the criminals to which she simply may not adhere.[18]

Instead, the author suggests:

> In attempting to understand recent changes in female crime patterns... it is perhaps more useful to conceive of these women as recipients of broad-based as well as micro-level societal changes, rather than themselves being responsible for a new era of sex role equality.[19]

Smart offers an alternative perspective of the 'women's movement' debate. She perceives those who argue that there is a positive relationship between the movement and female crime as plotting against the emancipation of women:

> The Women's Movement appears to have struck immense fear into the hearts of criminologists for generations past, even when the demands of such a movement were modest compared with claims for equality made today. As the Movement has now re-emerged and re-asserted itself again, it is being conceived once more as a threat to the stable character of female criminality and contemporary observers may be found to be expressing similar comments to Lombroso and Thomas about the dangers of allowing the same 'freedoms' as men.[20]

Viewing the 'emancipation leads to crime' thesis as the rantings of conservative men attempting to restrict women's role, Smart proceeds to attack their argument. The impression, however, is gained that the author in her enthusiasm to demolish such ideologically unsound reasoning, is myopically unwilling to concede any merit to the emancipation argument. In an attempt to undermine such theory from the start, Smart contends that there is no real increase in female crime — and therefore the emancipation argument must be wrong:

> ... the recent perception of changes in female delinquency is not so much indicative of actual changes in the frequency and character of female delinquency but denotes a new appraisal of the situation.[21]

What Smart is arguing is that:

> ... the police, social workers and other agents of social control are more

ready to define deviant behaviour by women and girls as violent or 'masculine' because of apparent changes in the social and economic position of women in society.[22]

However, finally Smart (perhaps more realistically in view of the consistency with which criminal statistics reveal an increase in female crime) contends the emancipation theory is too simplistic:

> The influence of 'emancipation' is extremely complex; it affects the material being and consciousness of not only the women who become 'emancipated' and the men whose lifestyles and consciousnesses may be transformed but also those women and men who reject the principles of liberation and yet are indirectly affected.[23]

Smart takes Giordano's idea that female criminals are '. . . recipients of broad-based. . . social changes' further in her attempt to identify the reasons for these changes. Asserting that it is unlikely that female offenders are politicised to the extent of embracing a feminist ideology, Smart points to a number of other factors which may have contributed to the increase in female crime:

> [Female offenders] may well be dissatisfied with the restrictions of the stereotypical feminine role and their limited opportunities in general but the changes in their consciousness are as likely to be caused by changing material conditions as by the principles of the Women's Movement.[24]

Structural changes in women's lifestyles are '. . . to some extent independent of demands for equality of the sexes.'[25] She cites as an example '. . . the demand for a female labour force [which] has arisen out of shortages of male labour during periods of national crises or during economic booms'.[26] Still wary that the women's movement could be blamed for the increase in reported female crime, Smart thus argues to the end that women have not precipitated their own emancipation but are victims of circumstances.

Although Smart is probably correct in asserting that women's emergence into the public sphere is the result of a complex set of factors, her persistence in denying the instrumentality of the movement in at least indirectly affecting the social structure of women's lives seems to belie the facts. The entry of women into a number of occupational areas — both professional and unskilled — has been a direct result of their struggle for equality. Notwithstanding the proliferation of women in low paid, low skilled jobs being a matter of economic (rather than ideological) expedience, the existence of women lawyers, bankers and bus drivers is still a clear indication of the growing acceptance of the ideas espoused by the women's movement.

Since emergence of the emancipation debate, an attempt has been made to empirically test the assertion that female delinquents perceive themselves as 'liberated' women. Leventhal reports on her survey into the sex role attitudes of female criminals compared with non-criminals.[27] Twenty-five subjects from both groups were given the Attitude Towards Women Scale, Open Subordination to Women Scale, and Minnesota Multiphasic Personality Inventory Mf Scale. It was found:

> ... the criminal sample's attitude toward women in general was that they were weak, less capable and unable to control their emotions. Moreover, they felt women should be submissive, faithful to their husbands, and should not drink, curse, or smoke. In short, that women's place was in the home.[28]

The criminal sample's reaction to the women's movement was consistent with this attitude toward women:

> Further evidence for this antifeminist stance is garnered by reviewing [their] open-ended answers about the Women's Liberation Movement. All but two responses were negative.[29]

The control sample, however, displayed more 'liberated' attitudes toward women and their role:

> [They] felt that women should assert themselves, play a leading role where applicable, and maintain their equality in social-sexual matters, employment, education, and family decisions. Their answers to the open-ended questions were positive and dealt with the issue of equality.[30]

Leventhal's findings support the arguments of Simon, Giordano and Smart that the female offender's motivation to commit a criminal act is unrelated to any aspirations for 'liberation'. On the contrary, the female offender possesses a highly traditional view of women's role.

Further evidence in support of the theory that female offenders do not view themselves as powerful rebels advancing the cause of women is provided by Bertrand, who asked female offenders and non-offenders 'What was the most important decision you have made in the last five years?' According to her:

The question... was based on a theory of Derek Erickson in his book *Responsibility* when he defines agents as against patients... the agent being the one who is really the author or (his action), who signs to his deeds, and the patient being the one to whom things happen, who is led to believe facts.[31]

She found that neither female offenders nor female non-offenders viewed themselves as the powerful agents of their own actions. There were no 'liberated' females. Decisions were consistently found to be trivial, '... domestically bound, also bound to appearance, to being loved, to being pretty, to remaining loved.'[32]

Bertrand was forced to conlude that:

... women and girls are deeply, profoundly convinced that they are absolutely powerless, they have absolutely no grip of what goes on in the world. That they have no political influence whatsoever [and] no economic value whatsoever.[33]

A Return to Role Theory?

In 1976 Smart, in her review of contemporary studies of female criminality, examined and expanded the role theory of female delinquency which had received little attention in criminological circles since the 1950s (Bertrand providing the exception). Smart commenced her analysis by detailing the major components of the theory:

Girls are generally more closely supervised than boys, and are taught to be passive and domesticated while boys are allowed greater freedom and are encouraged to be aggressive, ambitious and outward going... [Thus] both socialisation and the later development of consciousness and self perception does vary considerably between the sexes. As a result of this girls are usually expected to be non-violent and so are not allowed to learn how to fight or use weapons. Girls themselves tend to shrink from violence, and look for protection rather than seeking to learn the skills of self-defence, hence few women have the necessary technical ability or strength to engage in crimes of violence, armed robberies or gang fights.[34]

Smart builds on theoretical models of early criminologists concerned with the female sex role by highlighting the way in which opportunity structures predispose males rather than females to delinquency. She notes that girls have '... greater restrictions placed on [their] freedom of movement'; and women, due to the limitations of their sex role which is largely concerned with domesticity, are '... denied the opportunity to engage in anything other than petty or domestic offences.'[35]

Smart also comments on the failure of traditional role theory to examine the social origins of sex roles and calls for a revision of theory which will '... challenge the prevailing belief that sex roles and gender differences are "natural"'[36] by situating the study of the female offender in an historical, social and cultural context. Smart, however, is unwilling to do this herself; her discussion of role theory terminates with this heuristic comment.

In 1976 Scutt also considered whether role conditioning theory was a plausible explanation for the disparity in male and female criminality. For the purpose of her analysis, Scutt focused on Parsons' interpretation of role theory:

> Girls are encouraged to be passive and gentle; they are taught not to fight with each other or with their brothers... During childhood they are constantly reminded of the role expected to be adopted in the future; ever-present is a mother who represents the adult each will become. Not so with boys. Father is away from home at the office each day.[37]

The theory continues that boys, unable to envisage their father's role, but encouraged to be 'manly' and aggressive, cannot cope with the often sedentary tedium that their adult occupation imposes on them and, accordingly, rebel against this role by engaging in criminal behaviour.

In her evaluation, Scutt contends that a number of research studies have confirmed that the majority of women do in fact 'subscribe to the traditional view of the female.' She notes, however, that the family should not be viewed as the sole socialising agent. In Bettelheim's words:

> The little girl's first storybooks and primers, for example, hardly ever show a woman as working or active outside the home. It makes no difference that over five million American children under twelve have full-time working mothers. The little girl is expected to shape herself in the image of the maternal housekeeping women in these stories, and never mind what certain unfortunate mothers may be obliged to do.[38]

Thus the education system consistently promotes an image of women that the female child has already become familiar with at home.

Scutt also identifies a third area where females are subject to sex role socialisation: their peer culture. Moreover, Scutt asserts that the female adolescent's peer group may well be a complicating factor in her socialisation: peers do not always encourage the type of behaviour which is considered sex appropriate by the family. For example, the peer culture may incorporate sexual 'promiscuity' — behaviour which is strictly forbidden by the family. Scutt's final assessment of role theory is therefore:

> ... that although there may be some validity in [it] — girls are treated differently from boys, and their expectations appear to be affected by the difference in attitude — consideration must be given to additional factors.[39]

Both Smart and Scutt clearly have strong reservations about the value of role theory as an explanation for female criminality. Both attempt to update and diversify role theory by incorporating within this approach a number of social factors other than family: occupational opportunity structure, education and peer culture. In the end, however, one is left with a general feeling of dissatisfaction with role theory's conceptualisation of the female offender. Smart perhaps best sums up the reasons for this uneasiness in her recommendations on how role theory should be revised to provide a more complete explanation of female crime:

> To improve the status of the role theory approach the concept of role must itself be located within a theory which first can account for the existence of specifically differentiated roles as well as other features of human activity (like criminality) and second treats both as the outcome of socio-economic, political and historical factors, rather than treating one [crime] as the outcome of the other [sex roles].[40]

This, of course, begs the question: Why does Smart herself not attempt such theory building? In her review of Smart's book Peters comments on this failure to do nothing more than hint at a new theory:

> Why is there lacking any statement which brings together such insights into at least a rough adumbration for the reader to ponder?[41]

Symbolic Interactionism: A New Development for Role Theory

Smart demands a number of things from her improved role theory: first an explanation of sex roles — their origins and development; second, the location of this explanation within a theory which highlights the interactive, rather than the cause and effect, relationship between criminality and sex roles; and third (in line with this more sophisticated 'interactionist' treatment of female crime), the introduction of a number of social factors into this theoretical framework.

A 'symbolic interactionist' perspective may be applied to the study of the female offender with a view to meeting Smart's demands. The interactionist model of human behaviour may be a commonsense account of the individual's development of a social self modelled on sex role expectations. This interactionist analysis of the acquisition of a sex typed self image can form the basis of a tentative explanation of the behaviour of potential and actual female offenders: why females are loathe to acquire a criminal label and why, once embroiled in the criminal justice process, females experience difficulty coping with their deviant image.

The Symbolic Interactionist Perspective

> The special capacity for language not only differentiates humans from other species, but confers a distinctive quality on the relationship of a human being to his environment. The symbolic interactionist sees the world as essentially comprising not objective physical stimuli but subjective and symbolic meanings that are constructed and maintained in social interactions.[42]

The interactionist analysis of human behaviour thus focuses on the dynamic and reciprocal nature of social relations. Human development is explained in these terms: the infant child begins life as a creature of non-symbolic gestures — responding to direct, physical stimuli in an immediate, non-reflective manner (like animals). But with ongoing social interaction with significant others (parents) the child soon learns that human behaviour is more complex and there are underlying attitudes and feelings implicit in any human action. The vehicle by which the child acquires this appreciation of non-verbal cues and meanings is, ironically, language. For it is as the child learns to communicate with words instead of simple gestures that she acquires an ability to react less directly to any given situation. Words enable her to imagine situations — she can picture herself and others in different social contexts; she can imagine her behaviour; and she can imagine how others are likely to react to that behaviour. With imagination of such scenarios comes interpretation of their meaning. That is, by imaginatively playing at more than one part, or role, the child comes to view herself from the standpoint of others (she imaginatively interacts with herself as a social object) thereby arriving at some sort of evaluation of herself. From then on this evaluation colours her behaviour and the behaviour of others in any social situation. Communication becomes more than an exchange of simple gestures; it now consists of words, nuances and non-verbal gestures (or 'body language'). Words are no longer taken at face value — they are interpreted and situationalised.

Mead[43], founder of this theory of human development, labelled that ability which the individual acquires to imagine herself as others see her as 'the self' and the process by which it is acquired as 'role taking'. He then went on to characterise something which he called 'the generalised other': the amalgamation of the imagined evaluations of one's self by all significant others — or self image.

The Significance of Sex Roles

Mead contended that one of the most powerful determinants of self image was sex role. Given the plethora of roles an individual would take during self development, it was inevitable that roles would tend to group and be perceived as a stereotype; role grouping according to sex, for example, would be an obvious way of simplifying the role taking process.

Mead conceived this social stereotyping as basically a three stage process: first, the individual would have to obtain information on the characteristics considered appropriate to her/his sex; second, she/he would actually assume those characteristics; and third, she/he would then expect others to also act in sex appropriate ways.

Such a simplification of the role taking process does seem to occur in day to day social relations. We all carry preconceived notions of how other people, with certain social, sexual or racial attributes, should behave. These notions are based on our knowledge (both accurate and inaccurate) of social stereotypes. They are important to the extent that they alter our behaviour towards a person who fits a certain stereotype, and our behaviour, in turn, affects that person's reaction to us. In this way social stereotypes mould behaviour.

What are those distinctive qualities which characterise the sexes? Using the family as the smallest social unit suited to analysis,

Parsons contends that there is a division into fairly rigid 'functional' roles, along sex lines.[44] The husband-father is the breadwinner, while the wife-mother is the homemaker. By virtue of the importance of the male's occupational role, as a component of his familial role, the husband-father is designated the 'instrumental leader' of the family unit. Likewise, due to the fact that the female is home-centred and largely concerned with family relations, she is dubbed the 'sociometric star'; she adopts the expressive role. The essence of masculinity and femininity resides in this division of functions within the family.

Parsons also acknowledged that we associate certain behaviours with the different sex roles. The male as instrumental task leader, is associated with 'task' behaviour. More specifically, they involve giving suggestions, directions and opinions. The 'instrumental' person also tends to have certain attitudes such as inhibition of emotions, and the ability to accept hostile reactions from others in the process of pressing a point.

There are of course reciprocal behaviours and attitudes on the part of the 'expressive' person toward the task leader. These include the 'expression' of emotions, supportive behaviour to others, the desire to please and be liked, and a more generalised liking for other members of the family unit.

Despite Parsons' insight into the nature of current sex roles, his depiction of the family as an efficient social system implicitly stresses the functionality of such a sex role division. His method of differentiating the sexes is a thinly veiled appraisal and approval of the current stereotyped separation between women/home and men/work. This is clearly due to a failure to examine the origins of sex roles (in light of social, economic and political variables) which leaves his analysis flailing in the social vacuum.

Building on Parsons' analysis, Bertrand[45] develops a more critical picture of sex roles by situating them in their economic and social context. She describes the roles delegated to women in terms of their privatisation: that women's role dictates that their main concerns should be interpersonal ones within the family; they are effectively cut off from most extra-familial activities. Women are not expected to participate in the market economy other than via their husbands; they have no direct links. They are dependent on other people — usually their husbands — not only for financial support but also for their perceptions of the outside world. Women's home-centred role, which requires them to experience extra-familial life vicariously (through their husbands), means that '. . . their own class, status and privilege (is relegated) to a social function of their husband's work'.[46]

Amalgamating Parsons' functional division of sex roles (and the resultant personality characteristics of women) with Bertrand's notion of the 'privatisation' of females in our society, it is possible to construct a profile of the female self image. Given Mead's analysis of the development of self, and its assessment according to stereotyped notions of social groups (in this case, women), we can predict that females will learn to view themselves in terms of certain attitudinal and behavioural traits. These are likely to be characterised by excessive dependence on the opinions of others and the need to please and be liked.

Symbolic Interactionism and the Female Offender

The interactionist view of human development provides a commonsense explanation of the way in which the individual acquires a social self conditioned by sex role expectation. It highlights the fact that behaviour is inevitably modified by the way the individual imagines herself to be perceived by others which, in turn, is strongly influenced by social stereotypical notions of the sexes.

What does symbolic interactionism say about the female offender? First, it illuminates the self image of the non-offending female: it is weak and dependent. Second, it enables speculation on the effect of this self image on the offending female. That is, we surmise that women's dependent self image makes them particularly vulnerable to social disapproval. When placed in a social situation clearly attracting the displeasure of others they are likely therefore to internalise such negative reactions. Such displeasure is likely to be occasioned by apprehension for offending: the female offender is stigmatised both socially (family and friends) and officially (the criminal justice process).

An interactionist appreciation of the female self image thus says that the female delinquent (upon apprehension) is likely to internalise her criminal label and regard herself as a social failure — a pariah. Those who come in contact with the female offender during her processing by law enforcement officials are likely to find her in a state of extreme dependency: emotional, self-critical and highly sensitive to the opinions of others.

Testing the Thesis of the Negative Self Image of the Female Offender — Marie-Andree Bertrand: As previously stated, Bertrand found that both her criminal and non-criminal subjects were '... deeply, profoundly convinced that they are absolutely powerless, they have absolutely no grip of what goes on in the world.'

Bertrand's empirical work on the self perceptions of female delinquents lends support to the symbolic interactionist thesis that females develop a weak, dependent self image — and perceive themselves as helpless; and that the female offender, far from breaking away from this stereotype, comes to see herself as a manipulated object. Bertrand's investigations were precipitated by her conviction that there was a strong relationship between how women viewed themselves, how a culture viewed women and how the penal system treated its offenders. She predicted that emancipation would be a significant factor in moulding these perceptions.

From 1967 to 1970 Bertrand conducted her comparative analysis of the crime rates (according to sex), the penal codes and the 'self-image' of offenders in six countries — France and Belgium, Hungary and Poland, and Canada and Venezuela. Her hypotheses were:

> With regard to crime rates, that in the societies where women are less bound to their traditional roles of child-bearers and house-holders, we would observe a greater proportion of female criminality.
>
> With regard to penal codes, that those same countries which have favoured more formal equality between the sexes would have laid less ground for discriminatory procedures and differential treatment in the penal law.
>
> With regard to the self image of women, that there would be less tendency to perceive one's self in terms of object, victim and 'patient' in the societies where women have come to be more present in the economic structures and have achieved some degree of formal equality.[47]

Employing these hypotheses, Bertrand hoped to combine economic, political and legal variables and '... relate to the level of women's consciousness on matters concerning sexual equality and self-determination.'[48]

The results of her investigation were not as simple and coherent as predicted; in fact in many instances they were ambiguous and confusing. Whereas a number of the author's hypotheses tended to be proven — for instance, Venezuela as hypothesised had a very low rate of female criminality compared with Hungary (a more sexually 'liberated' country) — others were clearly falsified. As an example of this, the author found that in Canada, where women are relatively emancipated, the law enforcement agencies perceive female offenders as weak and 'sick'.

Notwithstanding the obscurity of the relationship observed between legal and penal policy, economic development and women's consciousness, Bertrand produced (unexpectedly) dramatic findings on the self assessment of women. Subjects were asked to respond to the question 'what was the most important decision you have made in the last five years?' Responses indicated the following:

> The universe of reference of women and girls, their Leitbild, as exhibited in response to my questionnaire, is significantly more narrow, more domestic, more homebound, more marriage and love-related, less politically informed than that of men and boys. The 'most important decision that (they) have taken in the course of the last four or five years', in the case of girls but more strikingly so in the case of adult women, illustrates their powerlessness, economically, politically, their relative lack of mobility and freedom and in many instances differ significantly from what boys and men see as their realm of decision.[49]

Bertrand's findings thus tend to confirm our prediction that women, in general, possess a weak, dependent, self image. An extrapolation from those findings is that women placed in situational crises, such as apprehension for offending, will suffer more than their male counterparts.

Implications for the Treatment of the Female Offender: An appreciation of the self perceptions of the female offender, upon the acquisition of her official criminal label (that is, her apprehension and/or detention), carries practical implications for her treatment. Police, probation and prison officers alike have noted the differential reaction of the female and male offender to the legal process. The female delinquent does appear to be more emotional and more dependent on authority figures than her male counterpart. As a rule, she seems less able to cope with her officially recognised criminality. This differential reaction has often, too simplistically, been attributed to assumed innate 'female' traits such as hysteria and inability to cope with crisis. Alternatively, a physiological explanation has been sought such as some irregularity in the menstrual cycle.[50]

By highlighting the effects of a sex typed self image on women, symbolic interactionism offers an alternative explanation for the reactions of the female offender to her criminal label. No longer focusing on the individual offender and her psychological or physiological problems, the reactions of female offenders are viewed in terms of their social interactions and sex role expectations implicit therein. The ongoing interactions between the offender and the various officials within the legal process thus serve as useful indicators to explain the offender's behaviour: her need to justify her behaviour to all around her. Unlike the male offender, the female delinquent may quite unrealistically, in view of the circumstances of her apprehension, deny the commission of any offence. Alternatively, she may be highly emotional in order to obtain support and protection from those involved in her criminal labelling. Both reactions are consistent with a symbolic interactionist interpretation of her behaviour. Moreover, they have received informal confirmation by personnel involved in the criminal justice process who frequently comment on the emotionalism of the female offender's response to criminal labelling.

An insight into the rationale underlying the female offender's behaviour should enable law enforcement officials to treat her in a more understanding and humane manner. If the offender's sensitivity to social disapproval leads her to react emotively to the advances of law enforcement officials, a supportive and non-judgemental approach may help to alleviate her fears of social disapproval and rejection. A similarly supportive approach should also help the female offender who is unable to cope with the fact that she has been detected offending and denies all knowledge of the incident.

Symbolic Interactionism and Alternative Forms of Female Deviance: A symbolic interactionist analysis of women's self image not only explains their reactions to situational crises where social approval is withdrawn but offers tentative solutions to the enigma of the relative insignificance (compared with males) of their offending.

Daunted by the prospect of social condemnation, the potential female offender may well turn to covert forms of deviance. Bertrand comments on the heuristic value of such a thesis when she suggests:

> . . . that women being defined [by men] as the functional harmonisers of conflicts within the family, the happiness provider — they could hardly be expected to act out their well repressed hostility.
>
> Mental illness as an alternative or female equivalent to male anti-social and aggressive behaviour could be explored as a promising (partial) explanation of the female crime rate and of the nature of female criminality.[51]

Conclusion

The failure of role theorists to produce an adequate account of female criminality is a symptom of the more general neglect of the female offender by criminologists and sociologists alike. Role theory, in its present form, is useful to the extent that it attempts to study the female delinquent in her (social) environment. It fails, however, in its refusal to recognise the complexity and dynamics of the process by which roles are acquired, and situate them in a social and economic context.

Symbolic interactionism provides the needs of a theory of female crime which both recognises the dynamic (and interactive) nature of role taking and imports a number of social factors into this process. It explains the way in which sex roles impinge on women's self assessment; how their resulting dependent self image makes them loath to place themselves in situations of social disapproval; and finally it explains the reactions of women who are unable to avoid social condemnation — female offenders confronted by the criminal justice process. As such, it represents a significant development in the sex role approach to female crime.

---

1. McCormack, Thelma, 'Toward a Non Sexist Perspective on Social and Political Change' in *Another Voice: Feminist Perspectives on Social Life and Social Service*, Marcia Millman and Rosabeth Moss Kanter (Eds.), Anchor Books, New York, 1975.

2. Heidensohn, Frances, 'The Deviance of Women: A Critique and an Enquiry', *British Journal of Sociology*, Vol. 19, No. 2, 1968, p. 170.

3. *Ibid.*, p. 171.

4. Parsons, Talcott, *Essays in Sociological Theory*, The Free Press, Glencoe, Ill., 1949.

5. Grosser, G.H., *Juvenile Delinquency and Contemporary American Sex Roles,* unpublished Ph.D. thesis, Harvard, 1951.
6. Cohen, A.K., *Delinquent Boys,* The Free Press, Glencoe, Ill., 1955.
7. Hartley, Ruth E., 'Children's Concepts of Male and Female Roles', *Merrill-Palmer Quarterly,* Vol. 6, No. 3, 1960, p. 153. Quoted by Scutt, Jocelynne A., 'Role Conditioning Theory: An Explanation for Disparity in Male and Female Criminality', *The Australian and New Zealand Journal of Criminology,* Vol. 9, No. 1, March 1976, p. 28.
8. Davis, R. and Olsen, Virginia, 'The Career Outlook of Professionally Educated Women', *Psychiatry,* No. 28, 1965, p. 334. Quoted by Scutt, *ibid.*
9. Douven, Elizabeth and Adelson, J., *The Adolescent Experience,* Wiley, New York, 1966.
10. Simon, Rita James, *Women and Crime,* Lexington Books, Lexington, Mass., 1975.
11. Bertrand, Marie-Andree, 'Self-Image and Delinquency: A Contribution to the Study of Female Criminality and Women's Image', *Acta Criminologica,* January 1969, p. 74.
12. *Ibid.*
13. *Ibid.*
14. Simon, *op. cit.,* p. 17.
15. *Ibid.,* p. 18.
16. *Ibid.*
17. Adler, Freda, *Sisters in Crime: The Rise of the New Female Criminal,* McGraw-Hill Book Company, New York, 1975, p. 15.
18. Giordano, Peggy C., 'Girls, Guys and Gangs: The Changing Social Context of Female Delinquency', *The Journal of Criminal Law and Criminology,* Vol. 69, No. 1, 1978, p. 127.
19. *Ibid.*
20. Smart, Carol, *Women, Crime and Criminology: A Feminist Critique,* Routledge and Kegan Paul, London, 1976, p. 71.
21. *Ibid.,* p. 73.
22. *Ibid.*
23. *Ibid.*
24. *Ibid.,* p. 74.
25. *Ibid.*
26. *Ibid.*
27. Leventhal, Gloria, 'Is 'Women's Lib' to Blame?', *Psychological Reports,* No. 41, 1977, p. 1179.
28. *Ibid.,* p. 1181.
29. *Ibid.*
30. *Ibid.*
31. Bertrand, *op. cit.,* presenting results of this research at a conference on 'Women and Deviance'.
32. *Ibid.*
33. *Ibid.*
34. Smart, *op. cit.,* p. 66.
35. *Ibid.,* p. 68.

36. *Ibid.*, p. 69.
37. Scutt, *op. cit.*, p. 26.
38. Bettelheim, Bruno, 'Growing Up Female', *Harper's Magazine*, October 1962, p. 121.
39. Scutt, *op. cit.*, p. 32.
40. Smart, *op. cit.*, p. 70.
41. Peters, Anne K., 'Carol Smart: Women, Crime and Criminology', *Crime and Social Justice*, No. 9, Spring-Summer 1978, p. 88.
42. Back, Kurt W., *Social Psychology*, John Wiley and Sons, Inc., New York, 1977.
43. Mead, George Herbert, *Mind, Self and Society*, University of Chicago Press, Chicago, 1934.
44. Parsons, Talcott and Bales, R.F., *Family, Socialisation and Interaction Process*, The Free Press, Glencoe, Ill., 1950.
45. Bertrand, *op. cit.*
46. *Ibid.*
47. *Ibid.*
48. *Ibid.*
49. *Ibid.*
50. See for example Scutt, Jocelynne A., 'A Factor in Female Crime', *The Criminologist*, Vol. 9, No. 34, 1974, pp. 56-71.
51. *Ibid.*

6 The Processing of Juveniles in Victoria

**ANNE EDWARDS HILLER AND
LINDA HANCOCK**

Historical Background of the Juvenile Court

The second half of the nineteenth century saw in America, England and elsewhere a gradual attempt to develop arrangements for juveniles separate from adults in relation to the definition of 'offences'; in the processing of offenders through the courts; and in the kinds of dispositions, especially custodial dispositions available. Previously children, even those as young as seven or eight, could be tried and convicted in adult criminal courts and committed to prison, though in practice it appears some allowance was made for age. At the same time, there was some recognition of the state's responsibility for homeless, destitute and neglected children for which purpose a variety of establishments (workhouses, industrial and reform schools, and others) had appeared along with provisions for children to be placed with 'suitable' persons.

This period which, as Platt has documented, was marked by the introduction of a new concept of juvenile delinquency, saw a shift, at least as far as the young were concerned, from an approach based on classical retributive justice towards notions of reform, reeducation and rehabilitation under the moral guidance of the state, acting *in parens patriae*:

> The reformatory system was based on the assumption that proper training can counteract the imposition of poor family life, a corrupt environment and poverty, while at the same time toughening and preparing delinquents for the struggle ahead.
>
> (Platt, 1969: 53)

First special institutions, and later separate courts and procedures for juveniles, followed from the acceptance of these ideas. Though the records show the first juvenile court was functioning in Adelaide in 1895, the children's court movement is more usually dated from the establishment of a juvenile court in Chicago in 1899, and such courts were then quickly set up in England and other states of America and Australia:

> The juvenile court was designed to be more than a court for children, however. It marked a conceptual change in the nature of the child's conduct, the child's responsibility for its conduct, and the state's role in dealing with that conduct.
> (Davis, 1974: 2)

Interestingly, about the same time, differentiation between female and male adult offenders was also being advocated, particularly with respect to types of disposition and places of detention. Women, like children, were believed to have special rehabilitative potential, to require special kinds of facilities and to benefit from longer or indeterminate sentences (Clements, 1972).[1]

The overriding welfare orientation of legislation dealing with juveniles at this time had a number of implications worth noting, since this general philosophy has persisted to the present day. Theoretically, a rehabilitation or treatment philosophy assumes the presence of 'disease' or maladjustment (by contrast with the classical notion of *mens rea*), crime or misconduct are seen as a problem deriving from the psychology and/or immediate environment of the individual, indicating the presence of some 'pathology'. Hence the remedy is seen as lying in supervision, character retraining, removal from contaminating influences and exposure to a superior moral and social climate, and the inculcation of a practical work ethic involving manual trades for boys and domestic skills for girls. 'The essence of rehabilitation is that punishments should fit the criminal not the crime.'[2] This seems to carry the indisputable corollaries that within certain age or time limits sentences to reformatories must be of a reasonable and preferably indefinite length, given the nature of the human material to be worked on and the reformative process being attempted, and that the sooner any symptoms are identified, the better the prognosis. Thus indeterminate sentences and the idea of pre- or potential delinquency or of 'delinquent tendencies' became part of the apparatus for controlling troublesome juveniles (Balch, 1975), consistent with this basically medical model of delinquency.

In turn these features of a treatment orientation have other legal and moral consequences for individuals brought into contact with a system based on such principles. Though in the case of treatment the object is to benefit the individual, while with punishment the aim is to exact penalties and/or to deter, and it is expected that what is meted out will not be appreciated by its recipient, as Packer[3] has argued, it does not follow that what we do to the 'patient' is any less painful or more welcome than what we do to the 'criminal'. The difference, if any, lies in how the treatment or punishment is presented by the legitimating ideology.[4] It is this which accounts for the fact that, whereas the criminal justice system contains a number of legal safeguards for the rights of the individual charged with a criminal offence because it is acknowledged that the interests of such a person are in conflict with those of the state, no such protections are required when it is a case of a sick person being offered help in the form of some appropriate remedy for his condition as recommended by those competent in that field. Indeed, the language itself reflects such a distinction, talking in the first case of 'rights' or 'interests' and in the second only of 'needs'.[5]

When the 'patient' is also a minor, whose dependent status is already recognised in law, he is regarded as a non-person in much the same way as are 'lunatics'. Even in contested cases between adults, usually parents, and children, the right to separate legal representation for children is not generally accepted or observed even now (the notable exception being custody following divorce). Kleinfeld, in an extensive survey of the 'balance of power between infants, their parents and the state', claims that as well as the argument that rehabilitation is not punitive and therefore not against the interests of those being subjected to it, is the historical accident that 'courts developed the notion, apparently simultaneously with the rise of the juvenile court system, that children had no right of liberty, and therefore no right to be heard on the question of whether their liberty should be taken.' (1970: 325). Children in law have traditionally been, and remain to a considerable extent, seen essentially as the property of their parents or guardians. Today this doctrine may speak more of the sanctity of the family than of parental rights over children, but the effect is the same, of disenfranchising the junior members of the family and of society. In many of the so-called 'status offences', parents are complainants against their wilful, disobedient or runaway children and there is little evidence that the law and the courts admit the possibility that parents may be as much at fault in such a situation as their children (though it seems, surprisingly, in earlier times they did).[6] Though *parens patriae* was intended to check parental misconduct or negligence, this has not eventuated.[7]

Around 1900 and progressively in the twentieth century, a second and significant development affecting the legal and judicial categorisation and handling of juveniles has occurred. Related to increasing acceptance of a treatment of rehabilitation philosophy, which provided the legitimation for the involvement of welfare agencies on behalf of the state in the lives of children and young people whose parents could not or would not care for and control, was the extension of the courts' jurisdiction and the provision of appropriate services over a wider range of types of 'need'.

Thus the turning of attention from offence to offender, from anti-social act to dubious moral character or undesirable social condition broadened enormously (perhaps even infinitely: Platt, 1969: 135) the range of situations in which a need for intervention and 'treatment' could be identified.

One major consequence or concomitant of the rehabilitative ideal promoted by the 'child-saving movement', as Platt described the organisations and interests concerned to change the approach to and the facilities for problem youth in America in the latter part of the last century, was the 'blurring of distinctions between "dependent" and "delinquent" children and the corresponding elimination of due process for juveniles, [which] served to make a social fact out of the norm of adolescent dependence.' (Platt, 1969: 135).[8] It was seen primarily as a question of the need to 'punish premature independence in children and restrict youthful autonomy' (p. 136), whatever form this took and, since all young persons coming under the jurisdiction of the court were not yet able to assume independent status of adult American citizenship, there was no question of any of them, criminal or not, needing or deserving the kinds of legal rights granted to offenders charged in adult criminal courts and contained in the due process clause of the Constitution: right to counsel, trial by jury, bail, scheduled hearings, proper notice, mandatory rules of evidence, and so on.

These trends have persisted throughout the twentieth century, with the steady increase in numbers and types of 'dependent' or 'needy' children coming under the jurisdiction of state welfare services and a continued commitment to differentiate between types of children in their care only for purposes of treatment, rather than classifying children according to whether they had committed a criminal offence or whether it was their unsatisfactory home situation causing them to be brought before the court. Recently, particularly in America, the idea that adherence to a rehabilitative philosophy renders irrelevant any arguments about the individual's right to certain legal safeguards has come under considerable criticism. The legal situation of juveniles processed by the courts and exposed to the attendant stigmatisation and, depending on the disposition, possible deprivation or curtailment of certain rights and freedoms, for their own good, has been reconsidered. Advocates for the reintroduction of some element of a legalistic justice model into juvenile court proceedings have claimed that:

> The juvenile court can easily become the instrument not only of arbitrariness but of oppression as well. Informality and compassion are not necessarily running mates. We may be doubly misled — first, into thinking that a benevolent purpose automatically ensures a beneficial result, and, second, into believing that the court always acts to benefit and protect its juvenile charges.
> (Starrs, cited in Clunies-Ross, 1968: 216)

Others (for example Balch, 1975) have observed that medical terminology and a treatment model can prove 'very efficient as a means to legitimise measures that otherwise would be extremely difficult to justify on strictly legal grounds.'[9] In one famous case (Gault, 1966) the judgment was made that due process requires that certain rights be protected even when the case involves intervention for the benefit of the child and where no criminal charge is being laid. This argument has been taken further in America by the application of the Equal Protection Clause which prohibits 'states from arbitrarily treating people differently under their laws' (Kleinfeld, 1970: 81) and which has resulted in closer correspondence between the legal and court procedures for juveniles and those for adults.

Of course, the whole question of whether equity or individualised treatment should constitute the basis for justice is much broader than simply how this issue affects the handling of juvenile misconduct. Kittrie (1971), the author of perhaps the most comprehensive analysis of the dangers of the 'therapeutic state', contends that modern welfare societies pose a major threat to the basic rights and freedoms of every individual by categorising all kinds of problems as social diseases and by advocating and justifying treatment programs for a variety of conditions without providing adequate legal safeguards, all in the name of the 'rehabilitative' ideal. This trend has for some time gone unchallenged because the treatment ideology underpinning it contains the presumption that rehabilitation is a 'self-evident good'[10], thus concealing the social control aspects of state intervention into people's lives behind a justifying rhetoric which combines science, medicine and humanism and emphasises prevention and cure rather than punishment.

The Current Situation

The current situation regarding the handling of 'needy', 'wayward' and 'delinquent' youth through juvenile courts, whether on criminal charges or care and protection applications, can best be understood as the logical outcome of the adoption of a rehabilitation philosophy and its implementation in juvenile court and welfare statutes in the late nineteenth and early twentieth centuries and with remarkably little substantial alteration.

Briefly, a child or young person under 17 or 18 years (varying by country and state) may appear in court for any of a number of reasons. These can be grouped into three main categories: (1) to face criminal charges in the same way as an adult might; (2) as a 'status offender', that is, as a result of conduct that is legally prohibited only for minors (such as non-attendance at school, running away, disobedience, uncontrollability or incorrigibility, sexual activity by girls, and maybe, smoking, drinking and staying out late at night); and (3) because of parental disappearance, inadequacy or ill-treatment. These three categories cannot in practice be so clearly differentiated and many courts deny the validity of such distinctions, preferring to operate on the presumption that all children appearing before them are in some sense 'in need of care, protection or control' (the *parens patriae* principle).

Despite the acknowledged problems associated with a welfare approach, there has as yet been no serious suggestion that the character or purpose of statutory services for the young should be altered in any significant way in the direction of a more legalistic system. Instead, our courts continue to administer what they regard as an individualised system, aimed at uncovering and remedying faults and inadequacies in the personality, family or immediate environment of the boy or girl. To this end, so-called 'non-offenders' (children before the courts on care applications), find themselves disposed of in similar ways to juveniles charged with criminal offences, including placement in the same institutions, though they have 'done nothing wrong'. Indeed, there is some evidence that the rehabilitation philosophy is responsible for non-delinquent but 'needy' children being sent to institutions more often, for longer periods and at younger ages than more seriously anti-social juvenile law-breakers. Since institutional sentences (whatever their rationale and character) involve removal from home and community, restrictions on movement, disruption of peer and other relationships, and enforced activities (educational, vocational and recreational) of various kinds and for considerable periods of time, they must be judged to be a more severe form of disposition than other non-institutional alternative.

An important consequence of the tendency to 'sentence' non- or status offenders in similar, if not more severe, ways than the delinquent offender is its differential effect on male and female juveniles. American research literature stresses the predominance of status offences (particularly those of a sexual kind) among female juvenile court appearances and of criminal law violations among males.[11] Grichting, in a nationwide survey of juvenile offenders, produces evidence both of status offenders receiving institutional placements (though he noted a greater likelihood for them to be sent to group homes and day centres while delinquents tended to go to institutions and training schools) and of the association between girls and status offences (1977: 140). Another recent study undertaken in Scotland (May, 1977) also supports these findings, though it is worth noting that the British situation differs from the American with respect to the proportion of females who are offenders. Whereas over half of court appearances of girls in America are concerned with status offences, in Britain only a minority of girls coming before the courts fall into this category, though the proportion is still markedly higher than that of boys.[12] Armstrong (1977: 116) produces data to support the contention that, compared with boys and given the varying nature of male and female delinquency, girls who less often commit criminal offences receive a disproportionately large number of institutional sentences and are detained for longer periods than are boys. Overall the issue of whether females are given more or less lenient treatment by the law and the justice system is a complex and confused one.[13]

This kind of sexual discrimination can be seen as a direct application of the protectionist philosophy contained in a rehabilitation approach, in which official intervention and disposition are determined not by a particular act (and the degree of damage, danger or social offensiveness involved) but by the perceived 'need' for help of the individual, particularly those individuals who happen to be young and female. In this spirit more 'treatment' is prescribed for the weaker and more vulnerable members of society. Put differently, and presumably by a writer who subscribes to this philosophy, 'Where the girl was perceived to be in some kind of moral danger the courts were inclined to adopt more positive [?] action' (May, 1977: 210); this entailed more use of probation and institutions compared with a greater resort to fines for boys.

A comparable picture emerges from available Australian data. The overall juvenile male:female sex ratio based on court appearances ranges between 4 and 6:1 and goes higher if welfare applications are excluded (Fielding, 1977: 155). A recent Queensland study found that 10 per cent of all appearances in 1973-74 for an offence were females, however, 51 per cent of care applications concerned girls. Higher proportions of girls than boys were committed to care and control or care and protection; fewer were either admonished and discharged or convicted and fined (Fielding, 1977: 180). A Victorian study of care applications in 1972 revealed girls outnumbering boys over the age of 12 years, and girls figured disproportionately in the categories implying moral or sexual risk (the 'exposed to moral danger' category was 80 per cent female and 'wandering' was applied in three quarters of cases to girls). Boys constituted over 50 per cent of cases only in the category 'lapsing or likely to lapse into a career of vice or crime', and of these over half had in fact already committed an offence. Neglect in its various manifestations affected boys and girls equally and particularly in the younger age groups. Regarding disposition, where the child's behaviour was deemed to be a significant element in the application, probation was more likely to be favoured, while, where parental circumstances seemed to be the problem, admission to the care of the Social Welfare Department was more common (Leaper, 1974).

These findings merit attention and explanation. Boys are primarily charged with committing the more serious offences in that they break criminal laws; girls predominantly find themselves in court on lesser charges relating to breaches of more general sexual and social behavioural codes of conduct (which are often 'offences' only when committed by those under a certain age). However, the bascially welfare-oriented model underlying the legislation, and the operation of the juvenile court system seem to result in young females receiving harsher sentences than their male counterparts, despite the finding that girls commonly appear on less serious charges than boys.

In looking for possible explanations of this situation, three main alternatives exist. First, there is the possibility that this differential attitude to and processing of young males and females is part of the **explicit and conscious intentions of the relevant pieces of legislation**, principally, in Victoria, the *Children's Court Act* 1958, amended 1973, and certain sections (that is, 31 and 34) of the *Social Welfare Acts,* 1970 and 1973. To establish whether or not this was the case, a careful examination of the particular legislation, and any associated or supportive legislation passed at the time, before or since, must be undertaken.

A second possibility would be that, although not clearly acknowledged as part of the explicit objectives of the legislation, those responsible for formulating legislative provisions, and/or those individuals and groups concerned about the problems the legislation was proposed to deal with, **intended that the measures** contained in legislation for the protection and control of wayward and delinquent juveniles **be interpreted differentially** for males and females in order to best meet different needs of the young members of the two sexes. Such a view would be consistent with a powerful though implicit **philosophy** favouring fairly traditional notions of family authority, adolescent behaviour, sexual morality and youthful susceptibility to temptation, and even corruption, in the absence of strong social and community controls. To test this argument, the basic philosophies of, and the major social influences operating on, those responsible for the relevant legislation would have to be uncovered.

Third, what we have termed sexual discrimination in the

treatment of juveniles may not be directly the result of the original intentions or provisions of the Acts nor of the underlying philosophy behind them, but of the fact that, as with all kinds of legislation couched in fairly general terms, the personnel whose task it is to implement it are left to interpret the provisions as they see fit, in the context usually of prevailing values, attitudes and expectations. That is, conceptions of male-female differences in relation to their biology, their personality development, their mental and moral capabilities and social roles, as well as popular or preferred approaches to problems of family inadequacy and juvenile misconduct as affecting the behaviour of such personnel. This kind of explanation requires an investigation of **perceptions and practices of a variety of persons and organisations** (police, social workers, teachers, court officials, magistrates), against a background of general community and media opinion and actions, in order to establish how each of these parties separately and often unintentionally, by acting in terms of their own goals, values, interests and knowledge, contributes to an overall pattern, which is based on, but not determined by, certain pieces of legislation and institutional machinery concerned with juvenile offenders.

The Legislation

In Victoria two main streams of legislation relate to the processing and disposing of children and young persons from the nineteenth century to the present day. On the one hand are specific children's court statutes, the most important being the 1906 Act establishing the children's court system and the 1958 Act (with some amendments in 1973). But second is a series of pieces of children's welfare legislation going back as far as the *Neglected and Criminal Children's Act* of 1864 and including significant developments in the Acts of 1928, 1958, 1960 and 1970. Although the various welfare and children's court Acts passed between the 1880s and 1970s in Victoria clearly constitute a relatively integrated package of attitudes and policies for state intervention in the families of certain categories of juveniles, it is convenient here to examine these two sets of statutes separately.

Perhaps the most important first observation is the remarkable degree of consistency and continuity (throughout approximately one hundred years) in the legislative provisions for delinquent and neglected youth, and how closely the situation in Victoria resembles the general picture drawn in the earlier part of this paper.

Starting with the welfare legislation, each of the various Acts contains a definition of 'neglected' or 'in need of care', procedures for apprehending and processing cases, a range of alternative dispositions, the kinds of institutions run or supervised by the government, and regulations governing institutions and private persons' dealings with state wards. Other less important sections deal with parental liability and maintenance arrangements for wards, the employment of children in care, the protection of infants, and other matters. Substantial additional provisions and an altered format are to be found in the 1960 Act which instituted subdivisions in the then Social Welfare Branch of the Chief Secretary's Department (a separate Social Welfare Department was set up only in 1970).

The definition of what constitutes 'neglect' or grounds for making a care application has not altered substantially.[14] Section 31 of the 1970 Act lists eleven separate reasons, with two additions in Sections 34 and 35, 100 and 104. In an abbreviated form they relate to children who:

Section 31   (a) are found begging or receiving alms. . .;

(b) are found wandering, abandoned, or sleeping, in any public place;

(c) have no visible means of support or no settled place of abode;

(d) are in a brothel or lodge, live or reside or wander about with known or reputed theives, drunkards, vagrants or prostitutes. . .;

(e) are employed in street trading in contravention of that Division or the regulations. . .;

(f) are not provided with sufficient or proper food, nursing, clothing, medical aid or lodging or who is ill-treated or exposed;

(g) take part in any public exhibition or performance . . . whereby the life or limbs of the child taking part is endangered;

(h) are in the care or custody of any person unfit. . .

to have the care or custody. . .;
- (i) are lapsing or likely to lapse into a career of vice or crime;
- (j) are exposed to moral danger;
- (k) are required by law to attend school and who without lawful excuse has habitually absented himself from school. . .

Subsection 34 (1) provides that any person having the care and custody of a child whom he believes to be beyond his ability to control may apply to a Children's Court for an order that the child is uncontrolled.

Subsection 35(1) provides that any parent, guardian, or person having the care and custody of a child may apply in the prescribed form to the Director-General that the child be admitted to the care of the Department.

Sections 100 and 104 duplicate the provisions of 34 and 35 but with reference to young persons between the ages of 15 and 17.

Section 13 of the original *Neglected and Criminal Children's Act*, 1864, covered categories (a), (b) and (c) together, (d), and an 'uncontrollable' category. The *Neglected Children's Acts* of 1887, 1890 and 1915 and the *Children's Welfare Act*, 1928 raised the age from 15 to 17 years, added a provision for criminal offenders and children working at nights to be considered as 'neglected', and separated the category residing in a brothel or associating with a prostitute from living or associating with other undesirables. The 1928 Act introduced for the first time a category of child whose parents admitted inability to support or who were referred by relatives or police for this reason.[15] Several new grounds were added in 1933 which correspond essentially to categories (e), (h) and (i) above, and broadened considerably the scope of the Department in removing children from unsuitable parents where the deficiency was largely moral, not material. In this vein there were also two categories directed expressly at **females** only:

(being a female) found soliciting men for prostitution or otherwise behaving in an indecent manner;

. (being a female) found habitually wandering about in a public place or public places at night without lawful cause. . .

These two clauses alone over the entire period refer specifically and only to girls. They disappeared, however, from the next Act, passed in 1954, which used almost exactly similar formulations as the 1958 Act and in the most recent legislation as quoted earlier. The 'moral danger' category, which does not mention females particularly, but which was presumably designed to replace the two provisions in the 1933 Act, has in fact, as has already been observed, been applied almost entirely to girls. The fact that the category of offender was dropped from the list of reasons for children being 'in need of care' in the 1954 Act seems a technical matter only, since children's court legislation provides for the juvenile law-breaker to be treated as either a neglected child or offender, and from 1956 a care and protection order was one of the admissible dispositions available to the courts in such cases.

Terminology used to describe the types of facility under the control of government welfare personnel reveals a mixture of penal and judicial elements with those relating to education and rehabilitation, of the kind already discussed above. 'Probationary' and 'reformatory schools', 'industrial schools' and 'receiving homes' (1884, 1887, 1915 and 1928 Acts) were the main places mentioned in the earlier legislation. Not until 1958 was a more unequivocal welfare orientation revealed by the classification of facilities into 'reception accommodation', 'homes', 'juvenile schools' and 'hostels'[16], and the explicit statement that each of these types of facility should be used both for juvenile offenders and for children admitted to care. In the description in the 1960 Act (and again in the 1970 Act) of the functions of the different Divisions in the Department, the Family Welfare Division was entrusted with the supervision of 'reception centres' and 'homes', while it was the concern of the Youth Welfare Division to manage 'remand centres' and 'youth training centres', as well as hostels and clubs. This showed an awareness of the existence of two different categories of juvenile under the Department's jurisdiction and the necessity for maintaining the notions of 'training' and 'detention' as well as 'care'. It appears that in part the problem of this dual function was solved by the introduction into the Department of these Divisions. In addition to the two already mentioned, a special Probation and Parole Division was instituted, predominantly to provide certain services for criminal offenders, both juvenile and adult and, because of alternative institutional provisions for criminals under the age of 21, a Prison's Division to be concerned with adult prisoners only.

A major innovation was the creation of separate Family and Youth Divisions. To the former was given prime responsibility for children taken into care (though young persons in need of care and protection were not excluded), a category which, by virtue of age and circumstances, was most suited to specifically welfare forms of aid. The latter was to be concerned with all young persons (that is adolescents aged between 15 and 21), including delinquents (who simply because of the age factor could be expected to present a more serious control problem).[17]

Thus, current welfare legislation, though indicating an acceptance of some differences between offenders and non-offenders in the types of services and institutional facilities required, primarily differentiates between categories of juvenile more in terms of age and type of need. The only reference to suggest any sort of sexual differentiation lies in the 1864 Act, which talks of 'superintendents' for boys' institutions and 'matrons' for girls' institutions, and suggests that a medical model of treatment at that time seemed more natural in the case of females than males.

Turning to the range of measures available for the 'treatment' of neglected children, these essentially covered a variety of institutions, public and private, and included reformatories up to as late as 1928; placements with private citizens for boarding and/or employment; and from 1928, in some cases, probation. Excluding special provisions, including probation, for uncontrollable children[18], no explicit directions were given as to which type of facility would be most appropriate for which type of child. This can be taken as strong indication of the acceptance of the principle of individualised treatment, matching disposition to the particular needs and circumstances of each child rather than attempting to prescribe a specific remedy for each type of presenting condition. In other words, the grounds for intervention were regarded as simply signs of underlying problems or pathologies, and not maladies in their own right. It is not therefore surprising that no recommendations are to be found which differentiate between boys and girls as to what form 'care' should take, though it is relevant to mention here that in one Act (1887 *Juvenile Offenders Act,* section 32), a specific injunction was placed on staff in reformatory schools to make sure females who had led an 'immoral or depraved life' were kept separate from other wards.

The only other sections of these welfare statutes pertinent here are those dealing with what constitute 'offences' against wards of the Department. Throughout the period, legislation prohibited communication between wards and 'outsiders', entry to premises under the control of the Department, and assistance or inducement to absconsion. Additionally, in the 1887, 1890, 1915 and 1928 Acts, special mention is made of sexual offences against young females in care of the Department: penalties are to be imposed on anyone who 'for the purpose of prostitution or defilement, inveigles or entices any unmarried female ward' under 18 years or 'who carnally knows' any female under 15 in his care or under 18 who is apprenticed or licensed to him.[19] The language used originally in the 1880s captures precisely the kind of special concern shown for girls. On the one hand girls are more likely to be considered to be harmed by inadequate moral supervision and to be more susceptible to the corrupting influence of undesirables. On the other hand, cases which came to official attention included girls who were themselves sexually procious if not active or who were judged to be already on the way to a life of 'immorality and depravity'.

Certain Acts were specifically concerned with the establishment and operation of children's courts in Victoria from 1906 to the present day. Basically the children's courts were set up, with support from probation officers and later a clinic (which operated from the 1940s), to adjudicate in as informal a manner as possible, and with the minimum of legalistic forms, cases of offences committed by males and females up to the age of seventeen.

From the earliest times, disposition of each case was to be decided in the light of extensive background information: specifically mentioned in the 1906, 1915 and 1928 Acts were the 'child's habits, conduct and mode of living' and from 1956 a longer list was given, covering 'the child's antecedents, home environment, companions, education, school attendance, employment, habits, recreations, character, disposition, medical history and physical or mental defects'.[20] The court is instructed to pay attention to any such report tendered and, where necessary, to adjourn the hearing for a report to be made.[21] Special reference is made in the 1958 Act (section 44) to reports supplied by the Children's Court Clinic.

The court in earlier Acts was explicitly empowered to treat any juvenile offender either as such or as a neglected child, but in 1958 this provision was replaced by a general direction that:

> ... the Court shall firstly have regard to the welfare of the child but shall also, where dealing with the child for an offence, have regard to the nature and circumstances of the offence, and to the child's character history and previous convictions (if any).[22]

To this was added in 1973:

> ... and shall make such recommendations as it considers necessary for the treatment or guidance of the child.[23]

The juvenile court has from its inception in Victoria been advised to be 'guided by the real justice of the case without regard for legal forms and solemnities' and to 'direct itself by the best evidence it can procure or that is laid before it'[24], and this same phrasing was used in the Acts of 1915 and 1928. Identical sentiments were expressed in later Acts:

> ... the court shall proceed without regard to legal forms and ceremonies and shall direct itself by the best information it can procure or that is laid before it.[25]

However in contrast to the earlier period[26], more recent legislation has reinstituted a stipulation that something like the usual legal rules of evidence be observed. This clause preceded the general advice quoted above and states:

> ... the court shall not be satisfied of the child's guilt except upon proof beyond reasonable doubt by relevant and admissible evidence.[27]

This is interesting in view of the generally controversial question of how courts, especially children's courts, balance legal rights and welfare needs. These considerations relate more specifically to the phase in the court's proceedings concerned with determining the guilt, innocence or 'need' of the child. Important also is a second major stage in which courts then decide on the most appropriate way of disposing of the case.

The welfare aim of individualised treatment, matched to characteristics and needs of each child rather than apportioned according to seriousness of offence or type of family problem, also requires a range of alternative dispositions and flexibility for the court in choosing between them. The 1958 and 1973 Acts permit the courts a number of alternatives for offenders, whether convicted or not, including commitment to the care of the Social Welfare Department, which effectively shifts the responsibility for ultimate disposition from the court to the Department.[28] These wide discretionary powers for the courts and the Department have not surprisingly attracted some negative comment.[29]

Another keenly debated issue relating to the legalism versus welfare question concerns the tendering of background reports. The child's social history is only supposed to be used in guiding the court in making the most suitable disposition, not on determining guilt or need.[30] But, as Johnston (1972: 248) points out, in parental neglect and ill-treatment cases and where girls are suspected of being 'exposed to moral danger', determining whether the child is in need of care and protection presumes some background information on the child and family. There are two relevant sections in the same Act, one prohibiting the use of social histories before a finding and the other admonishing the court to proceed on 'the best information' available.[31] Foreman (1975: 48-9) and Clunies-Ross (1968: 214-5) also draw attention to this problem. Johnston and Leaper (1974: 224) advocate consistency to the 'rehabilitative ideal' and hence argue for the admissibility of all available and pertinent information in the court from the start, but Johnston adds the proviso that, as in South Australia, the court should be satisfied not only that 'the child needs care and protection but that the state can in fact better meet the children's needs' than his current parents or guardians (1972: 249). Their answer to this dilemma then is not to reintroduce the kinds of legal safeguard provided in adult criminal courts but to increase the juvenile court's control over the welfare department regarding the ultimate dispositional outcome of the court granting a care application.[32]

In other words, the welfare of the child is better served by greater accountability of government departments and public facilities than by a strict formal adherence to the innocent before proven guilty rule and other legal safeguards. Others, however, see the solution in a sharper separation of predisposition and disposition phases of court hearings and/or the segregation of hearings and courts concerned with offenders from those dealing with care applications and welfare cases.[33]

The more practical aspects of the use of social reports by the courts will be discussed later, when we consider the ways in which the law and the court system actually work and turn our attention to the attitudes and practices of the various personnel involved in the 'social organisation of juvenile justice' (Cicourel, 1968).

This brief general analysis of the main provisions of the Victorian welfare and juvenile court legislation from the late nineteenth century to the present day has clearly established the existence of a welfare philosophy underlying the processing and disposal of children and young persons. The wide range of circumstances which can bring a child before the court; the kinds of considerations the court is enjoined to admit; and the instruction to select from the range of alternative measures according to the needs of the individual, as ascertained from a comprehensive social report, rather than by reference to the nature of his or her offence or the formal grounds for the care application, all point to a preference for a treatment over a legal or judicial model. Evidence for the blurring of the demarcation between 'delinquent' and 'dependent' youth can be found in the overlapping of legislative provisions, specific injunctions to the courts and similarities of disposition, including placement in the same institutions, for the various categories of juveniles.[34] Some problems, however, persist over how far therapy should be allowed to displace legality in determining the policy and practice of the courts. This seems, though, to be the kind of contentious issue that is never likely to be satisfactorily resolved.

It clearly appears that, from the late nineteenth century, a protectionist philosophy operated generally over a wide range of situations of juveniles 'in need' without any explicit sexual differentiation. The legislation was passed to ensure that all children and young persons coming under the care of the various government authorities would receive the benefits of welfare-oriented policies directed primarily at remedying material, social and moral deficiencies in their families or environment. The language, the types of facilities, and the avowed objectives of the legislation progressively over the period expressed a commitment to rehabilitative ideals rather than to a concern to find and punish wrongdoers, whether the offenders were law-breaking juveniles or negligent and irresponsible parents.

However, because the vast majority of juvenile offenders were and are male, whereas care applications deal equally with males and females up to the age of 10 or 12 years, but with greater numbers of teenage girls than boys (Leaper, 1974: 243), legislation devoted specifically to the welfare of 'needy' children developed (unchallenged from late last century) a strongly treatment-oriented approach. Delinquent boys could both be seen as less 'disturbed' and more justifiably disposed of in ways that related as much to their offence and prior delinquent record as to their current moral and social character and background. Society needed little persuading that young children and girls 'in need of care, protection and control' should be regarded as victims of their circumstances and treated accordingly.

Without overstating the case, there is also some evidence that young females present special problems and that some differences in policy and attitude are appropriate. Special extra provisions seem to be demanded, in the eyes of those responsible, because of the sexual nature of much female disturbance and deviance and the additional risks to girls of dubious or undesirable associations (whether with family members of others), compared with what is perceived as more 'normal' or 'healthy' male forms of adolescent protest or independence. Examples were given of clauses relating to a special need to protect girls from sexual abuse, but also shielding innocent girls in institutions from their more worldly peers, illustrating a somewhat ambivalent dual conception of the females in the care of the system.

Nevertheless, one must concede that the statutes themselves are in the main worded in a general way and that any selective enforcement along sexual (or any other, such as class, lines) cannot be attributed to the legislation as such. In any case, no conclusion could validly be drawn at this stage concerning the policies and practices of the courts and related personnel and organisations simply from an analysis of the relevant legislation.

The Underlying Philosophy

The gradual but steady conversion to the rehabilitative ideal of influential members of the professional middle class, politicians and legislators from the late nineteenth century in America and elsewhere and the implications of this for the processing and treatment of 'problem' youth has already been adequately covered, as has the prevalence of the associated notion that children cannot be assumed to have responsibility for their actions: they need to be helped to be good not punished for being bad. This latter premise is, of course, an essential element in any treatment-oriented model, though, as Clunies-Ross (1968: 221), among others, reminds us, no definite verdict has yet been reached as to whether we are dealing with partial or no responsibility. Further, if this is the case, then who or what is responsible?[35]

Platt sees the roots for the 'child-saving movement' as lying in middle class maternal but strict moralistic interests and values which were aimed at the moral and social reform of children from the poorer and immigrant sections of the urban working class. This was to be achieved, it was believed in the late nineteenth century, by committing wayward and neglected children to special, rurally located institutions which could provide, in isolation from the corrupting influence of the city and under disciplined and demanding but healthier conditions, for their moral as well as material welfare. Urbanism and industrialism were blamed for what was seen as general social disorganisation and widespread immorality and corruption, from which the young needed to be rescued for their own good and that of society as a whole.

This line of thinking, of course, opened up an unlimited number of possible excuses for outside intervention in the lives of the nation's (particularly lower class) families for the benefit of the child. Indeed juvenile welfare legislation and moral statutes have progressively both broadened the conception of 'need' and extended their scope over an ever wider range of types of cases considered to merit the court's attention. In fact this process has come in for critical comment just on these grounds. Platt has pointed out that it was the high value placed on home and family, facilitating the removal of children from families which failed to attain the standards set, that resulted in a situation in which 'almost any parent could be accused of not fulfilling the "proper function".' (1969: 135). Similarly, with regard to the 'status offence' concept (and taken in conjunction with the provisions for children whose parents lack the ability or inclination to restrain, control or instruct them in the proper way), almost no child or family is immune. Riback (1971) lists four ways in which the basic rehabilitation philosophy governing these statutes was deliberately used to justify legislation which offends other social norms. It was and is, she claims, 'unconstitutionally vague', 'impermissibly broad', 'unconstitutionally overbroad and subjective' and it 'impermissibly punishes a status', resulting in the arbitrary and discriminatory treatment of juveniles (on the basis of their age) and more particularly females. In this connection it is relevant to mention Clements' contention that discrimination based on a status (age, sex and so on) cannot be considered as a justifiable form of the exercise of discretion for the purpose of individualisation of treatment since it is based on group not individual characteristics (1972: 895).

It seems apparent that such discrimination was not only foreseen but deliberately intended by those drafting and supporting the legislation. Many provisions were clearly designed to give police, probation officers and social workers grounds to bring charges or a care application almost whenever or wherever they wished: 'the vague language incorporated within sex-neutral juvenile morals statutes', which was presumably deliberately adopted to permit the unrestricted application by professionals of a reform and treatment approach to juvenile misconduct and family inadequacy, 'invites, if not requires, sexist as well as subjective interpretations of morality' (Riback, 1971: 321).

Other factors obviously played a role. Johnston (1972: 242-3) attributed development of elaborate child welfare legislation and the shift from punishment and legalism to therapeutic aims particularly during the twentieth century, in part to the increase in knowledge of an expertise in child rearing and child management due to expansion and popularisation of the social and behavioural sciences. Different views as to the causes of problem behaviour in children and breakdown of relations between child and parent and the appropriate measures for dealing with such situations contributed to the changed role of the court and the increased emphasis on welfare measures and personnel.[36]

However, the application of biology, psychology and sociology has not necessarily made any serious impact on pre-existing notions about the different basic natures of males and females, about the different manifestations of disturbance, disorder or deviance among the young members of the two sexes and thus about their differing needs as regards treatment, therapy or rehabilitation. Rather, one could argue, such knowledge has added a further explanation of and legitimation for any sexual discrimination in these areas. Boys are aggressive and destructive, according to this line of thinking, which means their deviance mainly takes the form of law-breaking and, given the insecurities and frustrations of adolescence, such conduct in moderation can be understood and 'normalised'. Girls, however, need more careful and close guidance and supervision and those who come to official attention are more likely to be psychologically disturbed and to need more prolonged and substantial kinds of treatment. Exactly what is implied in the argument that women enjoy a different or greater rehabilitative capacity compared with men is often left unclear by those theoreticians and practitioners making use of it.[37]

Problems with girls are most likely to be associated with sexual precocity and their presumed greater vulnerability to temptation and corruption which, if not detected and checked, can lead to future promiscuity and unhappiness, even prostitution. Notions of pathology or 'innate moral perversity'[38] were, and still are, more likely to accompany explanations of female deviance than of male. Females, unlike males, were more frequently denied the 'classical concept of self-determinism'[39], the inference being that, since female criminality is statistically rare, female offenders are typically regarded as 'unnatural' or 'sick' members of their sex.[40] This perhaps helps account for the fact that, though criminal behaviour constitutes more of an obvious and direct danger to members of society, non-criminal female deviants may be subjected to more severe forms of sanction: premature or promiscuous sexual behaviour can evoke a more extreme reaction from the courts and welfare personnel. For this reason pre-delinquency intervention, care applications on the basis of 'exposure to moral danger', 'uncontrollability', and 'running away', and the use of indeterminate institutional sentences are regarded as more necessary and appropriate measures in the case of girls. In other words, in the past and continuing to the present, 'traditional stereotypes of women as the weaker and more dependent sex rationalise, indeed even legitimate, discriminatory correctional practices in the name of humanitarianism.'[41]

That this analysis is also applicable to Australia may be justified on twin grounds that we have evidence of a moral reformist and treatment-oriented approach to delinquency and problems of youth steadily replacing a more traditional correctional philosophy[42] and that Australia, like America, was a patriarchal society (reflecting the ideas of Victorian morality) subscribing to sexual stereotypes.

In particular, historical research shows that women in Australia were viewed in a somewhat contradictory light. On the one hand, their passive, dependent and suggestible nature demanded special vigilance and moral concern, lest they be led astray and in turn exercise a corrupting influence on others, specially their own children; on the other, they were respected, even revered, for their supposed superior moral and spiritual qualities.[43]

This belief appears to be deeply-rooted and widely found in human societies of all kinds. Its importance in this context lies in the effects of such a paradox on society's perception and treatment of females as compared with males, particularly those believed to be deprived, delinquent or in some way 'in need'. To sum up, these ideas permit, if not demand in the name of humanism and compassion, greater supervision and restriction of females, especially adolescent girls, even though their behaviour, whether actually or only potentially deviant, poses no serious threat to anyone or anything, except maybe themselves or a generalised but abstract entity such as the moral character of society. By contrast, the prosecution and penalisation of criminal offenders, who are predominantly male, can more readily be justified on the grounds that serious harm has been threatened or caused to property or person. Despite, therefore, the lack of direct or detailed evidence of the beliefs, attitudes and values relating to juvenile delinquency and dependency during this period in Australia, we maintain that conclusions drawn from the American context can be applied here. The general thesis that has been advanced is that legislation concerning neglected and delinquent children and their families reflected the prevailing state of moral concern about the effects of the 'urban-technological complex' (Platt, 1969: 72) and a decline in the traditional authority of religion, community and the family.

The Perceptions and Practices of Law Enforcement and Welfare Personnel

From a labelling perspective[44], deviant behaviour and social problems are to be viewed as social products not only in the sense that they have social antecedents but also in order to stress the fact that the perceptions and practices of particular persons and organisations in labelling and processing such phenomena play an important part. Social reaction, then, is considered to be instrumental in determining which of a broad range of possibly offensive or undesirable conditions and actions become 'deviant', that is, they are transformed into 'problems', 'crimes', 'diseases', 'disorders' or simply indicators of 'need'. The accompanying social control ideology can assume various forms. The two main contemporary examples are therapeutic (whether in a narrowly medical or broader social welfare version) and legalistic or correctional, both of which have already in this paper been seen to exercise important roles in the history of juvenile justice and children's welfare.

No account of the development and operation of the system for dealing with delinquent and dependent youth could, therefore, be complete without a consideration of how it works in practice. Certainly, we cannot assume that because politicians, legislators and others or the statutes themselves profess certain aims and philosophies that the resulting actions of the relevant institutions and personnel can or do put these into effect. Setting correctional or welfare goals and providing appropriate services are two quite separate things. As Bean (1976: 9) has noted, reform or rehabilitation and humanitarianism are not the same: reform may or may not have humanitarian aims; humanitarian policies may not be reformative. Some practical and administrative matters enter the picture too. Rehabilitation presumes the existence of a coherent body of knowledge, certain kinds of trained staff, particular types of institutional and other facilities, and so on.[45]

We have already established that females in general and adolescents in particular seem the prime candidates for the application of a treatment-oriented protectionist philosophy. For their own good the girls are brought to court on some moral charge, often resting more on the chance of future possible harm than on actual conduct or misconduct and with any sexual implications prominently featured as though these would, *ipso facto* and regardless of the circumstances, justify whatever judgment the court saw fit to make. Foreman (1975: 63) attributes this situation to 'a passive acceptance of the notion of "individualised justice" and adherence to the *parens patriae* philosophy' and goes on to raise the problems this can cause in threatening legality and more formal notions of equity justice. In pursuit of 'treatment', informality, subjectivity and flexibility are all encouraged with the effect that 'the medical analogy helps conceal abuses of the juvenile justice system.'[46]

What evidence supports this general thesis? Two main aspects of the operation of the Victorian children's court system are relevant: firstly, the question of how and why male and female juveniles are brought before the court and what dispositions are recommended by the courts and on what grounds; second, interpretation and assessment of the findings with the aid of comparable American material.

We have already made use of Leaper's 1972 study of care applications before the Victorian children's courts. Briefly her main findings were as follows. Out of 1,843 cases 60 per cent concerned children over the age of 12, the overall sex distribution was 62 per cent female and 38 per cent male, and the excess of females over males occurred in the older age-group. The two largest categories of application were 'exposed to moral danger' (26 per cent) and 'lapsing or likely to lapse' (22 per cent); over 95 per cent of the former were girls and two-thirds of the latter boys (1974: 243). Girls were also over-represented in the 'wandering' category and slightly over 50 per cent of the cases in the only other sizable categories ('no visible means' and 'in care of unfit person') were girls. Leaper notes a decline in the number of 16 year old girls on the various 'moral' charges which she associates with the age of consent (p. 13).

Except then for a minority of younger children and the 'neglect' categories, care applications predominantly concerned girls who were believed, because of their behaviour, character, family or associations, to present problems serious enough to warrant court intervention. The only category in which older boys were involved in any numbers was that of 'lapsing' (63 per cent), which, on the basis of the fact that over half had already had contact with the police and some 50 per cent (but not necessarily the same children) had criminal offences cited in support of the application, Leaper infers (pp. 184-6) were really a 'delinquent' group, which for reasons that were not entirely clear was being processed in this way rather than by proferring criminal charges Girls in 'moral danger' and 'found wandering' were as likely o even more likely to be referred by their families than by police, agencies or others and many of their home situations were characterised by high levels of conflict. By comparison children in the 'lapsing' group, who were more often male, were recorded as having less conflict with their parents.

The courts dealt with children of the various types somewhat differently. Approximately two-thirds of the cases falling into the 'neglect' categories were consigned to the care of the Social Welfare Department, compared with around one-third of those reported for behavioural or moral problems. For this latter group probation was the preferred measure in more than half of the cases (though for 'wandering' girls the figure was only around 30 per cent and another 30 per cent were adjourned).

Leaper thus paints a picture of the workings of the welfare and juvenile court systems as far as these affect non-delinquent problem youth which fits with our expectations based on current welfare thinking and the general intentions of the relevant legislation and which corresponds with what we know of the situation overseas. She raises doubts as to 'how far it is appropriate or efficacious to use the process of bringing a girl to Court and exposing her to the consequences of a Court appearance if her parents cannot, or do not, control her activities and make her behave in accordance with their own values and with community mores' (1974: 179). This present system results in some girls being committed to institutions also occupied by juvenile offenders which can hardly be considered to constitute 'rehabilitation' and where other kinds of social and community support for the girl either with her parents or in some other group setting would be far preferable.

Hancock examined a sample of 300 male and 141 female court appearances taken from cases involving police contact between January and June 1975.[47] Of these some 63 per cent of girls and 8 per cent of boys were brought to court on protection applications, the rest on criminal charges. This study too revealed sex differences in how juveniles attracted police notice. Higher proportions of females came to police attention by virtue of 'status offending', including being found drinking under age, wandering, hitchhiking, living away from parents or being in the company of undesirable persons. The proportion of girls apprehended in this category (34 per cent) far exceeded the proportion of boys (6 per cent). Also evident is that parents were responsible for occasioning police notice in far higher proportions of female cases (21 per cent compared with 1 per cent of males). Thus girls attracted police attention through status offending, parental complaints and, only in under 40 per cent of instances, criminal offences; boys overwhelmingly (over 90 per cent) came to police notice through their lawbreaking acts.

Further substantiation of the sexualisation of teenage misconduct was also found in that from the material contained in the police reports, it was evident that girls' sexual or moral behaviour was often a focus in cases where they actually came to notice through status offending or parental complaints. In addition a small proportion of females on protection applications came to police notice through their illegal behaviour but were presented on moral grounds because of other, sexual, kinds of deviance.

That actual offence rates were relatively equal for males and females in the 'status offence' categories, that parents were more likely to report daughters as missing, that police were more likely to apprehend girls than boys for 'status' offence behaviour and, finally, that some girls were 'known' to have behaved illegally but were still presented to court on a care and protection application indicate that police sexualise female behaviour and enforce different, and stricter, moral standards on girls than on boys. Thus the impression given by official figures that female offending is typically 'sexual' in nature may reflect more the police (and community) acceptance of a dual standard of morality and concern to reinforce conventional and respectable notions of morality and parental authority, rather than actual sex differences in behaviour.

The 1975 data also confirms that courts are more likely to choose rehabilitative measures (probation, supervision, institution) for girls (52 per cent:46 per cent) and favour more legalistic ones (bond, fine, adjournment) for boys. Cross-tabulation of type of offence and court disposition revealed that, if charged with illegal behaviour, girls were more likely than boys to receive lesser penalties, such as a warning or fine; for example, girls appearing in court for property offences were more likely to be given a non-supervisory sentence than were comparable boys (60 per cent:46 per cent). However, where females offended against moral standards, they were treated more harshly than males.

Analysis of police Form 276 brought to light direct evidence of sex differentiated judgments and selective emphasis in case presentation. Two examples only can be given here. Both truancy and unemployment seemed to be mentioned more often for females than for males and additional statements made implied that 'free' time was suspect in the sense that it provided opportunities for illegal or immoral behaviour. Secondly, as regards explicit mention of sexual history, although the numbers are too small for statistical tests, some explicit reference to sex-appropriate behaviour was found in 40 per cent of female cases but only 5 per cent of male, and 'sexual intercourse' in 29 per cent and 1 per cent of cases respectively. Further examination revealed that, whereas in the few male cases sexual history was directly related to an offence charge such as indecent exposure, a girl's sexual history was linked to a wider range of variables, including the girl's attitude to authority, cooperation with police, her credibility, home situation and moral reputation. Also involved was an acceptance of adolescent male sexual experimentation compared with the need to protect females from pre-marital activity and the definition of regular or frequent sex as 'promiscuity', a serious problem requiring official intervention. This too has different implications for girls from different socio-economic groups, in that, because lower class girls are socially and sexually 'precocious' in comparison with their middle class peers and spend more of their leisure time in public places they and therefore their behaviour is more likely to come to police notice and they are the ones most affected by a moralistic-welfare conception of adolescent female deviance.

Studies such as these reveal how the attitudes, values and actions of personnel entrusted with the tasks of child and family welfare and law enforcement affect the implementation of legislation. In relation to the operation of the juvenile court system in Victoria at least, the police play a key role. They make the decisions as to whether to deal informally with an incident or to bring the case to court, and whether under the relevant sections of the *Social Welfare Act* or as a criminal prosecution. They also prepare background social reports, a situation which has attracted criticism because of the legal implications of the police acting in the roles both of complainant and adviser to the court. Increasingly it is intended that the Social Welfare Department (both Court Advisory Service and Regional staff) should take over this latter function.

A number of writers in this field have concerned themselves

with the question of social reports. The very admission of such reports itself, of course, attests to the pursuit of treatment-oriented aims. Their purpose seems to have changed from that of offering relevant background information in mitigation of the offence committed to providing supportive evidence for and advice about sentencing with the objective of improving the appropriateness and effectiveness of court decisions.[48] However, as Davies (1974) points out, a dual system still obtains. For the young, for females and for first offenders, individual 'needs' may take precedence over more legalistic considerations, but even in these cases some balance between rehabilitation and the application of a tariff or equity principle must be set.[49] This places the writers of such reports, in most countries probation officers and social workers, in the powerful and invidious position of tendering their own social and moral judgments as to relevant factors and an individual's potential for reform in the name of offering 'objective' facts and technical or expert advice. Whether the probation officer tailors a report to suit the known practices and prejudices of a particular magistrate or whether over time the various parties come to share the same views, research shows that by and large the recommendations as to disposition of these specialist staff are followed by the courts.[50]

Whatever is the case, we badly need detailed sociological investigations, involving both interviewing and observation, into how and why police make their decisions about whether or not to prosecute and on what count, what effects different kinds of background information prepared by different categories of personnel have on the outcome of cases, and how courts determine guilt (or its equivalent) and choose between alternative dispositions. To date in Australia we have had to rely on suggestive evidence only such as that provided by the studies reported here.

Nonetheless, we can with some confidence assert that gender is an important factor in the minds of police, social workers and court officials whether or not they are aware of it, and that their attitudes and opinions do contribute significantly to the differential perception and treatment of young males and females by our welfare and juvenile justice systems. This picture broadly accords with the findings of comparable, historical[51] and contemporary, research from overseas. Scutt (1977) for one gives examples from one American juvenile court of the way any concern for due process still, despite Gault and other cases, fails to curb the licence afforded the court by the so-called protectionist principle. As Clements (1972: 896) concludes from his examination of sex and sentencing, '"protecting" women has resulted in women, in many cases, being denied equality of treatment'.

What this means, of course, is that to account adequately for the perceptions and practices of such specialist personnel we must look beyond them at the structural and institutional factors affecting them, the systems in which they work and society in general, and at general community attitudes and values relating to sex roles, the socialisation and education of the young, the family, norms governing adolescent behaviour and misbehaviour, strategies and ideologies of social control, and so on.

The history of welfare and children's court legislation in Victoria reveals few explicitly sexist references. However, the sexual climate surrounding this legislation, the protectionist stance adopted by children's court reformers and unequal implementation of vague juvenile-morals statutes has led to more frequent intervention of the state into the lives of females whose behaviour has contravened moral rather than criminal rules. What remains to be found is precisely under what conditions, as a result of what actions by what persons and with what consequences this victimisation occurs.

---

1. In this connection, Kleinfeld (1970: 411) has observed that it was only in the late eighteenth and nineteenth centuries that women, 'inferior' racial groups and the unpropertied classes were given full citizenship rights. Previously they shared in many respects the same kind of subordinate status which children still have.

2. Bean (1976: 16).

3. Bean (1976: 67).

4. Edelman develops this line of argument and talks of the different symbolic implications of using a language of 'reinforcement' and 'help' rather than of 'authority' and 'repression'. He contends that the language of the helping professions conceals the fact that their activities are nonetheless political: that is to say they 'create and reinforce popular beliefs about which kinds of people are worthy and which are unworthy: about who should be rewarded through governmental action and who controlled or repressed. Unexamined language and actions can help us understand more profoundly than legislative histories or administrative or judicial proceedings how we decide upon status, rewards, and controls for the wealthy, the poor, women, conformists, and non-conformists.' (1974: 297).

5. This and other elements of the justice approach, the welfare or

treatment approach and a third, which she terms a community approach, are outlined and compared in Parsloe (1976). See also Christie (1971).

6. For an extended analysis of the current state of the law in America regarding parental powers over children, see Kleinfeld (1970: 425-43).

7. See Kleinfeld (1977: 66-71).

8. As Platt has noted (1969: 176), both in the 'child-saving' period of the late nineteenth century and in the writings of the 1920s and 1930s 'social pathologists' analysed by Hills (1943), blame for most 'social disorganisation' and certainly the problems of adolescent disturbance and misconduct was laid at the door of urbanism and industrialism, and the general breakdown in family, religion and community that was believed to accompany such changes; the solutions that were advocated, particularly in the earlier period, centred around the re-creation in rural settings of the 'simple', 'natural', but disciplined and productive life.

9. Christie (1971: 364).

10. Bean (1976: 3).

11. See, for example, Chesney-Lind (1973: 55) and the President's Commission on Law Enforcement and the Administration of Justice (1967).

12. Despite this fact which is clearly demonstrated in annual Home Office Criminal Statistics on court appearances in England and Wales, English writers still cling to the notion that female delinquency is synonymous with sexual misconduct. See, for instance, Cockburn and Maclay (1965: 290).

13. See Smart (1976: 128-40). However the effects of this protectionism can be seen at no less than six points in the processing system: pre-trial detention, the granting of bail, the use of physical examinations, the grounds upon which institutional sentences are justified, the length of detention, and types of activities provided within institutions; and some evidence can be found that sexual discrimination in all these forms occurs.

14. Lemert, writing on the Californian situation, terms many of these same categories 'anachronisms' (1970: 82) and indeed very few cases nowadays are brought under some of them (Leaper, 1974: 243), but they remain on the statute books.

15. Section 24 of the *Children's Welfare Act*, 1928.

16. Section 12 of the *Children's Welfare Act*, 1958.

17. See the relevant sections of the 1960 and 1970 Welfare Acts, principally Sections 7, 9 and 10 of the 1960 Act and Sections 13, 27 and 92 of the 1970 Act.

18. Section 34(3), *Social Welfare Act*, 1970. It has already been noted (Leaper, 1974) that probation orders are more often made where the child's behaviour is a problem and Social Welfare Department care orders where family inadequacies are more to blame.

19. See Section 51 of the 1887 *Juvenile Offenders' Act*, Section 84 of the 1887 *Neglected Children's Act*, and Section 83 of the 1890 and 1915 *Neglected Children's Acts* and of the 1928 *Children's Welfare Act*.

20. See Section 12 of the *Children's Court Act*, 1958. Section 11 of the 1973 Act added to the above '. . . and any other relevant matters'.

21. See Section 27 of the 1958 Act and Section 25 of the 1973 Act.

22. Section 27(3) of the 1958 *Children's Court Act*.

23. Section 25(4) of the 1973 *Children's Court Act*.
24. Section 29 of the *Children's Court Act*, 1906.
25. Section 22(2) of the *Children's Court Act*, 1958. Section 20(2) of the 1973 Act.
26. In fact Alley (1976: 5) cites a proposed amendment to the 1906 Act (that failed to go through) which would have waived the usual rules of evidence altogether.
27. Section 22(1) of the 1958 Act, Section 20(1) of the 1973 Act.
28. Sections 28 and 29 of the 1958 Act and Sections 26 and 27 of the 1973 Act.
29. See, for example, Bean (1976: 143-7), Clunies-Ross (1968: 215) and May (1971: 366-8).
30. Section 27(1) of the 1958 Act and Section 25(1) of the 1973 Act.
31. Sections 12(4) and 22, *Children's Court Act*, 1958.
32. Bean (1975: 586) and Leaper (1974: 231) share this view.
33. See, for instance, Kittrie (1971: 148-56) and Clunies-Ross (1968: 220-3). In fact in many American states, arraignment and disposition in juvenile cases are determined at completely separate hearings.
34. Significant also, as Clunies-Ross (1968: 216) points out, is the fact that in different states neglect and uncontrollability may be handled as charges (South Australia and Tasmania), as bases for care applications (Victoria) or either (New South Wales). This suggests that whichever is the case is a relatively minor technical matter and what is important is the general uniformity of attitudes and provisions for all categories of children 'in need'.
35. For an insightful comparison of the underlying philosophies and the practical, moral and legal implications of a 'sickness' or medical model and a 'wickedness' or criminal justice one, see Aubert and Messinger (1958).
36. We should perhaps qualify this statement somewhat with respect to females. As a number of writers have pointed out (Rasche, 1974; Smart, 1976), a relatively simple biological or psychological deterministic theory about female behaviour and misbehaviour has dominated thinking and writing in the field of criminology particularly until very recent times.
37. Writers who deal with this issue and its bearing on the differential sentencing of the sexes include Armstrong (1977), Clements (1972), Riback (1971) and Schlossman and Wallach (1978).
38. Schlossman and Wallach (1978: 69).
39. Smart (1976: 5).
40. Smart (1976) devotes a whole chapter to the question of criminality, mental illness and female deviance (chapter 6). See Note 38 above for material relating to the implications of a 'sick' as opposed to a 'criminal' label. Rasche (1974: 312-3) comments on how in the 1920s legal and medical concerns became merged in the handling of female sexual deviance in America.
41. Schlossman and Wallach (1978: 67).
42. We should perhaps take care not to exaggerate the extent or the speed of this movement. Alley (1976: 12) quotes a report from the Melbourne *Argus* as late as 1939 to the effect that 'the substitution of parental for strictly judicial administration in Children's Courts' was still in the process of being accomplished.

124   Women and Crime

43. See Anne Summers, *Damned Whores and God's Police*, Penguin Books, Ringwood, 1975.

44. The main features of the labelling perspective are set out in Box (1971), Cicourel (1968), Kitsuse and Cicourel (1963) and Schur (1971). A reasonably comprehensive coverage of the major criticisms of this approach is to be found in Davis (1972) and Gove (1975).

45. Kraus (1973: 199) suggests that recent sentencing changes in relation to male delinquents in New South Wales may reflect an increasing permissiveness (lighter sentences) but shows no evidence of an increasing concern for treatment.

46. Balch (1975: 130).

47. A sample was also drawn of warnings, but that material is not included here. Excluded from the populations prior to sampling were cases of young children under the age of criminal responsibility and protection applications where no illegal or offensive behaviour of the child was mentioned.

48. Bean (1975).

49. Hardiker has contributed some interesting data on this subject. She found in one study (1979) that 'need' and 'tariff' factors were both associated, though independently, with sentence. She also (1977) after interviewing probation officers in England discovered that, though all made some use of a treatment philosophy, some seemed to favour such a model more than did others.

50. See Davies (1974). However this does not invariably happen; see the findings in a special study of 'moral danger' cases reported in Leaper (1974: 272-3).

51. Schlossman and Wallach (1978) present a well-documented account based on court records and secondary sources of how juvenile justice operated in the so-called 'progressive era' in America.

References

Alley, Diane (1976). 'The History and Development of the Children's Court in Victoria'. *The Probation Officer*, February: 2-18.

Armstrong, Gail (1977). 'Females Under the Law — "Protected" but Unequal'. *Crime and Delinquency*, 23(2): 109-20.

Aubert, Vilhelm and Messinger, Sheldon L. (1958). 'The Criminal and the Sick'. *Inquiry*, 1: 137-59.

Balch, Robert W. (1975). 'The Medical Model of Delinquency'. *Crime and Delinquency*, 21(2): 116-30.

Bean, Philip (1975). 'Social Inquiry Reports'. *Justice of the Peace*, 11 and 18 October: 568-9 and 585-7.

Bean, Philip (1976). *Rehabilitation and Deviance*. Routledge and Kegan Paul, London.

Box, Steven (1971). *Deviance, Reality and Society*. Holt, Rinehart and Winston, London.

Challinger, Dennis (1977). *Young Offenders*. NACRO, Melbourne.

Chesney-Lind, Meda (1973). 'Judicial Enforcement of the Female Sex Role: The Family Court and the Female Delinquent'. *Issues in Criminology*, 8(2): 51-69.

Christie, Nils (1971). 'Law and Medicine: The Case Against Role Blurring'. *Law and Society Review*, 5(3): 357-66.

Cicourel, Aaron V. (1968). *The Social Organization of Juvenile Justice*. Wiley, New York.

Clements, Mark C. (1972). 'Sex and Sentencing'. *Southwestern Law Journal*, 26: 890-904.

Clunies-Ross, Janet (1968). 'The Dilemma of the Child and the Law'. *The Australian and New Zealand Journal of Criminology*, 1(4): 212-24.

Cockburn, James L. and Maclay, Inga (1965). 'Sex Differential in Juvenile Delinquency'. *British Journal of Criminology*, 5: 289-308.

Davies, Martin (1974). 'Social Inquiry for the Courts'. *British Journal of Criminology*, 14: 18-33.

Davis, Nanette J. (1972). 'Labelling Theory in Deviance Research'. *Sociological Quarterly*, 13: 447-74.

Davis, Samuel M. (1974). *Rights of Juveniles: The Juvenile Justice System*. Clark Boardman, New York.

Edelman, Murray (1974). 'The Political Language of the Helping Professions'. *Politics and Society*, 4(3): 295-310.

Fielding, June (1977). 'Juvenile Delinquency'. In Paul R. Wilson (ed.), *Delinquency in Australia*. University of Queensland Press, Queensland. 153-90.

Foreman, Lynne (1975). *Children or Families?* Australian Government Social Welfare Commission, Canberra.

Grichting, Wolfgang L. (1977). 'On the State and Fate of Status Offenders'. *The Australian and New Zealand Journal of Criminology*, 10(3): 133-51.

Hardiker, Pauline (1977). 'Social Work Ideologies in the Probation Service'. *British Journal of Social Work*, 7(2): 131-54.

Hardiker, Pauline (1979). 'The Role of Probation Officers in Sentencing'. In H. Parker (ed.), *Social Work and the Courts*. Arnold, London. 117-34.

Gove, Walter R. (ed.) (1975). *The Labelling of Deviance: Evaluating a Perspective*. Wiley Halsted Press, New York.

Johnston, Stanley W. (1972). 'Strengthening the Children's Court Act in Victoria'. *The Australian and New Zealand Journal of Criminology*, 5(4): 241-9.

Kitsuse, John I. and Cicourel, Aaron V. (1963). 'A Note on the Uses of Official Statistics'. *Social Problems*, 11: 131-9.

Kittrie, Nicholas N. (1971). *The Right to be Different*. John Hopkins Press, Baltimore.

Kleinfeld, Andrew Jay (1970). 'The Balance of Power Among Infants, Their Parents and the State'. *Family Law Quarterly*, 4(3) and 4(4): 320-50 and 410-43.

Kleinfeld, Andrew Jay (1971). 'The Balance of Power Among Infants, Their Parents and the State'. *Family Law Quarterly*, 5(1): 64-107.

Kraus, J. (1973). 'Children's Court Policy in New South Wales'. *Australian Law Journal*, 47: 197-202.

Leaper, Patricia M. (1974). *Children in Need of Care and Protection*. University of Melbourne Criminology Department, Melbourne.

Lemert, Edwin M. (1970). *Social Action and Legal Change*. Aldine, Chicago.

Martin, Christopher A. (1977). 'Status Offenders and the Juvenile Justice System: Where do They Belong?'. *Juvenile Justice,* 28(1): 7-17.

May, David (1971). 'Delinquency Control and the Treatment Model: Some Implications of Recent Legislation'. *British Journal of Criminology,* 11: 359-70.

May, David (1977). 'Delinquent Girls Before the Courts'. *Medicine, Science and Law,* 17(3): 203-11.

Mills, C. Wright (1943). 'The Professional Ideology of Social Pathologists'. *American Journal of Sociology,* 49: 165-80.

Parsloe, Phyllis (1976). 'Social Work and the Justice Model'. *British Journal of Social Work,* 6(1): 71-89.

Platt, Anthony M. (1969). *The Child Savers.* University of Chicago Press, Chicago.

President's Commission on Law Enforcement and the Administration of Justice (1967). *Task Force Report: Juvenile Delinquency and Youth Crime.* U.S. Government Printing Office, Washington, D.C.

Rasche, Christine E. (1974). 'The Female Offender as an Object of Criminological Research'. *Criminal Justice and Behaviour,* 1(4): 301-20.

Riback, Linda (1971). 'Juvenile Delinquency Laws: Juvenile Women and the Double Standard of Morality'. *U.C.L.A. Law Review,* 19: 313-42.

Schlossman, Steven and Wallach, Stephanie (1978). 'The Crime of Precocious Sexuality: Female Juvenile Delinquency in the Progressive Era'. *Harvard Educational Review,* 48(1): 65-94.

Schur, Edwin M. (1971). *Labelling Deviant Behaviour.* Harper and Row, New York.

Scutt, Jocelynne A. (1977). 'Justice in a Juvenile Court: What Price Due Process?' *The Australian and New Zealand Journal of Criminology,* 10(3): 173-84.

Smart, Carol (1976). *Women, Crime and Criminology: A Feminist Critique.* Routledge and Kegan Paul, London.

Summers, Anne (1975). *Damned Whores and God's Police.* Penguin Books, Ringwood.

Victorian Statutes: *Neglected and Criminal Children's Act* 1864, No. 216; *Neglected Children's Act* 1887, No. 941; *Juvenile Offenders' Act* 1887, No. 951; *Neglected Children's Act* 1890, No. 1121; *Children's Court Act* 1906, No. 2058; *Children's Court Act* 1915, No. 2627; *Neglected Children's Act* 1915, No. 2703; *Children's Court Act* 1917, No. 2914; *Children's Welfare Act* 1924, No. 3351; *Children's Court Act* 1928, No. 3653; *Children's Welfare Act* 1928, No. 3654; *Children's Welfare Act* 1933, No. 4152; *Children's Welfare Act* 1954, No. 5817; *Children's Court Act* 1956, No. 6053; *Children's Court Act* 1958, No. 6218; *Children's Welfare Act* 1958, No. 6219; *Social Welfare Act* 1960, No. 6651; *Social Welfare Act* 1970, No. 8089; *Children's Court Act* 1973, No. 8477.

7 The Myth of Rising Female Crime

SATYANSHU K. MUKHERJEE AND
R. WILLIAM FITZGERALD

Review and Analysis of Previous Work

In recent years there has been a considerable interest in the subject of 'crimes by women'. Many writers seem to suggest that this subject is an issue warranting further investigation in the context of the changing status of women in society. This interest has coincided with the accelerated momentum of the feminist movement. In the light of the available evidence the seriousness of female crime presented by numerous writers of varied ideological persuasions and theoretical biases, the import of this issue is not adequately substantiated. The analysis and interpretations of evidence by some of the writers are inappropriate and misleading; others have presented purely conjectual opinions.

The earlier works on the subject concentrated mostly on convicted prisoners and delinquent girls in institutions and currently this work is being critically re-examined. Almost all of the work since earlier this century has been labelled as 'sexist, racist and classist in its implications'[1] by the so-called 'feminist' and 'radical' criminologist. One must appreciate that the writers of today are as value system bound as their forebears, but that the value systems have changed with time and are now seen to be inconsistent. Thus, to label the earlier work as Klein has done, is unwarranted and unscholarly. History is replete with incidents in which a particular work was acclaimed when it was written but severely criticised several years later. That the feminist and radical perspectives will meet a similar fate some years from now is highly probable, and this could happen to what we are now writing.

Recent work on female criminality places a greater emphasis on the study of the nature and extent of crime by women. These writers, who have invariably criticised earlier works, are themselves open to similar accusations. In all cases, with the possible exception of Simon[2], we consider that their selected uses of data, types of analytic techniques employed and derived interpretations are not consistent with the data they present. If the arguments posited by these writers are to be supported or rejected, then data of a larger time span than has been used will be necessary, coupled with more appropriate analysis.

Longitudinal studies on the nature and extent of crime are few and those which relate crime to socio-economic change are fewer still. There is no study to date which has systematically analysed the involvement of women in crime for a length of time that could reasonably be acceptable for trend analysis. Yet, to substantiate that the changes in the status of women are responsible for the increase in criminality by women requires longitudinal data. Moreover, even if we demonstrated an increase in female criminality along with augmented female participation in all spheres of human endeavour, our conclusions would at best lead to an imputation of relationship, causality in the social sciences being indeed a tenuous concept.[3]

Present knowledge on female involvement in crime is inadequate. The literature that existed until recently dealt with the etiology of female crime and delinquency, research on which relied primarily on data gathered from prisons and juvenile institutions. These researchers, while offering various explanations, placed heavy emphasis on biological characteristics of the female sex. Thus, most writers on the subject of female criminality, from Lombroso[4] to Thomas[5] and Pollak[6], devoted their investigations to the physiological and psychological aspects of female offenders.[7] This is not to deny the fact that all of them, and Thomas[8] in particular, analysed female delinquency in relation to the interaction between aspects of culture and social environment.

All of these writers have suggested that the violations by women were predominantly centred on promiscuity and prostitution. In this context, and on the basis of abundant case studies presented by the above authors, the modern critics of these works term them as sexist in approach. That the societies in the early part of this century placed heavy sanctions on sexual aberrations by females and that those who sanctioned these aberrations were predominantly males are beyond dispute. Although these earlier works in a sense considered the female sex inferior to the male, they did not necessarily lay the blame for this inferiority on the female sex. Lombroso, for example, in the preface to his book, *La donna delinquente, la prostituta e la donna normale,* remarks:

> Not one of the conclusions drawn from the history and examination of woman can justify the tyranny of which she has been and is still a victim, from the laws of savage peoples, which forbade her to eat meat and the flesh of the coconut, to those modern restrictions, which shut her out from the advantages of higher education and prevent her from exercising certain professions for which she is qualified. These ridiculous, cruel, and tyrannical prohibitions have certainly been largely instrumental in maintaining or, worse still, increasing her present state of inferiority and permitting her exploitation by the other sex. The very praises, not always sincere, alas, heaped on the docile victim, are often intended more as a preparation for further sacrifices than as an honour or reward.[9]

Similarly, Thomas sees individual aberrations as consequences of the total social environment:

> It is only as we understand behaviour as a whole that we can appreciate the failure of certain individuals to conform to the usual standards. And similarly, the unrest and maladjustment of the girl can be treated only as specifications of the general unrest and maladjustment.[10]

> All age levels have been affected by the feeling that much, too much, is being missed in life. This unrest is felt most by those who have, heretofore, been most excluded from general participation in life — the mature woman and the young girl. Sometimes it expresses itself in despair and depression, sometimes in breaking all bounds.[11]

Pollak, by contrast, emphatically asserts that 'the criminality of women reflects their biological nature in a given cultural setting'.[12]

Unlike the previous two authors, Pollak does not present any supporting evidence whatsoever to substantiate his own 'self deception'. Lombroso and Thomas have used numerous case studies, albeit with a lack of any contemporary sampling and statistical techniques, whereas Pollak uses neither.

Klein's criticism of Thomas ignores his overall approach to the concept of social change, through the institutionalisation of deviance, for example, 'redefinition of the situation'. In Thomas' own words:

> Every new invention, every chance acquaintanceship, every new environment, has the possibility of redefining the situation and of introducing

change, disorganisation or different types of organisation into the life of the individual or even of the whole world.[13]

Klein is decidedly uncharitable in her comments:

> [Thomas] rejects economic causes as a possibility at all, denying its importance in criminal activity with as much certainty as Lombroso, Freud, Davis, Pollak and most other writers.[14]

Quite to the contrary:

> The bad family life constantly evident in these pages and the consequent delinquency of children, as well as crime, prostitution and alcoholism, are largely due to the overdetermination of economic interests — to the tendency to produce or acquire the largest possible amount of economic values — because these interests are actually so universal and predominant and because economic success is a value convertible into new experience, recognition response, and security.[15]

Similarly, Lombroso did not reject 'economic causes as a possibility *at all*'[16]; an entire chapter is devoted to the examination of 'Influence of Economic Condition/Wealth'.[17]

Pollak does not mention economic causes at all. His idea of women's emancipation, however, is directly related to job opportunities for women. By asserting repeatedly, with inconsistent data from various countries, that criminality of women increased during the war years, Pollak implies that this was so because more women entered the job market. Curiously, his book supplies no corroborative evidence on employment of women.

In contrast, recent authors have examined official criminal statistics to assess the extent and significance of female criminality. Some of these have extended their analyses to encompass the possible effects of the emergence of the feminist movement. Furthermore, a number of authors have noted the paucity of literature in the area.[18] Recent writings have generated interest in the subject but have added very little, if any, to the body of substantive knowledge. Most of the authors have provided some data to support their arguments and ideological underpinnings; few have demonstrated an ability to analyse and interpret the data they present; fewer still, relate crime data to exogenous variables; and none express the increase or decrease of female crime as a function of population.

Pollak[19] is perhaps one of the earliest writers to assert that the criminality of women was increasing; he included in his work statistics from the United States and several European countries. However, his selective use of data, inappropriate analysis, and dubious interpretation based on false assumptions are hardly convincing.

Hoffman-Bustamante[20] with the help of arrest data from the *U.S. Uniform Crime Reports* and *California Crime Statistics* examines the nature of female crime. Although she presents data for 1958, 1964 and 1970 she does not make any attempt to demonstrate changes in the pattern of female criminality. For interpretation she relies heavily on works on specific offences by earlier writers. Unlike others, she has used proportion of male-female involvement in crime but unfortunately she, like most others, has not computed these proportions on population based rates.

Adler asserts that, 'Women are indeed committing more crimes than ever before. Those crimes involve a greater degree of violence.'[21] Her analysis is somewhat simplistic, and if we view the rise of female criminality in isolation then we cannot but agree that it is increasing. However, a simple percentage change in crime (as used by Adler) leads to an overstatement of the fluctuations in crime; a more precise and appropriate measure is to express crime data in relation to population, for example, rate per 100,000 population.

If we want to demonstrate the increase in female criminality in comparison to male criminality (as Adler intends) it seems to us that a more appropriate method will be to compare proportions (preferably computed from rate per 100,000 population) of total crime ascribed to male and female; since crime by women is numerically small any increase will produce an inflated picture in percentage terms.

Tables 1 and 2 illustrate the *UCR* crime data for the years 1960 and 1972 (used by Adler) in terms of the three basic methods of describing changes: percentages based on absolute numbers (column 7 — *UCR* presentation), sex-specific rates per 100,000 population (column 8), and proportion of male to female participation based on sex-specific rates per 100,000 population (column 9).

Percentage change within sex is a convenient method of demonstrating changes in the absolute numbers. It cannot provide a comparison of volume of participation in crime between sexes.

Table 1 — Assessment of Change in Arrest Data for Females for Serious Crimes, UCR 1960 and 1972

	Number of Crimes 1960 (1)	1972 (2)	Crime Rate/100,000 1960 (3)	1972 (4)	Proportion of Total 1960 (5)	1972 (6)	UCR Δ % (60-72) (7)	Rate Δ % (60-72) (8)	Proportion Δ % (60-72) (9)
Murder	740	1,585	1.96	3.61	.165	.154	114.2	84.2	-1.1
Manslaughter	173	196	0.46	0.45	.100	.130	13.3	-2.2	3.0
Robbery	1,423	5,368	3.78	12.22	.046	.065	277.2	223.3	1.9
Agg. Assault	7,459	14,191	19.80	32.31	.141	.135	90.3	63.2	-0.6
Burglary	3,545	9,505	9.41	21.64	.030	.049	168.1	130.0	1.9
Larceny	30,199	121,759	80.16	277.21	.160	.297	303.2	245.8	13.7
Auto Theft	1,904	4,736	5.05	10.78	.036	.055	148.7	113.5	1.9
TOTAL	45,443	157,340	120.63	358.22	.101	.177	246.2	197.0	7.6

Population 37,672,020 43,923,240

Table 2 — Assessment of Change in Arrest Data for Males for Serious Crimes, UCR 1960 and 1972

	Number of Crimes 1960 (1)	Number of Crimes 1972 (2)	Crime Rate/100,000 1960 (3)	Crime Rate/100,000 1972 (4)	Proportion of Total 1960 (5)	Proportion of Total 1972 (6)	UCR △% (60-72) (7)	Rate △% (60-72) (8)	Proportion △% (60-72) (9)
Murder	3,589	8,354	9.92	19.80	.835	.846	132.8	99.6	1.1
Manslaughter	1,502	1,273	4.15	3.02	.900	.870	-15.2	-27.2	-3.0
Robbery	28,519	73,990	78.79	175.33	.954	.935	159.4	122.5	-1.9
Agg. Assault	43,606	87,178	120.48	206.58	.859	.865	99.9	71.5	0.6
Burglary	108,930	177,417	300.96	430.41	.970	.951	62.9	39.7	-1.9
Larceny	152,157	277,419	420.38	657.38	.840	.703	82.3	56.4	-13.7
Auto Theft	49,200	78,397	135.93	185.77	.964	.945	-59.3	36.7	-1.9
TOTAL	387,503	704,028	1,070.61	1,668.28	.899	.823	81.7	55.8	-7.6

Population 36,194,686 42,200,760

Notes:
1. Between 1960 and 1972 the national population growth was 15.2548 per cent and we assume the same rate of population growth in reporting agencies.
2. Since no population data is reported in the 1960 UCR, we have used as our base the 1972 figures and worked our way backward using compound yearly rate of decline up to 1960 at a rate of 1.2712 per cent per year. The population presented in the 1972 UCR was 86,124,000 and by the above method of calculation the 1960 population comes to 73,866,706.
3. The average male:female ratio in the population from 1960 to 1972 is 49:51.

Source: United States Uniform Crime Reports 1972, Table 30, p. 124.

Also, by definition, percentage change will always be positive unless there has been a drop in the absolute numbers. Furthermore, the size of percentage change is directly related to the size of the absolute numbers. The above points are likely to be exacerbated by the seemingly haphazard selection of time-span.

The major weaknesses of using percentage change as a measure of the changing volume of crime, which Adler and Simon[22] do not seem to be aware of, is that it cannot be used to compare criminality between sexes. Standardising the absolute crime data to sex-specific rates per 100,000 population insures comparability. What the standardised crime rates do not produce, however, is a quantification of the relative participation by males and females in this changing volume of crime. This relative participation can be expressed by using proportions. Furthermore, these proportions, if based on sex-specific rates per 100,000 population, offer a powerful and clear tool for the analysis of the relative participation in crime by the sexes. Thus, rates and proportions used as two distinct measures of the volume of, and relative participation in crime respectively provide a much more meaningful assessment of the changing character of crime than do simple percentages.

Following the above discussion, if we pause to examine Tables 1 and 2 we observe a somewhat different picture to that presented by Adler and Simon. Both authors, by using simple percentage change, suggest that the volume and relative participation in crime by women have increased substantially. Adler maintains that between 1960 and 1972 the number of women arrested for robbery rose by 277 per cent.[23] The change in the volume of robbery by women, based on percentage change in rates, is 223.3 (Table 1, column 8); this has been matched by a proportional increase of only 1.9 per cent, in the number of women arrested (Table 1, column 9). The figures for men arrested for robbery are 159.4 per cent, 122.5 and -1.9 respectively (Table 2, columns 7, 8 and 9). The increase or decrease in rates does not necessarily reflect a concomitant change in proportions in the same direction; a case in point is manslaughter for males and females.[24] Data in these two tables also demonstrate that except for larceny, the male-female participation in crime has remained fairly stable within the range of approximately ± 3.0 per cent; the overall change in proportion for index crimes during this period was only approximately ± 7.6 per cent.

Crites[25] is the only contemporary writer who has identified similar flaws to those pointed out by the present authors in the interpretation given to official statistics by Adler and Simon. She recognised that 'we can more appropriately examine the issue by analysing changes in the female percentage of total arrest'[26], for example, proportions. By amassing data from a number of studies she disputes the relationship between 'the rise in female crime and the women's liberation movement'[27] and she observes that, 'the movement appears to have had little effect on female offenders and their peers.'[28] Crites further suggests that the benefits of the movement:

> ... for equal employment opportunities accrue predominantly to white, middle class females. The women's rights movement has largely swept over the sub-population group of poor, minority females into which the female offender falls.[29]

It must be noted, however, that Crites uses the three terms, women's rights movement, women's liberation movement and feminist movement, synonymously although there are discernible functional and ideological differences between the three.

A review of the recent literature on female criminality would not be complete without references to the works of some of the proponents of feminism and radical criminology, for example, Klein and Kress[30] and Smart.[31] Their contributions to the sparse body of substantive knowledge on female criminality are at best marginal; these works are characterised more by flowing rhetoric than by hard evidence.

Here in Australia there are no comparable works in the area. The literature which exists deals with the Australian woman in an historical perspective[32], and wherever reference is made to the criminality of women it is concerned either with women as convicts[33] or women in prison.[34]

The Present Study

The Data: The impetus for this study came from both the current controversy surrounding the subject of female criminality and a major research project on the crime trends in Australia recently completed by the senior author.[35] It is not the intent of the present study to test any theories on female criminality, nor does it endeavour to establish a relationship between crimes by women and their participation in activities which have until recently been the prerogatives of men. This study simply makes a modest contribution to the knowledge on the criminality of women during the past several decades.

Our study is based on official crime statistics. Undoubtedly there are limitations to these statistics; which are well documented in the literature. In spite of these limitations, researchers have consistently used such statistics for comparison purposes. Nonetheless, until better methods of record-keeping become practicable and other means of assessing the phenomenon of crime (for example, victim surveys) become viable, the existing official statistics are the best sources of data.

An examination of the changing patterns of crime in Australia, with particular emphasis on the nature and extent of crimes by women, is the central issue in this paper. The two general hypotheses to be tested are that: (i) female crime has increased since the turn of the century and (ii) this rate of increase has been greater than that for men. These two hypotheses will be tested in relation to offence type and jurisdiction.

Since the study utilises all cases appearing before Magistrates' Courts for each year 1900 to 1975, this constitutes the universe of cases; thus, the need for sampling procedures is obviated. Considering this unique characteristic of the data, some of the statistical procedures required for sampled data, for example, tests of significance and association, are not only unnecessary but inappropriate.

To address the dual concept of measuring the volume of, and relative participation in crime, our analysis will be based upon sex-specific crime rates per 100,000 population, and proportions across sex.

The study covers four States of Australia, that is, New South Wales (N.S.W.), Queensland (Qld.), South Australia (S.A.) and Western Australia (W.A.).[36] The States of Victoria (Vic.) and Tasmania (Tas.) have not been included because sex-specific data are not consistently available. The Northern Territory (N.T.) and the Australian Capital Territory (A.C.T.) have been excluded because they came into existence as separate entities in 1911 and therefore statistical records are incomplete. Table 3 provides essential population characteristics of the jurisdictions.

The study encompasses the first 76 years of the twentieth century, that is, 1900 to 1975. This long time span enables us to

Table 3 — Population Characteristics as at 31 December 1975

Jurisdiction	Percentage Population	Population Density/km^2	Masculinity
New South Wales	35.43	6.01	99.83
Queensland	14.80	1.17	101.39
South Australia	9.11	1.26	99.53
Western Australia	8.36	0.45	104.01
Victoria	27.11	16.46	99.68
Tasmania	3.01	6.03	100.02
Northern Territory	0.70	0.07	118.21
Australian Capital Territory	1.48	83.82	103.43
Australia	100.00	1.77	100.51

Source: Australian Bureau of Statistics, Canberra, Unpublished data.

examine a period in Australian history which has been transgressed, like many other countries, by the following major events:

World War I
The Great Depression
World War II
The Post-war Economic and Baby Booms
The Recessions of the 1960s and the 1970s

The selection of Magistrates' Courts[37] data in preference to police statistics was dictated by the following considerations: (i) the data relating to cases brought before the Magistrates' Courts have been available in a fairly consistent manner for the entire period under study for all the four jurisdictions; and (ii) these statistics provide a broad spectrum of analytic possibilities because they include:

- all cases in which charges were laid and persons brought before the courts by arrest, summons and private prosecution;
- sex distribution of cases;
- type of disposition, for example, convictions, committals to higher courts, and discharges.[38] (No sentencing data have been compiled.);

an almost identical classification of offences into five major categories[39] across the four jurisdictions.

Police statistics (crimes known to police) contain none of the advantages outlined above. Specifically, they contain no sex-specific data, they do not exist in all the four jurisdictions for the entire period under study for all offences and in a comparable manner.[40]

We are aware that, 'the value of a crime rate for index purposes decreases as the distance from the crime itself, in terms of procedure, increases.'[41] As neither crimes known to or cleared by police have sex-specific data, the next procedural level for which consistent data are available is arrest. The Magistrates' Courts data include all cases cleared by arrest or summons, along with additional privately instigated cases. In other words, the Magistrates' Courts are the closest procedural stage to the crime itself.

The yearly offence data for all the Magistrates' Courts include both adults and juveniles; these data have been organised, for the purposes of the paper, into the following categories: (i) offences against the person (excluding rape)[42]; (ii) offences against property[43]; (iii) offences against good order[44]; and (iv) total offences (i to iii above).[45]

From our analysis we have excluded the entire category 'petty offences', which are generally violations of State laws such as maintenance laws, liquor laws, gambling, gaming and lottery laws, broadcasting and television acts, income tax and revenue laws, railways acts, traffic and transport laws, etc. It must be pointed out that the violations of traffic and transport laws constitute, especially since the early 1950s, a substantial majority of the 'petty offences'.

We felt that the inclusion of these offences would have seriously confounded our analysis. The traffic offences presented in the court statistics include minor traffic offences, most of which could have been settled out of court. The annual reports of police administrations indicate that a much larger number of such offences are settled out of court in each jurisdiction by payment of on-the-spot fines of which no detailed statistics are maintained. Serious traffic offences, for example, auto theft and those resulting in death or injury, are incorporated in offences against property and person respectively.

A further methodological point is that in the 'petty offences' category there have been significant changes in the content of offences because of the introduction of automobiles, television, etc., which have given rise to a large number of offences which were not possible in the early part of this century; the inclusion of these, therefore, would make a false comparison over time.

This study will therefore deal only with major offences and those minor offences stated above. 'Petty offences' tend to inflate the crime statistics as they form a substantial proportion of *all known offences*; this is demonstrated in Table 4.

Table 4 — 'Petty Offences' as a Percentage of All Known Offences Charged by Sex, State and Decennial Year: 1910-1975

	N.S.W.		QLD.		S.A.		W.A.	
	M	F	M	F	M	F	M	F
1910	25.6	16.3	18.6	14.3	27.1	13.3	22.9	20.3
1920	41.7	23.2	27.1	26.8	44.9	41.3	23.4	20.3
1930	47.2	26.8	35.4	20.8	63.7	58.0	55.4	46.9
1940	52.2	32.6	51.0	34.0	69.2	66.8	67.9	56.9
1950	42.6	27.6	26.9	11.9	68.7	70.7	60.4	41.2
1960	56.2	38.0	54.9	59.4	80.1	82.1	70.3	58.5
1970	64.1	50.9	59.9	70.3	81.1	77.1	57.2	49.6
1975	na	na	60.5	61.6	83.7	73.3	65.4	49.6

A data set of this magnitude necessarily presents problems which may arise because of record-keeping procedures, offence classifications, etc. In this context the paramount consideration was to ensure the consistency of data over time and across jurisdictions. The task was accomplished by meticulously scrutinising the offence content of the major categories in each jurisdiction for each year. Wherever we observed a change in the content of the major categories, we have rectified the discrepancy.

Results: The analysis of data in relation to the three major categories of offences and the two general hypotheses, stated earlier, will proceed in terms of the following: (i) volume of crime; (ii) relative participation of males and females; and (iii) conclusions.

(i) Volume of Crime

An initial examination of the data for the four States yields the impression that the volume of crime in Australia[46] is about the same in recent years as it was at the turn of the century. If one were to consider the total picture of crime, especially during the last two decades, to be represented by the totality of *all known offences,* one could not escape the conclusion that crime was on the increase. However, as demonstrated by the data in Table 4, the rise in these offences in Australia has been primarily because of violations of traffic and other State laws. In every modern society this set of *known violations,* which could not be considered as crimes in the strict sense of the word, is dealt with differently from *known crimes* such as theft, assault, disorderly conduct, etc. In this respect, our previous arguments on the confounding influences of these violations are highly relevant. A vivid example of the contribution of *total offences* to *all known offences* is presented in Figure 1.

Clearly, therefore, these violations, such as traffic violations, have made up a substantial and increasing proportion of *all known offences,* and this increase has been explosive since the mid 1950s.

An examination of the data relating to total offences shows that the rates of crime have not been the highest during recent years in all parts of Australia; this is true for both males and females. The data also indicate that crime has not increased in a linear or monotonic fashion. In each of the four States the first two decades of this century show high crime rates followed by some of the lowest rates in this century for the next 20 to 30 years.

Figures 2 through 9 illustrate offence rates for the four States by sex and by offence categories. Considering the total offences in each State for males and females we observe no monotonic or linear patterns. However, the crime rates for females produce a discernible U-shaped distribution over the years and across jurisdictions. By contrast, such a pattern emerges for males only in Western Australia. It is interesting to note that for females the bottom of the curves fall between 1933 and 1940, approximately during the middle of the study period.

Initially we set out to test the hypothesis that female crime is increasing. With regard to total offences by females, in all States, it is difficult to accept or reject the hypothesis. If we were to study the pattern of crime during the first three decades of the century, we could not but come to the conclusion that female crime was declining. Equally, if we study the period 1940 to 1976, we would have most probably confirmed the hypothesis. Just as we would have been completely mistaken to predict that female crime would continue to decrease in the case of the former, we could be wrong in predicting that female crime will continue to increase in the latter case.

On the basis of our data we see several possible scenarios for female crime: (a) a repeat of the U-shaped cycle (the recurrence of the U-shaped cycle may be sudden or gradual depending upon the proximity of the end point of the present cycle and the origin of the incoming cycle, in time) as may already be evident in the case of New South Wales after the early 1960s (this pattern is similar to the one observed after 1907); (b) a plateauing effect as roughly

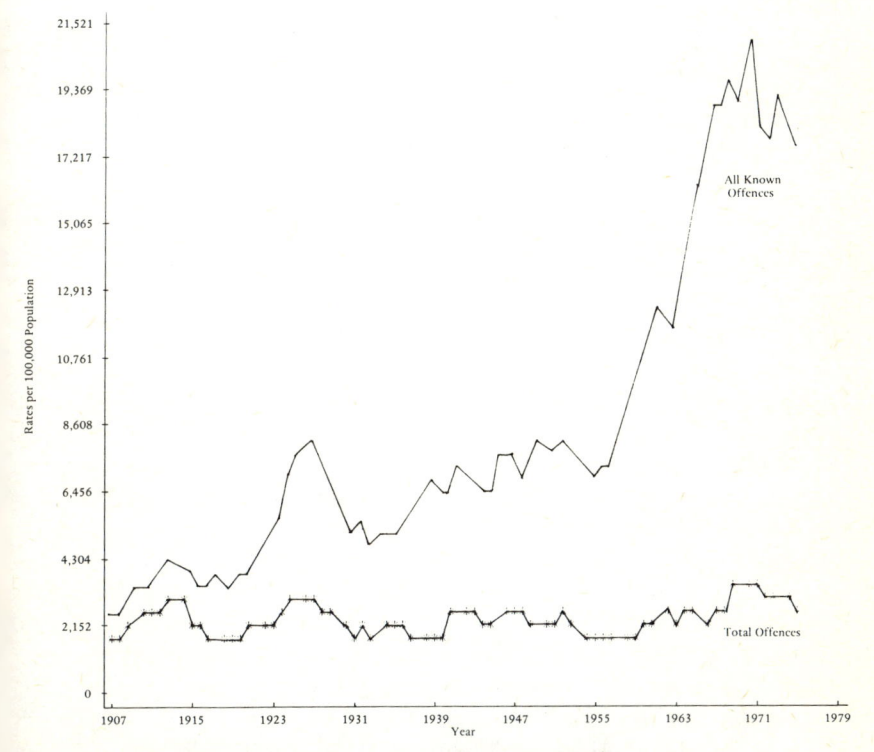

Figure 1 — Relationship of Total Offences to All Known Offences: South Australia, Males, 1907 to 1975

142 Women and Crime

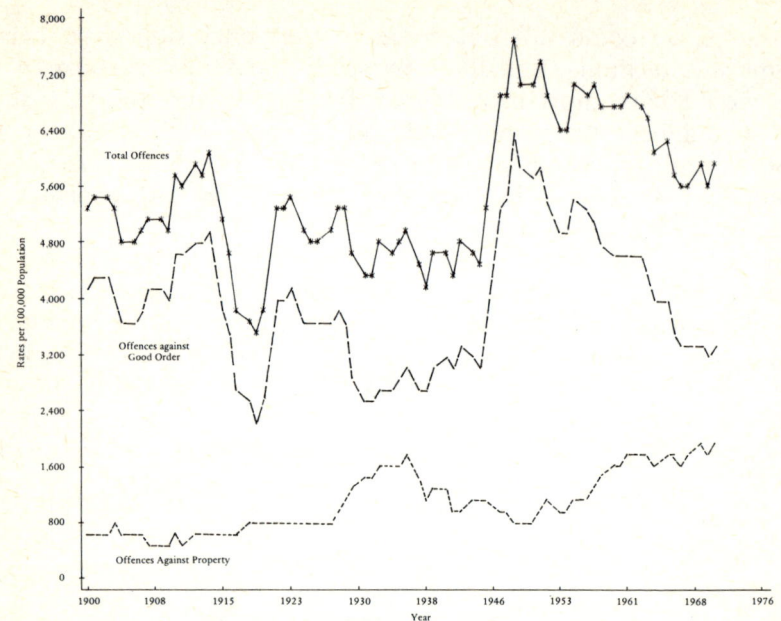

Figure 2 — Offence Rates: New South Wales, Males, 1900 to 1971

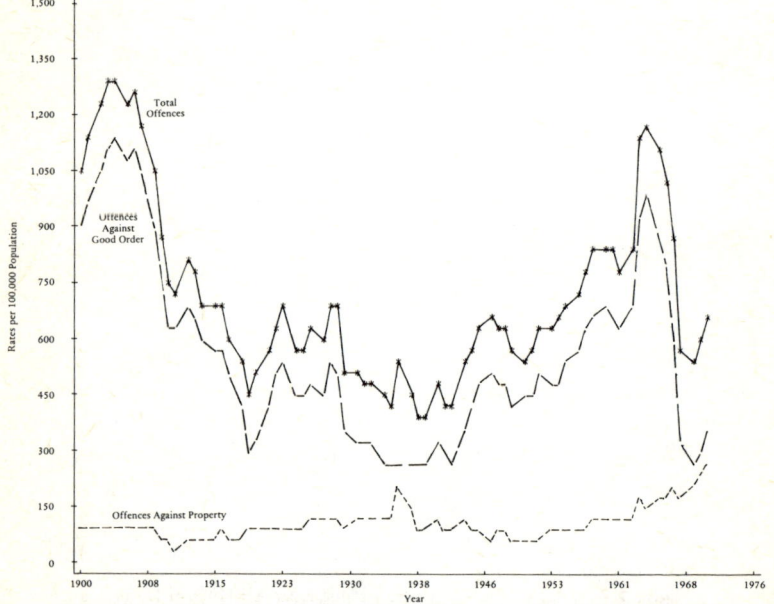

Figure 3 — Offence Rates: New South Wales, Females, 1900 to 1971

The Myth of Rising Female Crime 143

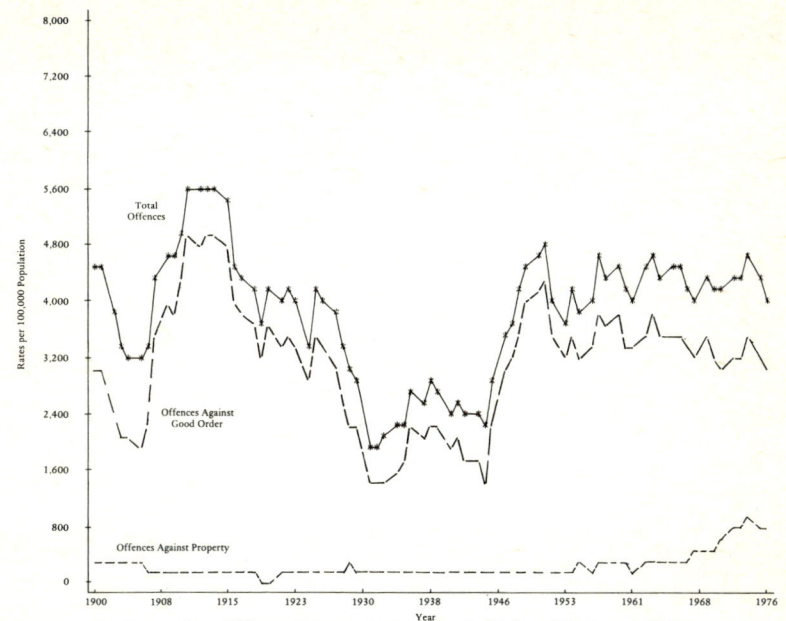

Figure 4 — Offence Rates: Queensland, Males, 1900 to 1976

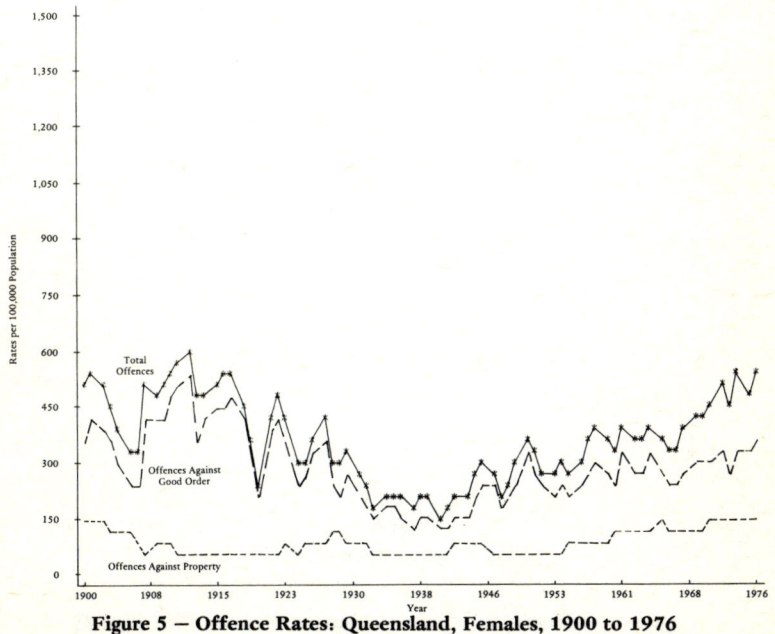

Figure 5 — Offence Rates: Queensland, Females, 1900 to 1976

144 Women and Crime

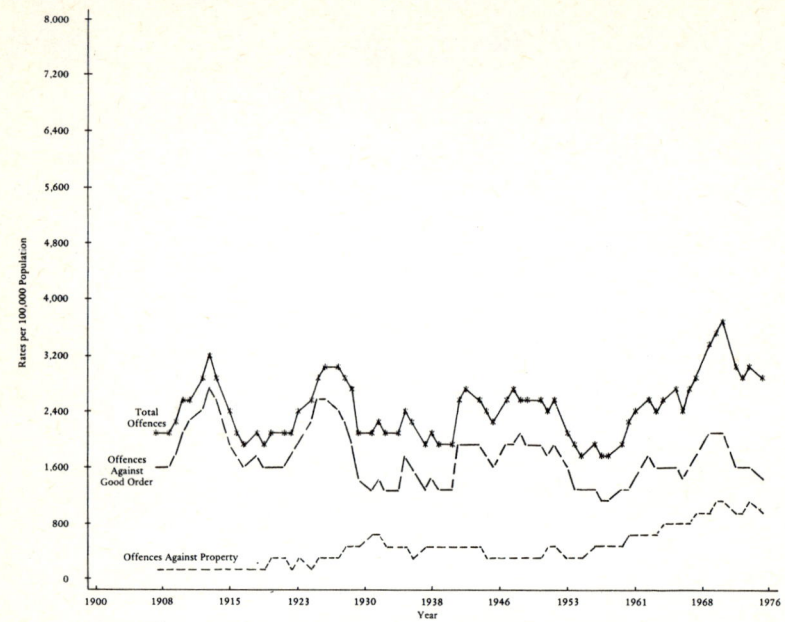

Figure 6 — Offence Rates: South Australia, Males, 1907 to 1975

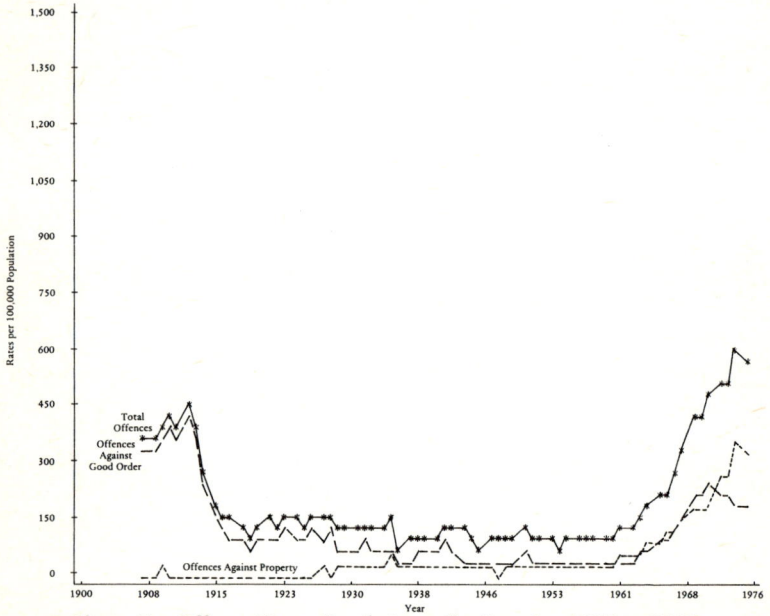

Figure 7 — Offence Rates: South Australia, Females, 1907 to 1975

The Myth of Rising Female Crime 145

Figure 8 — Offence Rates: Western Australia, Males, 1904 to 1975

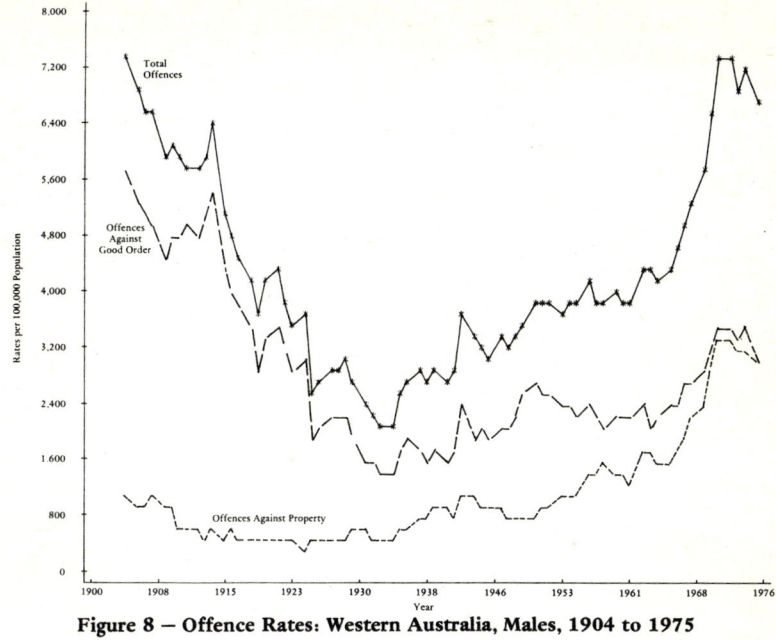

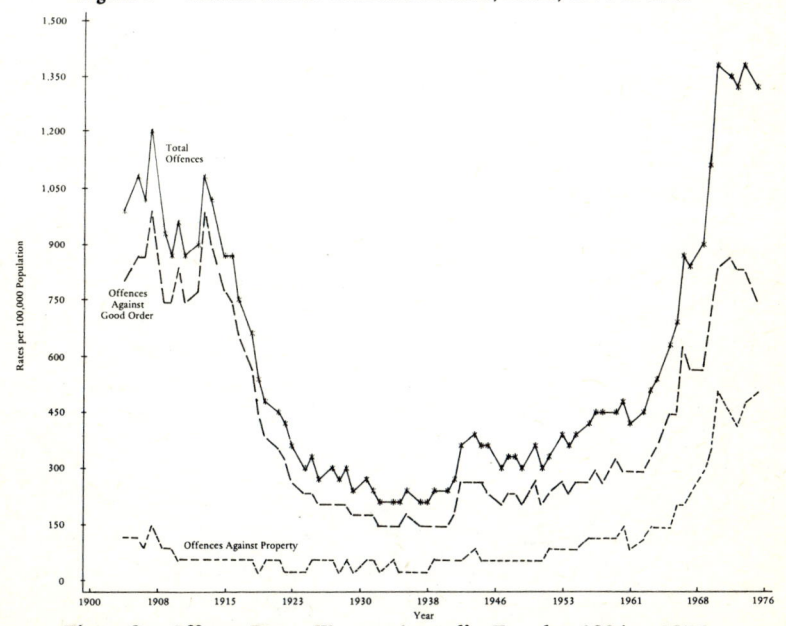

Figure 9 — Offence Rates: Western Australia, Females, 1904 to 1975

demonstrated in the other three States during the 1970s; (c) a continuing increase, etc. These scenarios not only demonstrate the severe limitations of using attenuated time-spans, but also suggest that a much more meaningful scenario could be drawn if data for a longer time period than our own were available.

With regard to males, the pattern of crime does not show the same consistency across jurisdictions as was observed for the females. Western Australia shows a U-shape distribution, New South Wales and Queensland show a declining pattern and plateau effect respectively, since the late 1940s, and South Australia shows a pattern of erratic fluctuations. The major increases or decreases, however, occurred simultaneously in all of the four States.

As may be observed, the volume of crime for the females has been consistently lower than that for males for the entire period and in every State. The highest female crime rate ever recorded was 1,400.7 in Western Australia in the year 1974. This, however, was much lower than the lowest crime rate ever recorded for males, which was 1,854.8 in South Australia in 1958.

The question of whether female crime is increasing at a faster rate than male crime may be answered only if we have agreed that female crime has been increasing; this we cannot definitively assert from the data for total offences. We feel that the two general hypotheses could be tested more meaningfully by examining the three offence categories.

The pattern for the offences against the person (Figures 10 and 11) exhibit similar characteristics to those observed for total offences, that is, the volume of crime in recent years is returning to levels comparable to those at the turn of the century. Notwithstanding these similarities, the curves for the offences against the person are far less complex in their behaviour. We could not fit a polynomial curve of a reasonable order in the case of total offences; the offences against the person were far more amenable in this respect.

In a study like this with a long time-span, it is always possible that the spread of the data might require a high order of polynomial to obtain a good fit. Our aim was to use the lowest order of polynomial which produced the highest F-ratio of regression and explained variance.

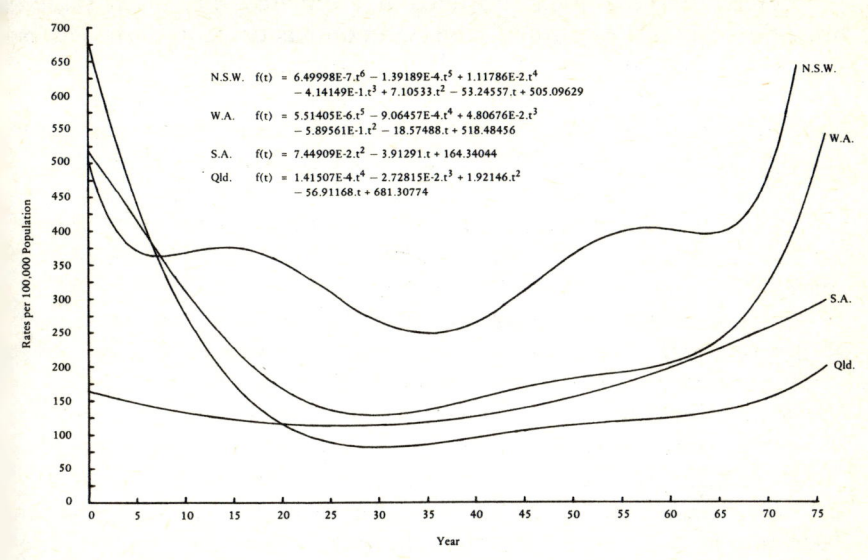

N.S.W. $f(t) = 6.49998\text{E-}7.t^6 - 1.39189\text{E-}4.t^5 + 1.11786\text{E-}2.t^4 - 4.14149\text{E-}1.t^3 + 7.10533.t^2 - 53.24557.t + 505.09629$

W.A. $f(t) = 5.51405\text{E-}6.t^5 - 9.06457\text{E-}4.t^4 + 4.80676\text{E-}2.t^3 - 5.89561\text{E-}1.t^2 - 18.57488.t + 518.48456$

S.A. $f(t) = 7.44909\text{E-}2.t^2 - 3.91291.t + 164.34044$

Qld. $f(t) = 1.41507\text{E-}4.t^4 - 2.72815\text{E-}2.t^3 + 1.92146.t^2 - 56.91168.t + 681.30774$

Figure 10 — Polynomial Curves of Best Fit for Offences Against The Person: Males

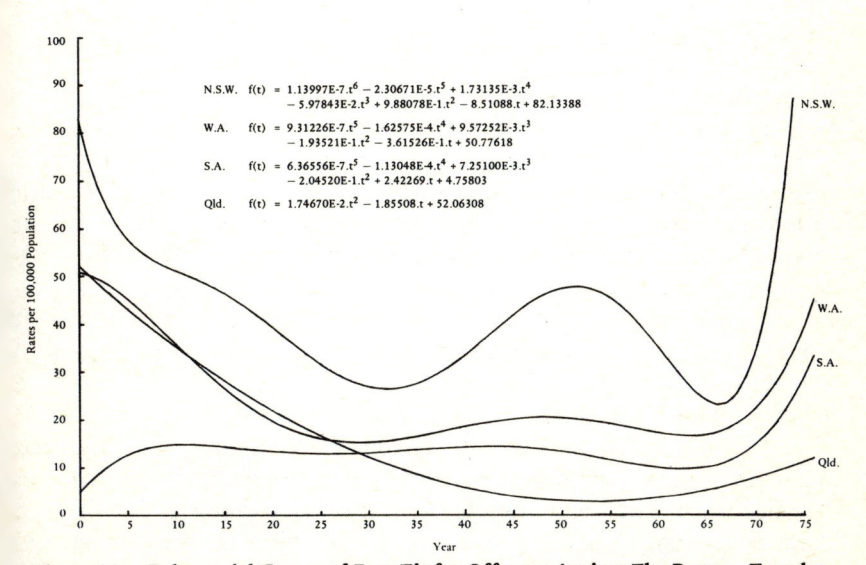

N.S.W. $f(t) = 1.13997\text{E-}7.t^6 - 2.30671\text{E-}5.t^5 + 1.73135\text{E-}3.t^4 - 5.97843\text{E-}2.t^3 + 9.88078\text{E-}1.t^2 - 8.51088.t + 82.13388$

W.A. $f(t) = 9.31226\text{E-}7.t^5 - 1.62575\text{E-}4.t^4 + 9.57252\text{E-}3.t^3 - 1.93521\text{E-}1.t^2 - 3.61526\text{E-}1.t + 50.77618$

S.A. $f(t) = 6.36556\text{E-}7.t^5 - 1.13048\text{E-}4.t^4 + 7.25100\text{E-}3.t^3 - 2.04520\text{E-}1.t^2 + 2.42269.t + 4.75803$

Qld. $f(t) = 1.74670\text{E-}2.t^2 - 1.85508.t + 52.06308$

Figure 11 — Polynomial Curves of Best Fit for Offences Against The Person: Females

Referring to the first hypothesis that 'female crime has increased since the turn of the century', the polynomials presented in Figures 10 and 11 illustrate the difficulties of testing this hypothesis for the entire period; we cannot accept or reject the hypothesis. It is possible, however, to test the hypothesis using time segments derived from the first differential of the equations to the curves.

The data in Table 6 identify distinct stationary points or turning points which divide the curve into time segments (at which $f'(t) = 0$, and $f''(t) \neq 0$). It may be noted that for some of the curves, the number of stationary points are fewer than the order of the polynomial suggests; the possible number of stationary points is equal to the order minus one. A polynomial may have turning points which do not fall within the time-span under study. A case in point is the curve for South Australia (Figure 10, Table 5) in which only one turning point occurs in the entire period.

In relation to the first hypothesis, by reference to Figure 10, it can be seen that in the three States, Western Australia, South Australia and Queensland, the curve for offences against the person by males reached the lowest point in the century between 1926 and 1931, and since then, it has been gradually increasing. New South Wales by contrast experienced a series of alternate decreases and increases, and reached the lowest point in the entire century in 1936.

With regard to females, all the States exhibit a varying number of time segments coinciding with alternate increases and decreases. Irrespective of the number of time segments, all the curves show an increase in the rate of crime since the most recent turning point which occurred between 1963 and 1965 in all States except Queensland. Furthermore, in New South Wales and Western Australia the present volume of crime is returning to the level experienced in the earlier part of the century, whereas in Queensland, it is far below the level at the turn of the century. Only in South Australia is the present volume of crime higher than at any time during the entire period.

Thus, for the entire century we reject the hypothesis. However, in terms of time segments, we can reject or accept the hypothesis depending on the segments chosen. For example, if we were to examine offences against the person by females since the mid 1960s, we can accept the hypothesis for New South Wales, Western

Australia and South Australia. Figure 12 can also be used to verify the above conclusions.

Table 5 — Measures of the Goodness of Fit and Polynomial Stationary Points for Offences Against the Person

State	Sex	F-ratio of Regression: $F^{df_1*\dagger}_{df_2}$	r^2	Order of $f(t)$	Polynomial Stationary Points: $f'(t)$ Year
W.A.	F	61.512^5_{66}	0.82332	5	1900 1930 1949 1964
	M	271.505^5_{66}	0.95364	5	1930 (1893)
S.A.	F	10.207^5_{63}	0.44756	5	1912 1927 1943 1963
	M	127.771^2_{66}	0.79474	2	1926
Qld.	F	89.606^2_{74}	0.70776	2	1953
	M	328.531^4_{72}	0.94806	4	1931
N.S.W.	F	52.705^6_{65}	0.82950	6	1932 1952 1965
	M	88.506^6_{65}	0.89095	6	1908 1915 1936 1958 1964

* df_1 and df_2 are the degrees of freedom of the regression and residuals respectively.

† All the F-ratios are significant at less than 0.001.

150 Women and Crime

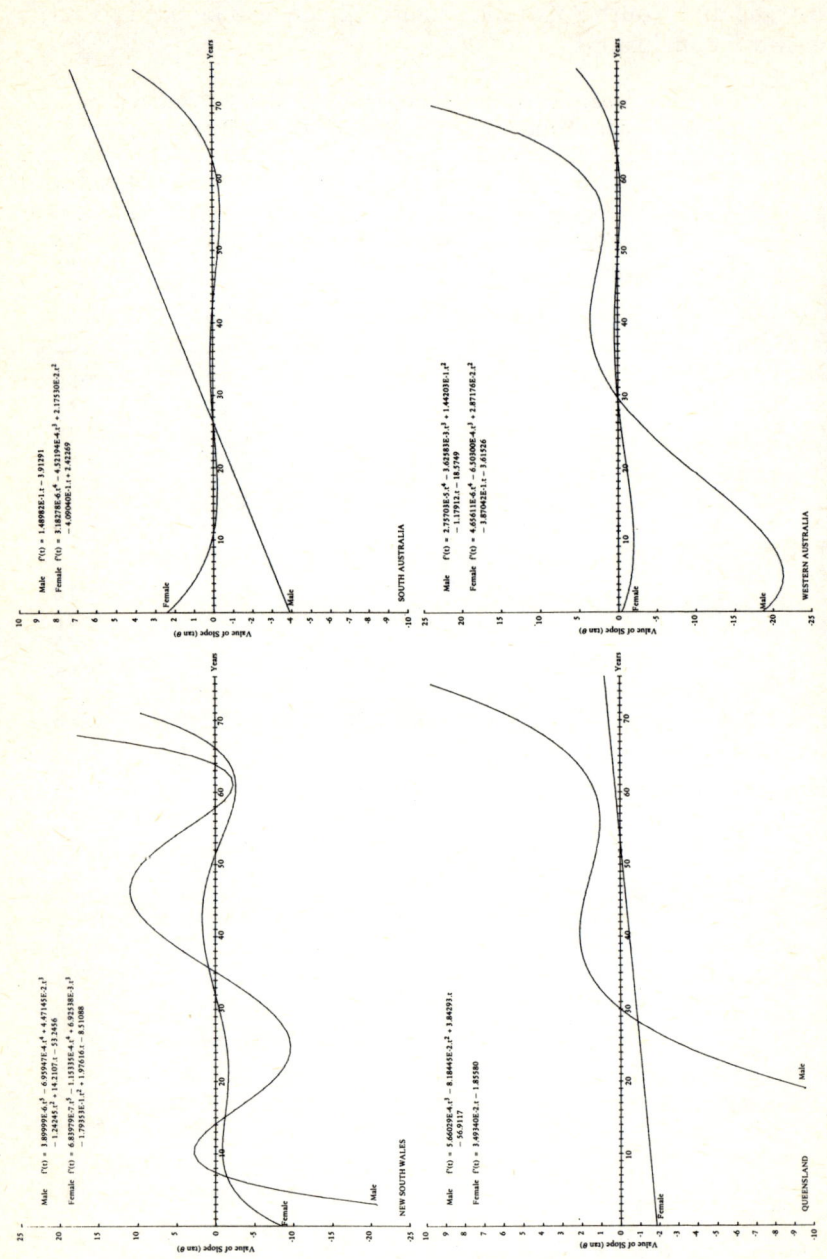

Figure 12 — Slopes of the Polynomial Curves (Value of f'(t)) for Offences Against The Person

Figure 12 represents the slopes (value of the first derivative, f'(t)) of the polynomial curves in Figures 10 and 11. These are especially helpful in testing the second hypothesis, that is, 'the rate of increase in female crime has been faster than that for males'. The y-axis represents the rate of change; if the value is positive then the crime rates are increasing, if it is 0 then there is no change, and if it is negative, the rate of crime is decreasing. From Figure 12, as in the case of the first hypothesis, we reject the second hypothesis for the entire time period. If, however, we read the y-axis as a continuum of the rate of increase (a legitimate technique) then the female rate of increase was faster than the male rate of increase for the period 1900 to 1926-31 in Queensland, Western Australia and South Australia, and for the remainder of the century the male rates of increase were faster than the female rates. Using a similar analogy in the case of New South Wales, we can also conclude that the male rate of increase was faster than the female rate since 1936 and during the period 1908 to 1915.

A similar analysis of property offences as illustrated in Figures 13 and 14 and Table 6 indicates that these crimes by females have been increasing in the most recent time segments and have reached their highest level this century in all four States. For males, both Western Australia and New South Wales have reached levels of crime higher than at any time during this century. While crimes by females in Western Australia have been increasing since 1928, New South Wales experienced a constant increase during the entire period of the study. In the remaining two States, the most recent period of increase has come to an end; the slope for both States is 0 in 1975 and the crime rate is about to decline. Thus, we reject the hypothesis for females in all States and males in all States except New South Wales. Figure 15 can also be used to verify the above conclusions.

Figure 15 indicates that if we consider the entire period of study we can reject the second hypothesis for all States except Western Australia. But as we have emphasised earlier, we must look into time segments. The analysis of the figure shows that we cannot make categoric statements. These slopes for property offences by males and females show that in Western Australia the rate of increase in property crimes by females has always been higher than those for males and we can definitively assert that property crimes by females have been increasing at a faster rate

152 Women and Crime

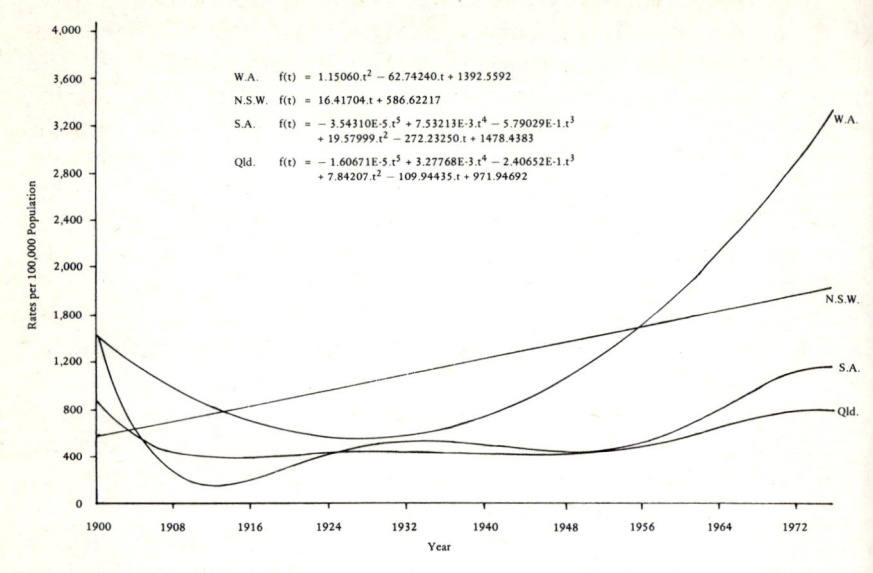

W.A. $f(t) = 1.15060 \cdot t^2 - 62.74240 \cdot t + 1392.5592$
N.S.W. $f(t) = 16.41704 \cdot t + 586.62217$
S.A. $f(t) = -3.54310\text{E-}5 \cdot t^5 + 7.53213\text{E-}3 \cdot t^4 - 5.79029\text{E-}1 \cdot t^3 + 19.57999 \cdot t^2 - 272.23250 \cdot t + 1478.4383$
Qld. $f(t) = -1.60671\text{E-}5 \cdot t^5 + 3.27768\text{E-}3 \cdot t^4 - 2.40652\text{E-}1 \cdot t^3 + 7.84207 \cdot t^2 - 109.94435 \cdot t + 971.94692$

Figure 13 — Polynomial Curves of Best Fit for Offences Against Property: Males

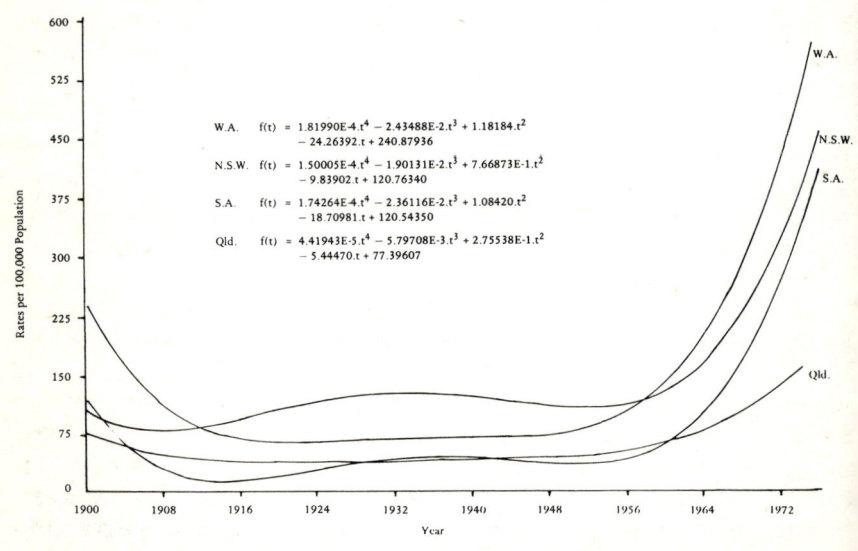

W.A. $f(t) = 1.81990\text{E-}4 \cdot t^4 - 2.43488\text{E-}2 \cdot t^3 + 1.18184 \cdot t^2 - 24.26392 \cdot t + 240.87936$
N.S.W. $f(t) = 1.50005\text{E-}4 \cdot t^4 - 1.90131\text{E-}2 \cdot t^3 + 7.66873\text{E-}1 \cdot t^2 - 9.83902 \cdot t + 120.76340$
S.A. $f(t) = 1.74264\text{E-}4 \cdot t^4 - 2.36116\text{E-}2 \cdot t^3 + 1.08420 \cdot t^2 - 18.70981 \cdot t + 120.54350$
Qld. $f(t) = 4.41943\text{E-}5 \cdot t^4 - 5.79708\text{E-}3 \cdot t^3 + 2.75538\text{E-}1 \cdot t^2 - 5.44470 \cdot t + 77.39607$

Figure 14 — Polynomial Curves of Best Fit for Offences Against Property: Females

Table 6 — Measures of the Goodness of Fit and Polynomial Stationary Points for Offences Against Property

State	Sex	F-ratio of Regression: $F^{df_1 *\dagger}_{df_2}$	r^2	Order of $f(t)$	Polynomial Stationary Points: $f'(t)$ Year
W.A.	F	366.216^4_{67}	0.95626	4	1908
	M	403.855^2_{69}	0.92130	2	1928
S.A.	F	703.805^4_{64}	0.97858	4	1915 1937 1951
	M	217.272^5_{63}	0.94519	5	1913 1934 1950 1975
Qld.	F	246.163^4_{72}	0.93186	4	1920
	M	72.767^5_{71}	0.83672	5	1914 1930 1946 1975
N.S.W.	F	76.232^4_{67}	0.81986	4	1910 1934 1952
	M	134.603^1_{70}	0.65787	1	

* df_1 and df_2 are the degrees of freedom of the regression and residuals respectively.

† All the F-ratios are significant at less than 0.001.

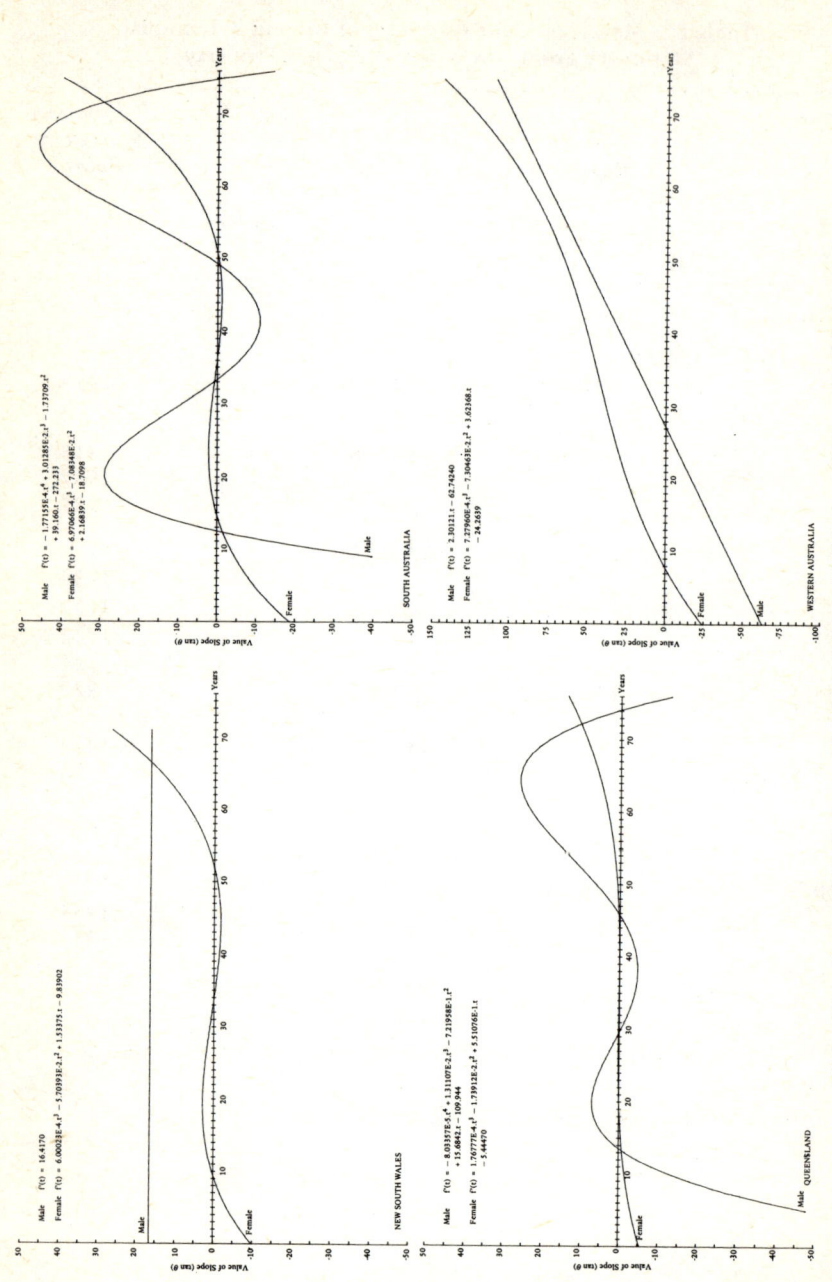

Figure 15 – Slopes of the Polynomial Curves (Value of F'(t)) for Offences Against Property

than property crimes by males during the entire period under study. The State of New South Wales presents a completely reverse situation until 1967, that is, a higher rate of increase for males. The remaining two States of Queensland and South Australia demonstrate a complex picture. At the beginning of this century, property crimes by females increased faster (that is, declined slower) than males; a similar pattern is observed during the period between 1930 and 1950. In the last time segment, however, we notice an interesting phenomenon. While in the first part of this time segment property crimes by both males and females increased, male rates being faster than female rates, in the later part of the time segment the male rate of increase declined and the female rate continued to increase to the extent that in the early 1970s the female rate of increase surpassed that of males. We could reasonably argue that the comparatively higher rate of increase for property offences by females is because of the decline in the rate of increase for males.

These findings are also subject to the limitations imposed by the varying lengths of the recent time segments; these are less constraining than those for the offences against the person. Although the lengths of the most recent time segments cause great concern in our making definitive statements, other writers at times have used not only shorter time-spans but have even gone to the extent of projecting future trends in crime on the basis of their scant data. We cannot be as authoritative as they.

This leaves us with the offences against good order. This offence category constitutes the largest proportion of total offences and by and large these have shaped the pattern of total offences, across jurisdiction, sex and over time (see Figures 2 through 9). During very recent years, however, the gap between the total offences and offences against good order has shown a tendency to become wider; this gap, in most cases, is accounted for by the changes in the offences against property and person.

Table 7, read in conjunction with Figure 16, shows the pattern of offences against good order. Except for South Australia, the pattern for males in all the States shows movements of much greater magnitude than those observed for females. Similar to our conclusions with regard to offences against the person and property, in the case of the present offence category we reject the hypothesis that 'female crime has increased since the turn of the century'.

Table 7 — Measures of the Goodness of Fit and Polynomial Stationary Points for Offences Against Good Order

State	Sex	F-ratio of Regression: $F^{df_1 *\dagger}_{df_2}$	r^2	Order of $f(t)$	Polynomial Stationary Points: $f'(t)$ Year
W.A.	F	238.817^2_{69}	0.87377	2	1942
	M	213.867^2_{69}	0.86109	2	1946
S.A.	F	125.160^2_{66}	0.79135	2	1945
	M	10.599^1_{67}	0.13659	1	
Qld.	F	32.963^6_{70}	0.73859	6	1903 1914 1940 1961 1970
	M	34.005^7_{69}	0.77527	7	1903 1915 1935 1956 1969 1972
N.S.W.	F	59.532^6_{65}	0.84604	6	1903 1939 1964
	M	18.944^6_{65}	0.63619	6	1904 1912 1932 1954 1971

* df_1 and df_2 are the degrees of freedom of the regression and residuals respectively.
† All the F-ratios, except South Australia males, are significant at less than 0.001. The F-ratio for South Australia males is significant at less than 0.05.

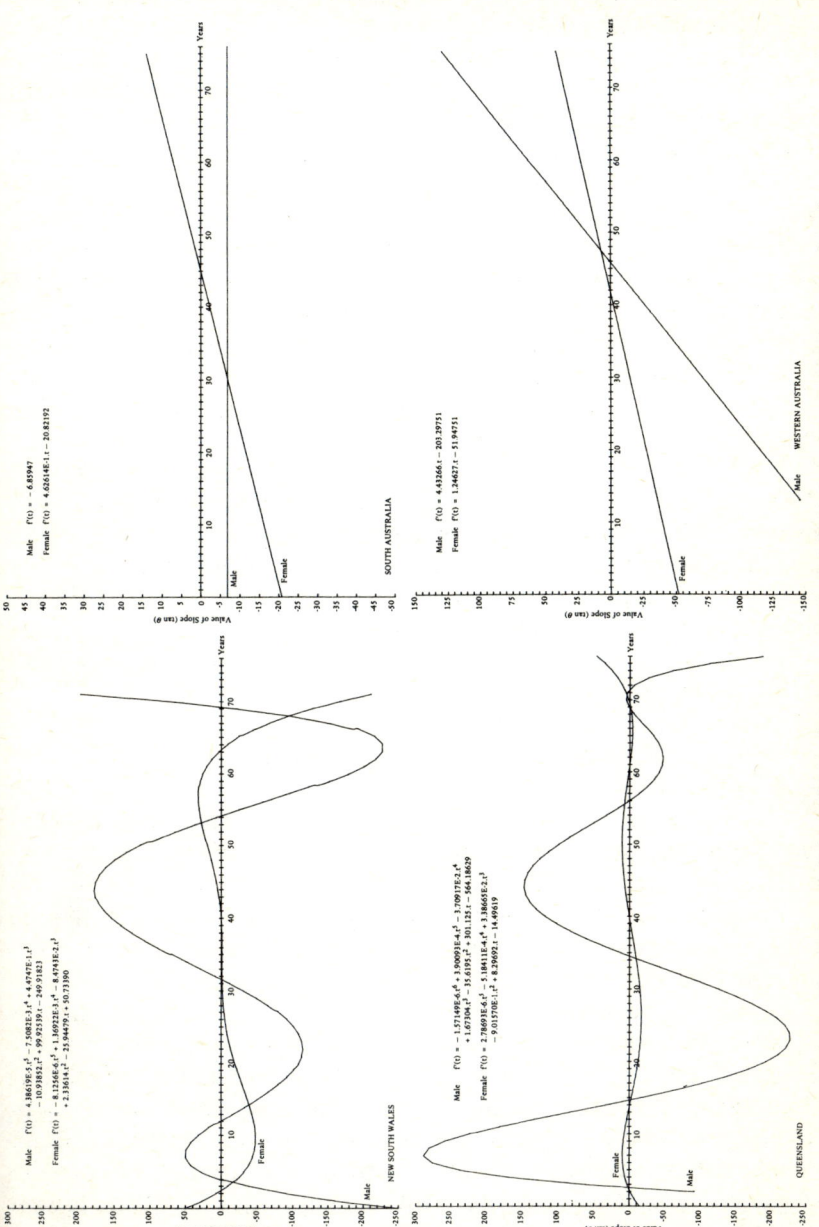

Figure 16 – Slopes of the Polynomial Curves (Value of f'(t)) for Offences Against Good Order

But if we look at the most recent time segment we do not obtain as consistent patterns as we have observed for the other two offence categories; in Queensland, South Australia and Western Australia there was an increase in crimes by females whereas in New South Wales it declined.

Considering the rate of increase in female crime, we observe no single pattern for the entire period under study in any jurisdiction and thus we reject the second hypothesis. In New South Wales and Queensland the magnitude of the changes in slope for males is always larger than that for females. By comparison, the changes in females have been far more gradual as reflected in the distance between turning points and the magnitude of the slopes. Since the mid 1950s the rate of increase for females has been faster than for males but in recent years this pattern is reversed in New South Wales. In Western Australia the male rate of increase has been faster than the rate of increase for females since the late 1940s. In the case of South Australia, although the figure shows that the rate of increase for females in crimes against good order has been faster than that for males since 1930, we must exercise caution in making this statement. As can be seen from Table 7, the explained variance of the curve to the male data is only one-sixth that of the curve to the female data, which seriously jeopardises any comparison between males and females.

(ii) Relative Participation of Males and Females

In the above section we have demonstrated that the two hypotheses could not be verified for the entire time period under study. Our findings showed that a more meaningful result could be obtained by examining the specific time segments. Having analysed the dynamics of the volume of change in crime it might also be useful to link these dynamics to the relative participation of males and females in crime.

Figure 17 presents the female to male ratio in offences against the person for the four States during this century. It is unmistakably clear that the relative participation of females has been declining since the end of the Second World War and that the ratio of female to male since then is lower than any that existed prior to the mid 1940s. (A higher female to male ratio means fewer males per female and *vice versa*.) It is interesting to note that the lowest female to male ratio in offences against the person occurred in all the four States during the mid 1960s and although in most recent years a higher ratio is obtained, this is still lower than most of the years under study.[47] The highest and lowest female to male ratios in these offences are presented in Table 8.

In the earlier section on the volume of offences against the person, we have shown that the rate of crime for both sexes has been increasing during recent years and that the male rate of increase was faster than the female rate in all the States since the early 1930s. The lower female to male ratio in all the States since the Second World War is quite consistent with the above findings. Before the early 1930s the rate of increases for both males and females declined; the female rate of decline being slower than that of male. This is reflected in the higher female to male ratio for the period (Figure 17).

The offences against property, on the other hand, demonstrated a reverse pattern, that is, a higher female to male ratio since the Second World War (Figure 18). Furthermore, the period since the

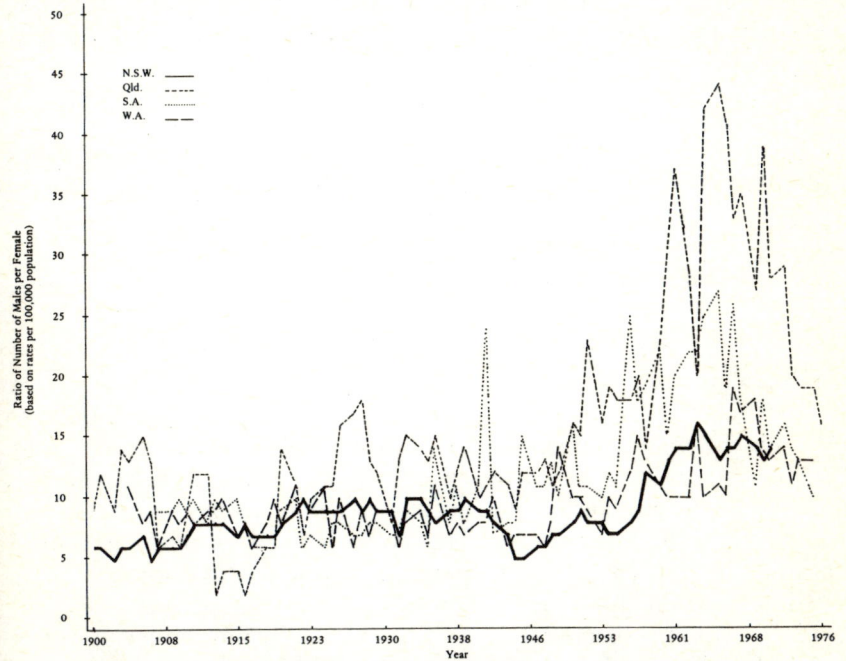

Figure 17 — Relative Female-Male Participation in Offences Against The Person for the Four States, 1900 to 1976

Table 8 — Female to Male Ratio in Offences Against the Person: 1900 to 1976

State	Highest Year	Value	Lowest Year	Value
New South Wales	1945	5.732	1963	16.011
Queensland	1913	2.370	1965	44.606
South Australia	1918	6.135	1965	28.000
Western Australia	1947	6.175	1967	19.434

mid 1960s experienced the most rapid and sustained rise in the female to male ratio in all the States. This is consistent with the high relative rate of increase in crimes against property by females, as shown in Figure 15.

The relative participation of males and females in offences against property and person remained fairly close up to the mid 1950s. Since then this participation in offences against property has increased and presently is more than twice as high as in offences against the person.

For offences against good order the female to male ratio has in recent years returned to the level experienced during the first decade of the century in all jurisdictions (Figure 19). This pattern is distinctly different from those observed in the other two offence categories. Except for South Australia we did not observe any substantial changes in the relative participation of males and females in offences against good order in the entire period under study.

(iii) Conclusions

Issues relating to crime and criminal justice have never been so prominent in the nation's affairs as they have been in recent years. Increasing criticism of the functioning of the criminal justice system and debates on new legislation and other measures are but a few of the indicators of concern. This concern focuses on the extent of criminality which in many quarters is felt to be unprecedented. Although there have been increases in crime in recent years, the present volume of crime, in all States, is returning to levels experienced earlier in the century. In most instances we have observed that the volume of crime was highest at the beginning of the

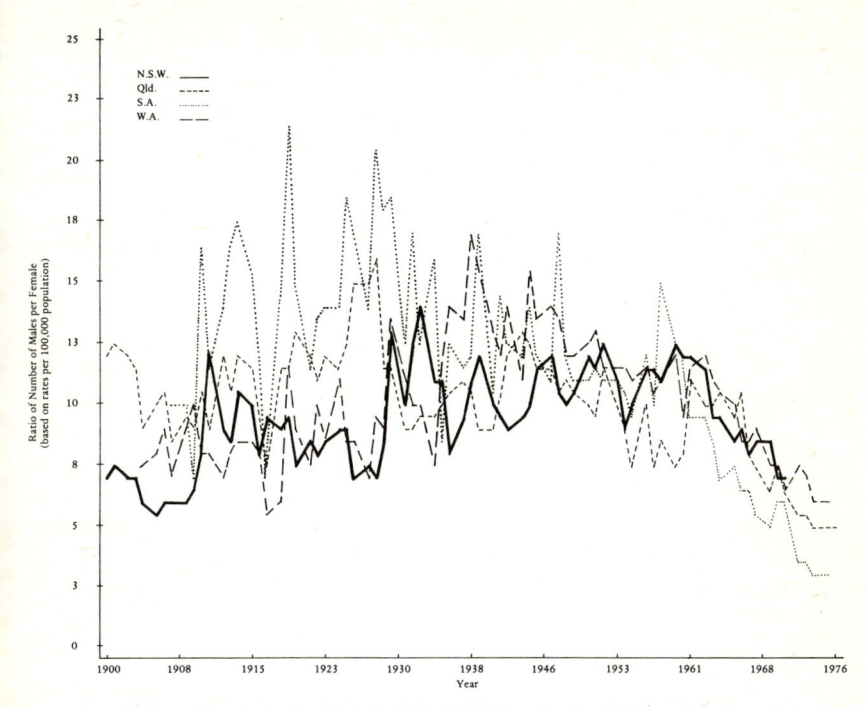

Figure 18 — **Relative Female-Male Participation in Offences Against Property for the Four States, 1900 to 1976**

century and it has reached its present level after a series of major and minor fluctuations. These general observations apply equally to offences by males as well as females.

Total crime: One of the phenomenon which we observed frequently in all States and across sex, was that the volume of crime declined rather sharply during the first two decades of the century. As compared to this, the current increase in the volume of crime demonstrates a completely reverse pattern. The rate of change in both instances has not only been equally rapid, but the most rapid.

Offences against the person: Our findings are that while these offences by both sexes have been increasing since the mid 1930s, the rate of increase for males has been much faster than the rate of increase for females in all States. Furthermore, the magnitude

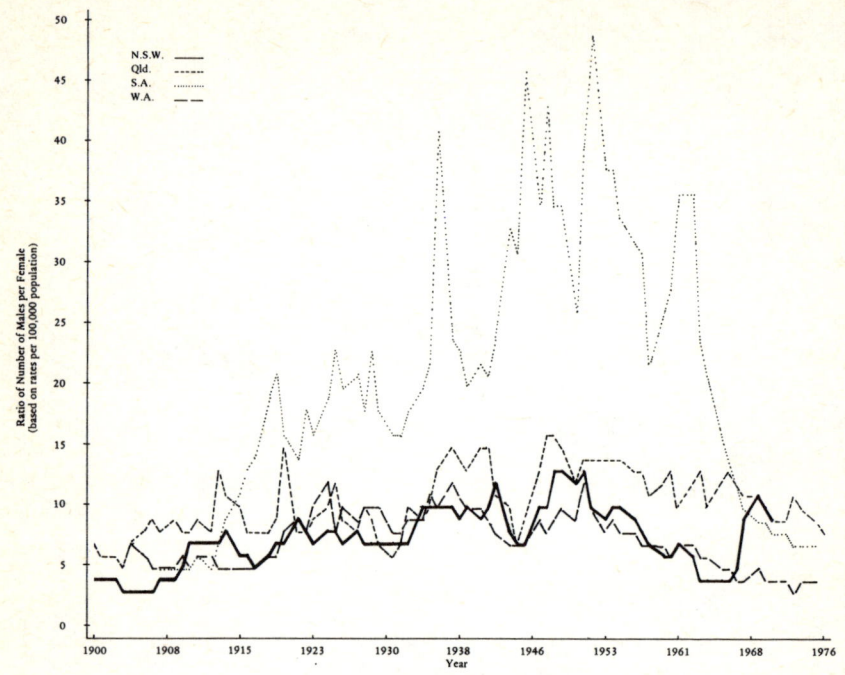

Figure 19 — Relative Female-Male Participation in Offences Against Good Order for the Four States, 1900 to 1976

of the rate of change for males was far larger than females. These findings are contrary to those of some recent writers. Data on relative participation convincingly support the above findings, that is, the female to male ratio since the end of the Second World War has been declining and is the lowest this century.

Offences against property: Here we observed a different pattern from that of offences against the person. Since the early 1950s, the volume of offences against property by both sexes and in all States have been increasing continually. Except in the case of Western Australia, the rate of increase for females has been faster than males only since the mid 1960s; in Western Australia the female rate of increase has always been faster than that of males. The relative participation by females in this offence category is the highest since the mid 1960s than any time before.

General: The present study covers a period of three-quarters of a century. In spite of this extensive data set we have desisted from making any forecasts of crime, although one could reasonably expect some indications of criminality in society from such a study and other writers have done so with far less data at their disposal. Our main reservation for not predicting future patterns of crime in the four selected States is that we have taken into account only two independent variables, that is, time and population. We believe that the phenomenon of crime is sensitive to socio-economic and political changes which constitute a large set of exogenous variables outside the scope of the present study. If one disregards the relationship between exogenous variables and crime, which is entirely unacceptable, and predicts on the basis of curves fitted to the available data the predictions will be merely artifacts of the curve fitting equations.

In a forthcoming publication, we intend to examine criminal statistics in relation to a range of exogenous variables. This exercise would hopefully lend itself to the development of a model for predicting criminality. Some of the earlier writers[48] on the subject of criminal statistics have noted the effect of certain major historical events, for example, world wars, depressions, etc., on criminality. It would be possible to examine our own data set in terms of major historical events in this century. An economic history of Australia testifies that unemployment reached an all time high of 20 per cent during the Great Depression of the 1930s. If the relationship between crime and unemployment observed by many writers has any validity, intuitively we would expect some impact of the Depression on criminality to be reflected in the criminal statistics. Similarly, during the height of the Second World War, there were approximately 720,000 young Australians, mostly males, fighting the war outside Australia; this represents a very high proportion of the then Australian population. Again, intuitively, one would expect some impact of the absence of this population group to be manifested in the criminal statistics.

Data for the major study of which the present study is an offshoot, will take into consideration the effect of these historical events. However, there are many major methodological hurdles to be overcome, least of which is the effect of time lag[49]; an initial analysis of our own data suggests that females are lagged three years behind males. To localise the lag effects to their source it is necessary to examine the interaction of crime with other major socio-economic variables.

The study suggests that the claim that there has been a substantial increase in the volume of crimes by females in recent years is somewhat tenuous. Certainly in the case of offences against the person and good order, volumes of female crime comparable to present levels have been observed at other times. The volume of property offences by females, on the other hand, has reached the highest level in all States in recent years; this is also the case for males.

---

1. D. Klein, 'The Etiology of Female Crime: A Review of the Literature', *Issues in Criminology*, Vol. 8, No. 2, Fall 1973, pp. 3-30.
2. R. Simon, *Women and Crime*, Lexington Books, Lexington, Mass., 1975.
3. A. Kaplan, *The Conduct of Enquiry*, Chandler Publishing Co., San Francisco, 1964.
4. C. Lombroso, *The Female Offender*, T. Fisher Unwin, London, 1895.
5. W. Thomas, *The Unadjusted Girl*, Harper and Row, New York, 1923.
6. O. Pollak, *The Criminality of Women*, University of Pennsylvania Press, Philadelphia, 1950.
7. There are several others whose works are of relevance, for example, S. Freud, *Female Sexuality*, 1931, and *New Introductory Lectures on Psychoanalysis*, W.W. Norton, New York, 1933; S. and E. Glueck, *Four Hundred Delinquent Women*, Alfred A. Knopf, New York, 1934; K. Davis, 'Prostitution', in R.K. Merton and R.A. Nisbet (eds.), *Contemporary Social Problems*, Harcourt, Brace, Jovanovich, New York, 1961; J. and V. Cowie, E. Slater, *Delinquency in Girls*, Heinemann, London, 1968; D.A. Ward, Maurice Jackson and R.E. Ward, 'Crimes of Violence by Women', in D.J. Mulvihill, *et al.*, *Crimes of Violence*, Vol. 13, U.S. Government Printing Office, Washington, D.C., 1969. Because of limitations of space and considerations of direct relevance to the paper in hand, these works have not been reviewed; extensive reviews of these authors appear in D. Klein, *supra* note 1; C. Smart, *Women, Crime and Criminology: A Feminist Critique*, Routledge and Kegan Paul, London, 1976; and J.G. Weis, 'Liberation and Crime: The Invention of the New Female Criminal', *Crime and Social Justice*, Fall-Winter 1976, pp. 17-27.
8. Thomas, *op. cit.*
9. C. Lombroso with Guglielmo Ferrero, *La donna delinquente, la prostituta e la donna normale*, Bocca, Turin, 1903. Extracted from G. Lombroso-Ferrero, *Criminal Man*, Patterson Smith, Montclair, NJ, 1972, p. 294.
10. Thomas, *op. cit.*, p. 2.
11. *Ibid.*, p. 72.
12. Pollak, *op. cit.*, p. 161.
13. Thomas, *op. cit.*, p. 71.

14. Klein, *op. cit.*, p. 16.
15. Thomas, *op. cit.*, p. 256.
16. Our emphasis.
17. C. Lombroso, *Crime: Its Causes and Remedies*, Patterson Smith, Montclair, NJ, 1968.
18. D.A. Ward, *et al.*, *op. cit.*, p. 847; F. Heidensohn, 'The Deviance of Women: a Critique and an Enquiry', *British Journal of Sociology*, Vol. 19, No. 2, 1968, p. 160; C. Smart, *op. cit.*, p. 1; D. Klein and J. Kress, 'Any Woman's Blues: A Critical Overview of Women, Crime and the Criminal Justice System', *Crime and Social Justice*, Spring-Summer 1976, pp. 34-5.
19. Pollak, *op. cit.*
20. D. Hoffman-Bustamante, 'The Nature of Female Criminality', *Issues in Criminology*, Vol. 8, No. 2, Fall 1973, pp. 117-36.
21. F. Adler, *Sisters in Crime*, McGraw-Hill Book Co., New York, 1975, p. 3.
22. Simon, *op. cit.*
23. Adler, *op. cit.*, p. 16.
24. The absolute percentage change for women was 13.3 but as the rise in female population was 15.2548 per cent during this 12 year period, the per cent rate change is -2.2.
25. L. Crites, 'Women Offenders: Myth vs. Reality', in L. Crites (ed.), *The Female Offender*, Lexington Books, Lexington, Mass., 1976, pp. 33-40.
26. *Ibid.*, p. 35.
27. *Ibid.*, p. 36.
28. *Ibid.*, p. 38.
29. *Ibid.*, pp. 36-37.
30. Klein and Kress, *op. cit.*
31. Smart, *op. cit.*
32. M. Dixon, *The Real Matilda: Women and Identity in Australia, 1788-1975*, Pelican Books, Sydney, 1976, and A. Summers, *Damned Whores and God's Police*, Penguin Books, Ringwood, Vic., 1975.
33. P. Robinson, 'Women and the Law: The First Forty Years' in *In Pursuit of Justice*, Mackinolty and Radi (eds.), Hale and Iremonger, Sydney, 1979, pp. 1-17.
34. Summers, *op. cit.*
35. The study on crime trends in Australia was initiated in mid 1977. This study, utilising police, court and prison statistics for the period 1900 to 1976 in every State of Australia, examines crime in relation to selected socio-economic variables. The study is expected to be published in early 1981.
36. Australia presently consists of six States and two Territories; the population of Australia, as at the 1976 census, was 13,991,059.
37. Including Courts of Summary Jurisdiction, Petty Sessions and Children's Courts, but excluding Coroners' Courts.
38. Discharges include withdrawn, dismissed, not guilty, remanded, etc.
39. The five major categories are: offences against the person; offences against property; forgery, uttering and other currency offences; offences against good order; and other miscellaneous offences.

40. As far as we have been able to ascertain the jurisdictions started publishing police data in the present format in the years set out below and containing the following information:

S.A. 1913-14 All reported offences.
N.S.W. 1953 Only serious reported offences.
Qld. 1970-71 All reported offences excluding traffic and street offences.
W.A. 1964 Selected crimes reported.

41. T. Sellin, 'The Basis of a Crime Index', *Journal of Criminal Law and Criminology*, Vol. 22, No. 3, September 1931, p. 346.

42. These include: murder, attempted murder, manslaughter, manslaughter by driving, assault, unnatural offences, etc.

43. These include: robbery, break and enter, larceny, wilful/malicious damage, fraud, false pretences, forgery, uttering, other currency offences, etc.

44. These include: drunkenness, disorderly conduct, public mischief, riotous or indecent behaviour, offensive behaviour, etc.

45. It is important for the reader to note that in the context of this paper this aggregation of offences which will be studied will be referred to as *total offences*, whereas the term *all known offences* will be used to represent the totality of crimes in the generic sense.

46. Henceforth Australia will be used to describe all the four States under study.

47. During the period 1913 to 1919 in Queensland, the female to male ratio for this offence category was the highest for any State at any time. A careful scrutiny of the raw data in conjunction with prison statistics revealed that an unspecified number of offences, usually placed in offences against good order, were inexplicably included in the offences against the person category. We were unable to rectify this recording aberration.

48. T. Sellin, *Research Memorandum on Crime in the Depression*, Social Science Research Council, New York, 1937; T.R. Gurr, et al., *The Politics of Crime and Conflict*, Sage Publications, Beverly Hills, Calif., 1977; P.N Grabosky, *Sydney in Ferment*, ANU Press, Canberra, 1977; M.H. Brenner *Estimating the Social Costs of National Economic Policy: Implications for Mental and Physical Health, and Criminal Aggression*, U.S. Government Printing Office, Washington, D.C., 1976.

49. Brenner, op. cit.; J.A. Fox, *Forecasting Crime Data*, Lexington Books Lexington, Mass., 1978.

8 Women in Constraints

JANETTE HARTZ-KARP

Introduction

All societies have cultural rules, and as a last resort formal social mechanisms, which control the behaviour of their members. However, in order to understand the making of a publicly labelled deviant one must examine a complex interactional process between the actions of the deviant and societal reaction. In western societies, at least, it appears that men and women are differentially affected by this interactional process determining deviancy. Recorded crime rates and mental illness rates show that while men are more likely to become involved in criminal careers[1], women are more likely to embark upon mental illness careers.[2]

While sex role socialisation may have some effect on female/male deviant outcomes, the making of a fully fledged deviant (prisoner or mental patient) is a dynamic process involving deviant action and societal reaction. Recorded crime and mental illness rates available in Western Australia over the last decade will be examined from this perspective.

The focus here is on crime and mental illness. This is not to imply that the criminal justice system and the mental health system are the only or even the most efficient forms of social constraint. For instance, it has been suggested that women's relegation to the private sector, 'the private prison'[3] and her dependence upon the social welfare system[4] are most effective mechanisms of social control and constraint. The available crime and mental illness rates (court, prison and mental hospitalisation data) are not representative of deviance in the community. The funnelling processes of formal social control mechanisms operate to channel only a small percentage of deviants into stigmatised and segregated deviant roles. Finally, imprisonment and mental institutionalisation may not be directly comparable as alternative forms of social constraint because of differences in entrance and exit criteria and the probable covert versus overt social passage through the mental health system compared with the criminal justice system. Nonetheless, their essential similarity — the possibility of involuntary incarceration — is sufficient to warrant comparison.

Women and Crime

All available indices of recorded world crime rates — police, courts and prisons — indicate that female crime rates are far lower than male crime rates.[5] In Australia, statistics from Magistrates' Courts show that in four states examined — New South Wales, Queensland, South Australia and Western Australia — offence rates for women are consistently lower than male offence rates.[6] Moreover, the highest female crime rate ever recorded (1,400.7 per 100,000 population in Western Australia in 1974) is much lower than the lowest male crime rate ever recorded (1,854.8 per 100,000 population in South Australia in 1958).[7] Fewer women are imprisoned than men. In Western Australia since the beginning of the decade, women prisoner receivals have accounted for approximately 12 per cent of total prisoner receivals.[8]

Although Western Australia has an unusual population in that males outnumber females[9], nonetheless, this does not account for the high male:female crime rate ratio. It has often been hypothesised that women are inherently less criminal than males (that is, inherently good[10] or less evolved than men[11]) or alternatively equally criminal but inherently less likely than males to get caught (that is, inherently devious, clever or manipulative[12]). However, this hypothesis is premised upon assumptions (or myths) about woman's 'nature' which cannot be substantiated and hence it has little research value. An alternative hypothesis is that the different socialisation of men and women leads to sex-differentiated paths of deviance. Although this hypothesis is difficult to substantiate empirically, nonetheless it generates several interesting research problems, for example, the extent to which characteristics of crime statistics may be sex-related and associated with sex role socialisation, and the impact of the Women's Liberation Movement on crime rates.

However the production of a publicly labelled deviant is a

function of a complex interactional process between the deviant actor and societal reaction. Hence, socialisation is an inadequate explanation of recorded rates of crime. It is simply one link in a chain of processes which, in the case of Western Australian crime statistics, must also include racial discrimination and the changing practices of the criminal justice system authorities.

Interpreting Female Court and Prison Statistics:
1. Sex role socialisation:
    a. **The importance of sex-related offences.** Crime statistics from the United States of America and the United Kingdom have consistently indicated that offences are sex-related; the numbers of persons who commit that crime are predominantly of one sex or the other. The sex-relatedness of crime has then been associated with traditional sex role socialisation.[13] Unfortunately, the data necessary to substantiate this proposition are not available in Western Australia. Police statistics contain no sex-specific data. Court statistics do not indicate whether offenders are Aboriginal or non-Aboriginal, however the variable of race is vital to a meaningful interpretation of Western Australian crime statistics. (Aboriginal women are largely excluded from the mainstream of 'white' Australian culture upon which the notion of sex role socialisation has been based. In Western Australia their crime statistics are quite distinct. Aboriginal women are convicted and imprisoned at higher rates than non-Aboriginal women and generally for different types of crime — predominantly drink-related offences.) Nonetheless, the limited data available — prison offences statistics — lend support to the thesis that offences are sex-related and can be understood as a function of sex role socialisation.[14]

    From Table 1 it is clear that total offence commitments for female prisoners are lower than male totals in all offences indicated. There is, however, considerable variation in the extent of female to male participation in different offence categories. Non-Aboriginal women are rarely indicted for what have been called 'masculine' offences — physical aggression against other persons, breaking and entering, drunkenness, car stealing and driving offences (making up

Table 1 — Offences for Which Non-Aboriginal Prisoners were Committed Based on Total Commitments for Penal Imprisonment 1977-78

Offence	Male Non-Aboriginal	Female Non-Aboriginal	Non-Aboriginal Female as percentage of Non-Aboriginal Total
Offences Against the Person	263	2	0.75
Breaking and Entering	688	6	0.86
Unlawful Use of Motor Vehicle	445	7	1.55
Traffic Act	1,672	14	0.83
Drunkenness	54	1	1.82
Disorderly Conduct and Obscene Language	139	13	8.55
Drug Offences	198	11	5.26
Stealing and Receiving	673	31	4.40
False Pretences, Fraud, Forgery and Uttering	1,027	286	21.78
Prisons Act	21	10	32.26

approximately 1 per cent of the male total). Women are more likely to be indicted for stealing and receiving — particularly shoplifting and receiving stolen goods — (making up 4 per cent of the male total), drug offences (5 per cent of the male total) and false pretences, fraud, forgery and uttering — particularly welfare fraud, false cheques and credit cards — (22 per cent of the male total). These offences are quite compatible with the helper, consumer, often dependent, passive role of the 'feminine' woman. Women form larger proportions of persons indicted for disorderly conduct and obscene language (9 per cent of the total) and prison act offences — usually behaviour problems within the prison — (32 per cent of the total). These statistics could well reflect traditional sex role attitudes held by those in authority who may deny chivalrous or preferential treatment to women who do not act in appropriately 'feminine' ways.

While sex role socialisation gives some insight into crime statistics it cannot be postulated as the single explanatory variable of female crime rates. Apart from oversimplifying the complex problem of crime, it leads to spurious debates such as 'what went wrong with the socialisation of women who were indicted for 'masculine' type offences?' Similarly, it has led to erroneous conclusions that changes in female sex role socialisation, brought about by the Women's Liberation Movement, have increased female criminality.

b. **The impact of the Women's Liberation Movement.** It has been suggested that the Women's Liberation Movement has 'emancipated' women over the last decade, so they are now more likely to participate in crime. In the United States and the United Kingdom rises in reported crime rate statistics have been blamed on 'the darker side' of the Women's Liberation Movement.[15] In Western Australia, much media attention has been devoted to the rise in female criminality and the increasing tendency for women to participate in more violent, 'masculine' types of crime. Increasing female criminality has now become a 'social fact', causing considerable public alarm and reaction.[16] However, in terms of Western Australian court and prison statistics this theory cannot be supported, for the following reasons.

   i. The structural data available tell little about community life. There is neither empirical evidence of the impact of the Women's Liberation Movement, nor true prevalence rates of female criminality.[17]

   ii. One would expect women prisoners to be increasingly those affected by the Women's Liberation Movement. However, the great majority of female prisoners in Western Australia always have been and continue to be Aborigines — generally tribal women or fringe dwellers — for whom the Women's Liberation Movement has no meaning.

   iii. One would expect female prisoners to be increasingly persons employed in the work force who subsequently have greater access to economic crimes. However, at the time of data collection, March 1979, the few women prisoners who were actually employed at time of arrest were involved in menial labour.

iv. One would expect to find more females indicted for 'masculine' types of crimes, that is, aggressive and violent offences. However, from the available court data, female rates of violent crimes have been rising at a much slower pace than male rates.[18]

v. Finally, the theory that the Women's Liberation Movement has induced rising female crime rates cannot be substantiated because it cannot be stated categorically that the female crime rate has risen significantly over the last decade. Statistics from the Western Australian Magistrates' Courts over the past century show that the rate of increase in offences by males has been faster than the rate of increase in offences by females except for property offences. Comparing female imprisonment rates with those of males, Table 2, it can be seen that on all indices — total commitments, prisoners received and distinct persons received[19] — female imprisonment rates have not risen to the same extent as male imprisonment rates.

Both statistically and theoretically the proposition that the Women's Liberation Movement has resulted in increased female criminality cannot be supported. Statistically, the 'social fact' of the rising female crime rate cannot be substantiated by the available evidence. In fact, from the imprisonment data (Table 2) it is apparent that fewer women are being imprisoned for fewer offences since 1970-71.

2. Racial discrimination: Second to the Northern Territory, Western Australia imprisons more persons per capita population than any other state in Australia.[20] In the case of female imprisonment rates, the relatively high numbers appear to be a function of the large number of Aborigines imprisoned. For instance, at the beginning of the decade, in 1970-71, Aboriginal women accounted for 91 per cent of female prisoners received and still in 1977-78 they accounted for 89 per cent of prisoners

Table 2 – Total Commitments, Prisoners and Distinct Persons Received in Western Australia: 1970-71 to 1977-78

	1970-71	1971-72	1972-73	1973-74	1974-75	1975-76	1976-77	1977-78
TOTAL COMMITMENTS								
Male	10,200	12,010	11,937	10,209	10,307	9,276	9,538	9,560
Female	1,499	1,676	1,541	1,358	1,159	905	753	990
Female percentage of Total	13	12	11	12	10	9	7	9
PRISONERS RECEIVED								
Male	6,396	7,393	6,913	5,742	5,531	4,140	3,437	3,025
Female	1,157	1,328	1,239	1,025	928	522	466	423
Female percentage of Total	15	15	15	15	14	11	12	12
DISTINCT PERSONS								
Male	3,353	4,784	4,027	3,420	3,306	2,365	2,398	2,115
Female	600	631	526	454	434	328	254	220
Female percentage of Total	15	12	12	12	12	12	10	9

received.[21] These figures are totally disproportionate considering that Aboriginals account for only 2 per cent of the total population of Western Australia.

Typically, the population of the Western Australian women's prison, Bandyup Training Centre, has been comprised of approximately 50 per cent Aborigines while the women's sections in the male prisons to the north and east have held predominantly Aboriginal women. Geraldton Regional Prison for example, received 109 female prisoners between 1974 and 1979, only six of whom were white. Female admissions to prisons in the far north are almost exclusively Aborigines. For example, Wyndham Regional Prison received 234 female prisoners between 1975 and 1979, only one of whom was white.[22]

Aboriginal women are afforded little protection by the law (an informal personal perusal of prisoner offence records, between 1975 and the present, showed that Aboriginal men accused, prosecuted and sentenced for raping and otherwise assaulting Aboriginal women, received relatively short sentences — apparently a token gesture of white 'hands off' Aboriginal affairs). Moreover, not only are Aboriginal women unprotected by law, they are victimised by law enforcement agencies being apprehended and imprisoned in disproportionate numbers for offences (for example, drunkenness) which are usually regarded as unsuitable for criminal sanctions.

Court sentencing patterns clearly reflect the differential treatment Aborigines receive at the hands of the law. From Table 3 it is apparent that Aborigines are far more likely than non-Aborigines to receive an outcome of imprisonment for drunkenness and disorderly conduct charges, rather than an alternative outcome such as fine, probation, bound over, dismissed and the like.[23]

A common belief throughout the criminal justice system is that women receive preferential treatment at the hands of the law.[24] However, the data in Table 3 clearly indicates that race is a far more important variable than sex in determining sentencing outcomes. The clear line of division demarcating

Table 3 — Outcomes of Drunkenness and Disorderly Conduct Charges By Sex and Race, 1975-1977

	Drunkenness				Disorderly Conduct			
	Aborigines		Non-Aborigines		Aborigines		Non-Aborigines	
Outcomes of Charges by Year	Male	Female	Male	Female	Male	Female	Male	Female
1975 Number of charges resulting in imprisonment	833	357	126	5	444	162	43	8
Percentage of total charges resulting in imprisonment	14	16	3	2	24	15	2	5
1976 Number of charges resulting in imprisonment	840	327	115	3	447	185	51	12
Percentage of total charges resulting in imprisonment	18	17	3	1	27	18	3	6
1977 Number of charges resulting in imprisonment	1,486	58	197	3	624	29	89	1
Percentage of total charges resulting in imprisonment	21	13	5	12	24	12	4	3

apparent preferential treatment is along non-Aboriginal/Aboriginal lines, not along female/male lines.

Western Australian court and prison statistics cannot be meaningfully interpreted without examining the variable of race. Aboriginal women consistently account for a disproportionately large percentage of the known criminal population. An analytic explanation of these statistics will not be developed here. Possibly it is suffice to say that they reflect a tradition of *de facto* and *de jure* racial discrimination practices in Western Australia.[25]

It is misleading to examine crime statistics solely from the perspective of the deviant. The criminal justice system plays an important part in determining what behaviour shall merit criminal sanctions, who shall be sanctioned and the extent of those sanctions.

3. Changing practices of the criminal justice system: From Figure 1 it is apparent that while the number of prisoner receivals at the women's prison, Bandyup, has been declining over the last five years, the prison muster has been steadily rising. For the first time in its history, Bandyup is filling to capacity. The current high prison muster reflects an unchanging policy of sentencing a comparatively large number of the population, especially Aborigines, compounded by an apparent increase in lengths of prisoners' terms of imprisonment, Figure 2.[26]

The noted increase in lengths of prisoners' sentences reflects an interplay between the authorities and those termed deviant. That is, changes in the criminal justice system affect and are affected by the behaviour and perceptions of those called criminals.

Designations of what is to be termed criminal behaviour change over time. Changes in offence statistics, in particular from drunk offences to drug offences, highlight the impact that altering designations of deviance may have on the criminal justice system. The following statistics of offences for which prisoners were committed (based on total commitments for penal imprisonment) illustrate these changes.[27]

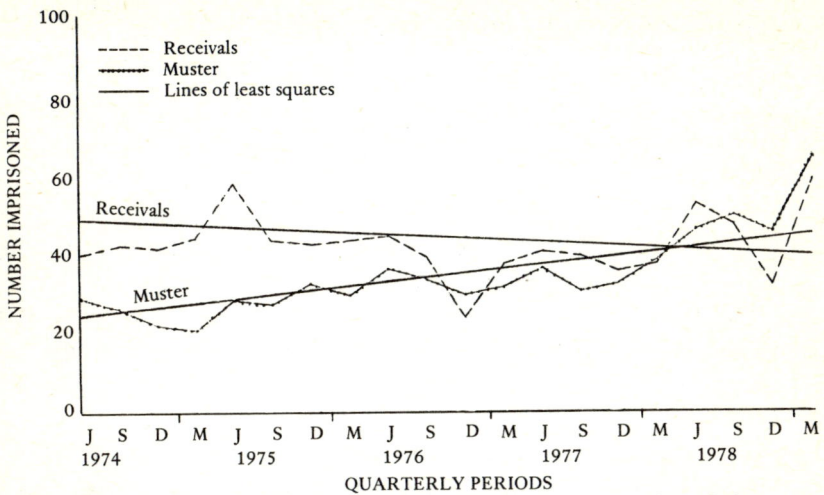

Figure 1 — Bandyup Prison Muster and Receivals Over Quarterly Periods From 1-4-74 to 31-3-79

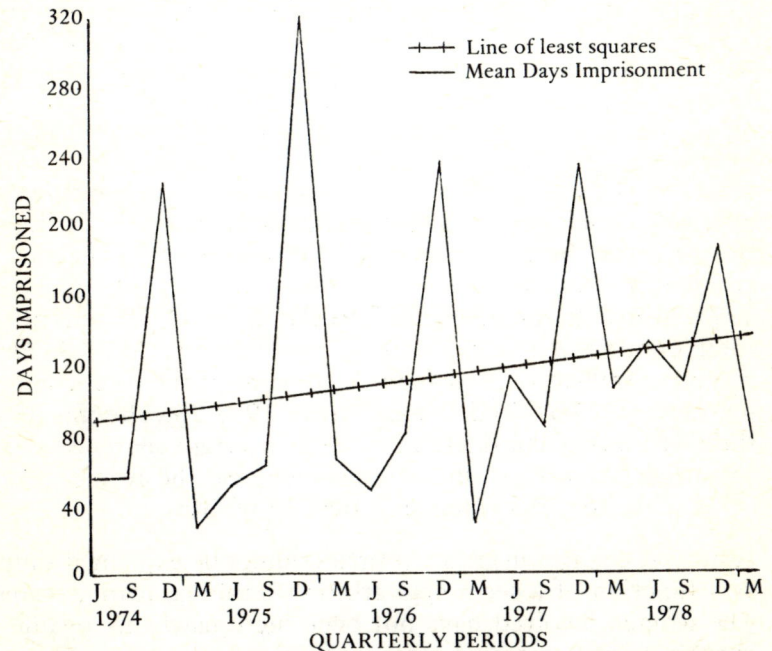

Figure 2 — Mean Number of Days of Female Sentences Over Quarterly Periods From 1-4-74 to 31-3-79

Female total commitment rates have fallen considerably over the decade. In 1967-68 the total number of commitments was 1,138, while in 1977-78, it was 990.[28] The decrease in total female commitments in Western Australia has largely been a function of changes in designations of criminality. Of the 1,138 female commitments during the 1967-68 financial year, 995 were Aboriginal commitments (87 per cent of the total) of which 897 were for drunkenness and disorderly conduct (76 per cent of female commitments overall). During the 1977-78 financial year, of the 990 total number of female commitments, 560 were Aboriginal commitments (57 per cent of the total) of which 307 were for drunkenness and disorderly conduct (31 per cent of female commitments overall).

Since there were no apparent significant changes in the situation of Aboriginal women over this period, it seems reasonable to conclude that the procedures of prosecuting authorities had changed and not the actual (criminal) behaviour of Aboriginal women. Indeed, during this time period, in 1975, as a result of a Supreme Court decision there was a change in the traditional practice of sentencing alcoholics to prison; alcoholics were to be designated as 'a serious social problem, the solution to which must be found outside the criminal law'.[29]

While on the one hand there has been official recognition that drunkenness should no longer be regarded as a criminal offence, on the other there has been a concerted effort on the part of criminal justice authorities to prosecute drug offenders. In 1973-74 drunk commitments accounted for 21 per cent of the total commitments and only 6 per cent in 1977-78. Drug commitments accounted for 0.5 per cent of the total commitments in 1973-74 and 2 per cent in 1977-78. The impact of these changes is considerable since the average sentence length for drunk offences is under 8 days whereas the average length of sentence for drug offences is over 18 months.

However, changes in crime statistics cannot be explained simply as a function of a seemingly arbitrary criminal justice system. The women involved have not been mere pawns in a game of chance. Female rates of offences against property are a case in point. According to court statistics in Australia, property crimes by females have been increasing, reaching their highest level this century. In Western Australia, female rates have been increasing at higher rates than those for males.[30] Total prison commitment statistics reflect the trend of increasing female property offences. For instance, in 1967-68, in the category of false pretences, fraud, forgery and uttering, 5 per cent were committed by females (846 by men and 38 by women), while 10 years later, in 1977-78, 21 per cent of those offences were committed by women (1,076 by men and 289 by women).[31]

These examples of changes in offence statistics highlight the fact that while it may be useful to examine the idiosyncracies of the deviant (the criminal), this is a futile exercise unless the practices of those who have authority to label those persons as deviant are examined concurrently. Functional theorists and labelling theorists alike have the unfortunate habit of concentrating on one side of the system to the exclusion of the other. While functional theorists examine 'what went wrong' with those designated deviant, labelling theorists concentrate on deviants as 'victims' — determined pawns in an arbitrary labelling system. However, clearly there is an interactive process between deviants and labelling authorities, each actively affecting the other.

The effects of this interactive process may snowball. It is quite possible that the 'social fact' of women's rising crime rate may prove to be a self-fulfilling prophecy. The current 'moral panic' about women's unprecedented advent into crime may result in women offenders being treated differently by prosecuting agencies — the police, courts and parole board. Women suspects may be more likely to be apprehended, sentenced, given longer finite and parole sentences, re-imprisoned for breach of parole or denied parole at greater rates than in earlier periods.

Unfortunately, there is insufficient statistical data available in Western Australia to examine this proportion empirically. There is definitely a more restrictive trend. However, it is not possible to determine the extent to which it is specific to females. For instance, women are receiving longer prison sentences, but so too are the men.[32] Similarly, Parole Board practices have become more restrictive; the proportion of parole releases decreased from 45 per cent in 1974 to 32 per cent in 1978 while parole denials increased from 7 per cent in 1974 to 13 per cent in 1978.[33] Separate statistics were not available for women. For the time being, the proposition of a backlash by the criminal justice system shall have to remain in the realm of the possible but as yet unknown.

In sum, statistical data available on female crime can be interpreted as a function of traditional sex role socialisation, a tradition of racial discrimination against Aborigines and the interaction of changing practices of the criminal justice system and changing patterns of criminal behaviour. Contrary to popular opinion, women in Western Australia are not becoming more criminal — at least not according to recorded court and prison statistics.

It has been suggested that the relatively low female crime rate may be a function of sex role socialisation wherein women learn behaviours and take on roles which tend to exclude them from participating in criminal activities or from being seen by the relevant authorities as criminal. On the other hand, the relatively high female mental hospitalisation rates may also reflect sex role socialisation in that female socialisation patterns may actually produce high rates of mental illness among women or alternatively, may cause women to be labelled mentally ill. Mental illness institutionalisation is seen here as an alternative form of social constraint to imprisonment.

Women and Mental Illness

While many more males than females are imprisoned, more females than males are admitted to psychiatric wards and hospitals. Statistics from the United States and England have shown that female rates of mental illness are significantly higher than male rates on all indices.[34] Available statistics from 1971 to 1978 show that in Western Australia female in-patient admissions outnumbered those of males up to 1977 but since that year the situation has been reversed (see Table 4).[35]

Interpreting Mental Hospitalisation Statistics:
1. Problems of data collection: Unfortunately, Western Australian statistics of mental hospitalisation are not comparable with

Table 4 — Male and Female Mental Patient Admissions to Mental Health Services and General and Private Hospitals, 1970-1978

Mental Health Services	1970-71	1971-72	1972-73	1973-74	1974-75	1975-76	1976-77	1977-78
Males	1,137	1,495	1,469	1,359	1,317	1,029	908	837
Females	1,036	1,140	1,163	1,128	942	919	769	681
Female Percentage of Total	44	43	44	45	42	47	47	45

Hospital In-patients under mental disorders, senility and ill-defined diseases*	1971	1972	1973	1974	1975	1976	1977	1978
Males	2,825	3,083	3,261	3,736	4,349	4,542	5,609	6,364
Females	3,860	4,286	4,688	4,819	4,817	4,941	5,372	5,966
Female Percentage of Total	58	58	59	56	53	52	49	48

* Note: The category senility and ill-defined diseases includes some possibly non psychiatric hospital admissions. Moreover, since the average female lives considerably longer than the average male, the senility category is likely to be weighted in favour of females.

data from the United States and England. Noticeably, the category of alcohol related conditions which are included in the Western Australian mental hospitalisation statistics are excluded from the United States statistics. However, if the alcoholism category were omitted from the Western Australian 1977-78 Mental Health Services statistics, women would make up 50 per cent of the total admissions and 59 per cent of the total psychiatric admissions to general and private hospitals in 1978.[36] The Western Australian data tend to conceal female rates of mental hospitalisation. For instance, whereas 'masculine' disorders — psychoses and alcoholism — are documented, 'feminine' disorders — depression and neuroses — are frequently subsumed under other categories such as physical disorders. In addition, comparative data reveal that women are more likely than men to be treated privately or on an out-patient basis.[37]

2. Sex role socialisation and labelling: Despite the problems of data collection, it is clear that women make up a considerable proportion of psychiatric hospitalisation admissions, that is, recorded mental illness in Western Australia. It has been suggested that high rates of mental illness among women are the result of female socialisation processes. Women have been taught to be self-destructive rather than other-destructive[38], the sick role is appropriate to expectations of the traditional feminine role[39], and finally women are socialised to take on roles as wives which are unstructured, invisible and unclear and the role strain thus induced drives women crazy whereas the role of husband 'preserves' men.[40]

From a labelling perspective, it has been argued that women's high rates of mental illness are an artifact of sex-biased diagnostic and/or treatment processes. It has been demonstrated that the ethic of health is masculine and hence typically feminine behaviours tend to be seen and labelled by the appropriate authorities as 'not healthy'.[41] However, wives who partake in typically masculine behaviours are more likely to be mentally institutionalised by their husbands than wives who perform domestically though they may be extremely docile, dependent and child-like.[42] Women are in a double bind — damned if they do (act feminine) and damned if they don't. As a variant on the labelling theme, it has been argued that women are more likely to see themselves as crazy and voluntarily label themselves, self reporting their deviance.[43] Finally, because women have been taught to be accommodative and nurturant they may be less likely to see their men as crazy or to hospitalise them.[44] Hence, true prevalence rates of male mental illness may be high, but men may be less likely to be labelled mentally ill.

The available statistics do support the proposition of a relationship between sex role socialisation and mental hospitalisation. For instance, male:female ratios of mental hospital admissions vary according to the type of admission involved. Women are more likely than men to be mentally institutionalised under the category of voluntary admissions — apparently more willing to seek and obey medical advice, take on the sick role and volunteer themselves for mental hospitalisation. Men on the other hand are more likely than women to enter the mental health system through agencies of formal control, Table 5.[45] Formal control agencies (police, courts, prisons and some medical referrals) may order persons to be received into a mental hospital where they are to be kept under varying degrees of restrictive custody. (The wording of these admission categories can be misleading. Not only persons admitted through formal agents of control are held voluntarily in mental hospitals. A person who voluntarily admits herself cannot necessarily voluntarily discharge herself — her status may be altered during the course of hospitalisation and she may be retained involuntarily.)

Although sex role socialisation provides an insightful starting point, it is an inadequate explanation of mental institutionalisation rates. Mental hospital admissions are influenced by a complex, dynamic relationship between community attitudes, the actions of those called deviant and authorities' changing policies.

3. Societal attitudes and changing policies: Societal attitudes towards mental hospitalisation affect admission rates stigmatising and excluding or alternatively medicalising and encouraging mental hospitalisation as a viable option to deal with stress and problematic behaviour.

Table 5 — Types of Admissions to Mental Health Services with Male/Female Ratios from 1970-71 to 1977-78

Type of Admission	1970-71	1971-72	1972-73	1973-74	1974-75	1975-76	1976-77	1977-78
All Admissions —								
Male	1,137	1,495	1,469	1,359	1,317	1,029	908	837
Female	1,036	1,140	1,163	1,128	942	919	796	681
Reception and Security Orders —								
Male	256	272	276	206	226	164	116	213
Female	83	94	83	67	62	78	23	86
Female Percentage of Total Reception and Security Orders	24	28	23	25	22	32	17	29
Female Reception and Security Orders as Percentage of All Admissions	6	4	3	3	3	4	1	6
Male Reception and Security Orders as Percentage of All Admissions	19	10	10	8	12	8	7	14
Female Reception and Security Orders as Percentage of Total Female Admissions	8	8	7	6	7	8	3	13
Male Reception and Security Orders as Percentage of Total Male Admissions	23	24	19	15	17	16	13	26

Hospital admission criteria have considerable effect on numbers of persons institutionalised by facilitating or hindering access to the mental health system. Tighter admission criteria to Mental Health Services appear to have affected general and private hospital in-patient psychiatric admission rates. While Mental Health Services admission rates have been falling, in-patient hospital psychiatric admissions have been rising (Table 4). One explanation for this may be that there has been a shift in populations, changing from specific (possibly stigmatising) public care to general (possibly covert) and private care.

Availability of medical benefits may affect admission rates by virtue of financial implications for prospective patients as well as doctors admitting.

The development of a private hospital system is likely to affect admission rates by enabling some persons under stress to adopt the sick role and virtually take a holiday without the implications of stigma.

Changing definitions of deviance may have considerable impact on hospitalisation rates. The disputed problem of alcoholism is a case in point. From Table 4 it would appear that compared with males, female rates of psychiatric hospitalisation have declined over the last decade. However, the changing female: male ratio does not seem to be a function of changes in the female population. Rather, it may be due to a dramatic increase in the numbers of male alcoholic admissions. Unfortunately, the available data are not sufficiently specific to allow for strict empirical testing. Nonetheless, it is notable that the psychiatric category including male alcoholics has risen dramatically while imprisonment rates for alcoholic offences has declined.

One explanation of the high rates of female mental hospitalisation has been sex role socialisation and sex-biased labelling and/or diagnostic procedures. However, in order to interpret the psychiatric hospitalisation statistics in Western Australia (problematic as they are), it is necessary to examine the interplay between societal attitudes towards mental illness, availability and accessibility of facilities and designations of deviance. The apparent decrease in the female:male ratio of psychiatric hospital admissions over the last decade in Western Australia should be understood in the light of these factors.

The Interrelationship Between Imprisonment and Mental Hospitalisation

If imprisonment and mental hospitalisation can be understood as alternative forms of social constraint, it seems reasonable to hypothesise a relationship between the two over time. As early as 1939 there were attempts to test the hypothesis of an inverse relationship between rates of mental hospitalisation and rates of imprisonment, that is, as imprisonment rates increase, mental hospitalisation rates will decrease or *vice versa*.[46] The underlying assumption of this hypothesis would appear to be that there is a malleable pool of deviants to be channelled into some sort of restrictive custody — mental hospitals or prisons — depending upon prevailing societal ideologies. A recent reformulation of the inverse relationship hypothesis is the proposal that with changing sex role socialisation, broadening economic opportunities and changing societal attitudes over the last decade, women may be more likely to be imprisoned and less likely to be mentally institutionalised.[47] However, in order to investigate the possiblity of an inverse relationship specific to women, the overall relationship must first be examined.

While Mental Health Services admission rates have been declining psychiatric admissions to general and private hospitals have been increasing. Overall, mental hospitalisation rates would appear to be rising (Table 5). During the same time period, imprisonment rates appear to be declining.

It is virtually impossible, however, to accept an hypothesis of an inverse relationship between mental hospitalisation and imprisonment since there are numerous intervening variables. Prison and hospital admission rates may depend upon the availability of alternative facilities (one case in point would be Community Centres providing a service for one system and not the other). Prevailing policies of the criminal justice and medical systems at any one time may totally distort a simple correlation between the two. For example, the open door policy of Mental Health Services (known more descriptively as the 'revolving door policy' — in, out and in again) boosts up hospital admission rates while the current trend to impose long sentences on criminals lowers prison admission rates.

Attempts to ascertain an inverse relationship between female participation in the mental health system and criminal justice are similarly hazardous. Females appear to be forming a slightly smaller percentage of both mental hospital and prison admissions over the last decade, but given the wide range of intervening variables and paucity of relevant data one can only guess possible reasons for this decline. It may be more useful to examine what happens to persons caught between the criminal justice and mental health systems. More insight into the relationship between mental hospitalisation and imprisonment may be gained by taking the underlying assumption of the inverse relationship hypothesis literally, and examining the malleable pool of deviants channelled into mental health or prisons depending upon prevailing contingencies.

Admissions to Mental Health Services Via Formal Agencies of Control: Female percentage of total admissions to Mental Health Services via formal agencies of control has shown an intermittent pattern of rises and falls over the period 1970-71 to 1977-78 (Table 5). Over the last financial year, however, there has been a dramatic increase in the number of females referred via formal agencies of control compared to female admission rates overall. Once again, the attempt to relate this finding to a change specific to women proves to be problematic. At the same time there was also a rise (though not so dramatic) in male hospital admissions via formal agencies of control. Moreover, these statistics may be reflecting changes in hospital populations referred to earlier, with more patients being admitted to Mental Health Services via formal agencies of control and more voluntary patients being admitted to general and private hospitals. Since changing rates of types of admissions to Mental Health Services are not easily interpreted, they offer little insight into the relationships between rates of imprisonment and mental hospitalisation.

The Borderline Cases — 'Mad' or 'Bad'?: Some women float between the mental health and criminal justice systems, labelled alternatively 'mad', 'bad' or both. Included in this category are persons thought to be unfit to stand trial at or before trial, prison transfers to mental hospitals and persons found not guilty on the grounds of unsound mind.[48]

1. **Unfit to stand trial at or before trial**: Persons thought to be unfit to stand trial at or before trial may be remanded to Mental Health Services for observation. The ratio of males: females on remand in Mental Health Services during the 1977-78 financial year approximated the ratio of males:females within the criminal justice system. If anything, there were less women on remand in Mental Health Services than would be expected, that is, in 1977-78 women made up 10 per cent of persons remanded to Mental Health Services and 12 per cent of persons admitted to prison. From Table 6, given the male rates, one would expect fewer women remanded to Mental Health Services to be fit to plead within the time period specified by the court. Although numbers are too small to form generalisations, tentatively, it would seem that women are more likely than their male counterparts to be directed into the courts and out of the Mental Health Services.

Details of the 30 June 1978 bed-census (including persons caught between mental health and the law for long periods of time) reveals that females on remand may spend shorter periods of time institutionalised in mental hospitals than their male counterparts. Once again, however, numbers are too small to form generalisations.

Table 6 — Types of Disposition by Sex of Remandees
To Mental Health Services During 1977-78

Disposition	Male Remands	Female Remands
Fit to Plead	68	8
Charges withdrawn	*15	1
Adjourned *sine die*	*21	2
Total	102	11

* Two remands whose charges were adjourned *sine die* later had their charges withdrawn without going to court. Hence, these two persons have been included in both the charges withdrawn category and the *sine die* category.

It would seem that women remands, compared with males, are not likely to receive preferential treatment, that is, they are not being given a way out of the criminal justice system by being classified as 'mad' as opposed to 'bad'. Once admitted to Mental Health Services, however, women seem to be released earlier than their male counterparts — possibly an instance of perceived lack of dangerousness and hence preferential treatment.

2. Prison transfers to Mental Health Services: Females in prison are not more likely to be transferred to Mental Health Services than males. In the 1977-78 financial year, 16 males and two females were transferred from prison to Mental Health Services. It should be noted that these persons do not necessarily reflect prisoners in need of mental hospitalisation, but rather persons acceptable to Mental Health Services.[49] Thus, it seems that female prisoners are not seen to be more appropriate mental health patients than their male counterparts by Mental Health Services authorities.

3. Persons found not guilty on the grounds of unsound mind: Women found not guilty on the grounds of unsound mind represent the only category of forensic patients who appear to be treated somewhat preferentially by both the courts and mental health authorities. At the bed-census of 30 June 1978, there were 22 persons in prison and Mental Health Services who had been found not guilty on the grounds of unsound mind. Their offences and the location to which they were ordered are given in Table 7.

While males found not guilty on the grounds of unsound mind had committed a variety of offences, all women found not guilty on the grounds of unsound mind had committed murder. One might postulate that if murder is seen as totally inappropriate to the feminine role (especially since most women have murdered family members including their children), women murderers may be more likely to be seen as 'mad' rather than 'bad'. However, since there are no readily available estimates of male and female murderers found not guilty on the grounds of unsound mind compared with persons found guilty and sentenced to death, this proposal cannot be substantiated.

Table 7 — Offences of Persons Found Not Guilty on the Grounds of Unsound Mind by Location and Sex

	Within Mental Health Services		Within Prison	
Offence	Male	Female	Male	Female
Wilful Murder	5	3	2	0
Murder, Unlawful Killing	2	0	0	0
Attempted Murder, Attempted Killing	2	0	1	0
Assault, Grievous Bodily Harm	3	0	0	0
Armed and Violent	1	0	0	0
Arson	0	0	1	0
Housebreaking	1	0	0	0
Damaging Buildings	1	0	0	0
Total	15	3	4	0

Women found not guilty on the grounds of unsound mind are far more likely than men to be sent to Mental Health Services rather than to prison. Possibly, the assumption that women are less dangerous than men operates informally to create this situation. Finally, women found not guilty on grounds of unsound mind spend shorter periods of time incarcerated than their male counterparts.[50]

An examination of forensic patients in 1977-78 financial year reveals that except in the case of those found not guilty on the grounds of unsound mind, women are as likely or more likely than their male counterparts to be channelled into prisons rather than Mental Health Services. Available data indicate that women on remand in Mental Health Services and women found not guilty on the grounds of unsound mind spend shorter periods of time incarcerated than their male counterparts. It is possible to postulate tentatively that while women may be as likely or more likely than men to be seen as 'bad' as opposed to 'mad', once designated 'mad' they may receive preferential treatment in terms of shorter periods of incarceration.

The borderline cases, 'mad' or 'bad', give some insight into the labelling process but add little to the understanding of the deviant actors involved. In fact, the quantitative statistics available are simply not useful for testing broad theoretical propositions such as changing sex roles in the community. A more useful endeavour would be to qualitatively examine careers of individual women who manage to escape the labelling process as well as those designated criminal and mentally ill to determine if there are similarities or turning points in their careers which could have led to either criminal or mentally ill careers.

Conclusion

From available statistics it would seem that rates of female incarceration (in prisons and mental hospitals) compared to male rates have declined slightly over the last decade. It is apparent that the hypothesis that the Women's Liberation Movement has led to a rise in female crime rates is not supported. Similarly, the hypothesis that the emancipation of women has resulted in rising female imprisonment rates and declining female mental hospitalisation rates is not supported. Even given the noted decline in female imprisonment and mental hospitalisation rates over the last decade one cannot conclude that women are becoming less criminal or less mentally ill. Not only are available statistics inadequate to formulate such a conclusion but the measurement itself — changes in incarceration rates — is not a useful measure of changing sex roles or behaviour in the community.

Although the theory of sex role socialisation provides insight into female/male deviant outcomes, it cannot bridge the gap between behaviour in the community (changing sex roles) and rates of incarceration. The making of a deviant (prisoner or mental patient) is a dynamic process involving the actions of the deviant as well as societal reaction. Hence, in order to interpret the Western Australian crime and mental illness statistics available, variables such as changing designations of deviance, changing policies, available facilities, prevailing societal attitudes as well as changing deviant behaviour must be examined. Qualitative rather than quantitative research would be necessary to examine changing deviant behaviour and the reaction to it as a separate variable in the complex process which results in women in constraints.

---

1. L. Radzinowicz and J. King, *The Growth of Crime: The International Experience*, Basic Books Inc., New York, 1977, p. 13. The authors state that

men and boys are found guilty of crimes six to eight times as often as women and girls.

2. W. Gove and J. Tudor, 'Adult Sex Roles and Mental Illness', *American Journal of Sociology*, 1978, pp. 812-25; C. Smart, *Women, Crime and Criminology: A Feminist Critique*, Routledge and Kegan Paul, London, 1977, pp. 152-3.

3. T. Stang Dahl and A. Snare, 'The Coercion of Privacy: A Feminist Perspective' in C. Smart and B. Smart, *Women, Sexuality and Social Control*, Routledge and Kegan Paul, London, 1978, pp. 21-3.

4. H. Land, 'Women: Supporters or Supported?' in D. Leonard Barker and S. Allen (Eds.), *Sexual Divisions and Society: Process and Change*, Tavistock, London, 1976.

5. Note, for example, the Home Office Criminal Statistics for England and Wales recorded in C. Smart, *op. cit.*; the F.B.I. Uniform Crime Reports reprinted in D. Hoffman-Bustamante, 'The Nature of Female Criminality', *Issues in Criminology*, Vol. 8, No. 2, 1973; and also the Norwegian Official Criminal Statistics noted in T. Stang Dahl and A. Snare, *op. cit.*

6. S.K. Mukherjee and R.W. Fitzgerald, 'The Myth of Rising Female Crime', see page 127.

7. *Ibid.*, p. 146.

8. Western Australia. Department of Corrections Annual Reports, 1970 to 1978.

9. According to the Australian Bureau of Statistics, as at 31 December 1978 there were 626,897 males and 604,789 females in Western Australia, that is, males made up 51 per cent of the total population. (The figures had been adjusted for undernumeration.)

10. J. Cowie, V. Cowie and E. Slater, *Delinquency in Girls*, Heinemann, London, 1968, pp. 176-7.

11. C. Lombroso and W. Ferrero, *The Female Offender*, Fisher Unwin, London, 1895.

12. O. Pollak, *The Criminality of Women*, A.S. Barnes, New York, 1961.

13. C. Smart, *op. cit.*, pp. 10-18.

14. The offence statistics were taken from the Western Australia Department of Corrections Annual Report 1977-78. For the sake of brevity and clarity, some categories have been collapsed (that is, offences against the person), others omitted and percentages added to the table given in the Annual Report.

15. F. Adler, *Sisters in Crime: The Rise of the New Female Criminal*, McGraw-Hill, New York, 1975; R.J. Simon, *Women and Crime*, Lexington Books, Massachusetts, 1974; T. Hart, 'The New Adolescent Offender', unpublished paper presented at the Institute for the Study and Treatment of Delinquency Spring Conference, 1975.

16. A pertinent example was, *The Daily Telegraph*, 22 June 1979, report on the Australian Institute of Criminology 'Women and Crime' Conference, Canberra, which stated incorrectly that the conference found that women were prosecuted less and received lighter penalties for their crimes than men, and that crime in Australia had reached its highest level this century.

17. Recorded rates of crime are particularly poor indicators of the extent of crime in the community as noted, for example, by P.N.P. Wiles, 'Criminal

Statistics and Sociological Explanations of Crime' in P.N.P. Wiles and W.G. Carson (Eds.), *Crime and Delinquency in Britain*, Martin Robertson, London, 1970. In relation to women offenders' official statistics, note D. Hoffman-Bustamante, *op. cit.*

18. S.K. Mukherjee and R.W. Fitzgerald, 'Overview of Research in Female Crime', unpublished paper presented at the Australian Institute of Criminology 'Women and Crime' Conference, Canberra, June 1979.

19. The categories used by the Western Australia Department of Corrections to measure imprisonment rates are not used universally and hence may need some clarification. Total commitments refer to the total number of *offences* for which prisoners are committed per annum to the Western Australian prison system. Prisoners received refers to the total number of prisoners received per annum by the Western Australian prison system whereby one prisoner may be received more than once. Distinct persons refer to the total number of distinct individuals received per annum by the Western Australian prison system.

20. Statistics provided monthly by the Australian Institute of Criminology.

21. It is not possible to examine Aboriginal:non-Aboriginal prison statistics over the last decade since separate statistics for Aboriginals and non-Aboriginals were not kept between 1971 and 1977.

22. Statistics were collected from the individual institutional records.

23. Unpublished statistics from the Australian Bureau of Statistics.

24. This has, however, been rejected by Jocelynne A. Scutt, 'The Myth of the 'Chivalry Factor' in Female Crime', *Australian Journal of Social Issues*, Vol. 14, No. 1, February 1979, pp. 3-20.

25. Note, for example, F.S. Stevens (Ed.), *Racism: The Australian Experience, Volume I, Prejudice and Xenophobia*, Taplinger Publishing Co. Inc., New York, 1972; also *Volume II, Black Versus White* and *Volume III, Colonialism*.

26. Lengths of imprisonment (including time spent on remand) from 1974 to 1978 were collected from institutional records and cross-checked where necessary with Departmental Central Records' data. The increase in lengths of imprisonment is underestimated in that the earliest possible release date was used to calculate incomplete maximum/minimum sentences even though prisoners may be held beyond that date and, moreover, the date of data collections was used to calculate sentences for women who have been imprisoned indefinitely at the Governor's Pleasure.

27. It should be noted that total commitment prison statistics are not a stable measure of crime rates in that they measure the total number of offences for which persons are committed rather than distinct persons imprisoned. (For example, one person indicted for hundreds of offences could alone account for large yearly variations in offence statistics.)

28. Western Australia. Department of Corrections Annual Reports 1967-68 and 1977-78.

29. Supreme Court decision, 18, 19 June, 19 July 1974, *Murphy, Davidson and Ward* v *Watson*. The women appellants contested that their six month sentences for drunkenness and disorderly conduct were excessive. The appeals were allowed and a fine of $10 substituted in each case. Since the Supreme Court is the highest court in the state the lower courts were expected to

comply with this decision. This expectation has been only partially fulfilled.
30. S.K. Mukherjee and R.W. Fitzgerald, *op. cit.,* p. 158.
31. Western Australia. Department of Corrections Annual Reports 1967-68 and 1977-78.
32. In the absence of more accurate data an approximate mean sentence length can be calculated by taking the median of each sentence length category tabulated in the Western Australia Department of Corrections Annual Reports, multiplied by the number of receivals for that year and averaged.

Year	Average Length of Sentence
1973-74	3.7 months
1974-75	4.1 months
1975-76	5.6 months
1976-77	6.8 months
1977-78	7.4 months

33. Western Australia. Parole Reports 1974 to 1978.
34. P. Chesler, *Women and Madness,* Allen Lane, London, 1974, pp. 42-3; C. Smart, *op. cit.,* pp. 146-50; W. Gove and J. Tudor, *op. cit.*
35. These statistics were collected from Mental Health Services Annual Reports from 1970-71 to 1977-78; statistics of hospital in-patients psychiatric categories for 1971, 1972 and 1978 were made available in tabulated form by the Australian Bureau of Statistics, Western Australian Office; and finally, Hospital In-patient Statistics Catalogues for 1973 to 1977.
36. The hospital in-patient calculation is an approximation only, since the Australian Bureau of Statistics category which includes alcoholism is all-inclusive, that is, 'neuroses, personality disorders and other non-psychotic mental disorders'.
37. W. Gove and J. Tudor, *op. cit.,* p. 823.
38. P. Chesler, *op. cit.,* pp. 38-9, 54-5.
39. D. Mechanic, 'Perceptions of Parental Response to Illness: A Research Note', *Journal of Health and Human Behaviour,* Vol. 6, 1965, pp. 253 8; H.R. Geertsen and R. Gray, 'Familistic Orientation and Inclination Toward Adopting the Sick Role', *Journal of Marriage and the Family,* Vol. 6, November 1970, pp. 638-45.
40. W. Gove and J. Tudor, *op. cit.*
41. I.K. Broverman, S.R. Vogel, D. Broverman, F. Clarkson and P.S. Rosenkrantz, 'Sex Role Stereotypes and Clinical Judgements of Mental Health', *Journal of Consulting and Clinical Psychology,* Vol. 34, 1970, pp. 1-7; B. Fabrikant, 'The Psychotherapist and the Female Patient: Misperceptions and Change' in Franks and Burtle (Eds.), *Women in Therapy,* Brunner Maxel, New York, 1974.
42. S. Angrist, S. Dinitz, M. Lefton and B. Pasamanick, *Women After Treatment,* Appleton-Century-Crofts, New York, 1968.
43. D.L. Phillips and B.E. Segal, 'Sexual Status and Psychiatric Symptoms', *American Sociological Review,* Vol. 34, No. 1, 1969, p. 59.
44. Statistical information which would appear to support this notion can be found in C.A. Taube, 'Admission Rates by Marital Status: Outpatient Psych-

iatric Services', Statistical Note 35, *N.I.M.H. Survey and Reports Section*, December 1970; qualitative support can be found in C.G. Schwartz, 'Perspective on Deviance — Wives' Definitions of Their Husbands' Mental Illness', *Psychiatry*, Vol. 20, 1957, pp. 275-91.

45. Total numbers of admission types were collected from Mental Health Services Annual Reports from 1970-71 to 1977-78 and percentages were added to demonstrate proportional changes over time.

46. L.S. Penrose, 'Mental Disease and Crime: Outline of a Comparative Study of European Statistics', *British Journal of Medical Psychology*, Vol. 18, 1939, pp. 1-15. For a more recent discussion see J. Gunn, 'Criminal Behaviour and Mental Disorder', *The British Journal of Psychiatry*, Vol. 130, April 1977, pp. 317-29.

47. C. Smart, *op. cit.*, pp. 146-75.

48. These Mental Health Services statistics were made available in the form of computer print-outs from the Statistical Research Unit. Where necessary, cross-checks were made with records at the hospitals concerned.

49. This statement was made by Dr Rollo, the Psychiatric Superintendent of the Western Australia Department of Corrections in personal communication, January 1979.

50. A. Freiberg and D. Biles, *The Meaning of 'Life': A Study of Life Sentences in Australia*, Australian Institute of Criminology, Canberra, July 1975, p. 57.

9 Prisons, Prisoners and the Community

SANDRA A.K. WILLSON

Interest in women's prisons has been stirred by the television program 'Prisoner', and many people ask 'are there any Veras or Megs, or Beas?'. From my experience 'inside', I can affirm there are: just as a macrocosm of the free world, the world 'inside' has its good and its bad, its violence and its leaders, its faults and its advantages. Unfortunately, these are not equally distributed and good intentions are often outweighed by bad consequences.

Many 'happenings' in the system are consequences emanating from prison directives, prison management and the day-to-day life of prisoners. For example, no matter how much the staff might be kindly intentioned, there is a directive that staff are **not** allowed to 'gossip' to prisoners. Even good, honest, person to person conversation can be regarded as 'gossiping'. Therefore the staff prefer not to be seen talking to prisoners and this inadvertently aids in keeping alive the age-old feud between staff and prisoners. Prisoners invariably hate the staff and feel threatened by anyone seen talking to staff, believing them to be 'lagging in' someone for something and therefore, the second prisoner is labelled an informer, a 'dog': this can lead to that prisoner sustaining a black eye as the result of violence by other prisoners. Thus a cause as far removed from the prison as a rule hidden away in directives for staff behaviour can lead directly to violence in the prison.

There are cases when one person looks hungrily at the fence, total gaol security is tightened and all prisoners, good, bad and indifferent, suffer the consequences. Resentment increases, hostility rises and confrontations between staff and inmates result. This is particularly noticeable when a woman imprisoned for drug offences succeeds in smuggling drugs into the gaol. Security is tightened, privileges such as contact visits are withdrawn from the good behaved as well as the bad. All suffer. Alternatively, visits are conducted under such tight restraint and supervision that the feeling of privilege is lost.

Prisoners at Mulawa[1]

This may be one of the system's greatest failings — treating all insiders similarly, regardless of behaviour, attitudes and criminality. Here, 'criminality' is relevant, because not everyone in gaol is a criminal. A woman going in for one or two weeks out of her whole life, who is never to reoffend, is **not** a criminal although a gaol sentence usually means that to the community. As soon as such a woman is released, friends and neighbours shy away from her as though she were contaminated. At this point, the chances are high that such a woman might reoffend because of community attitudes.

There are other women in gaol who come in with monotonous regularity. They are not dangerous or violent and are not vicious criminals, but are lonely, institutionalised and totally unable to cope with the free world. This is the result of another failing of the authorities. The gaol tends to function as smoothly as possible, with staff in charge giving orders, making decisions and being obeyed. The prisoner striking out on her own, making her own decisions and in consequence 'making waves', upsets the delicate balance of the gaol and is soon suppressed. If the prisoner does not submerge quietly, is a 'troublemaker', confrontation usually results between herself and the staff. Thus the total result of imprisonment is to manufacture quiet and happy prisoners who can cope quite well in gaol, getting along with the staff and never having a bad report. The moment these 'happy little prisoners' are released, they have become so dependent and institutionalised, the pressures of outside life are intolerable. They reoffend by choice so they may go 'back' to an environment they can handle (although they do not enjoy it) and where decision making is taken from them.

Another type of female prisoner in gaol today is the mentally disturbed individual. She has a history of psychiatric admissions, been released, and unintentionally commits an offence. In accordance with law, she is sent to prison and once there cannot be helped. There is no treatment. First, custodial staff have no psychiatric training; they are unable to deal with the mentally disturbed. Second, the consultant psychiatrist has a heavy case load and consequently interviews the woman for five minutes every week — if she's lucky. In reality, she is hardly ever seen and when she is, is put onto heavy doses of tranquillizers. If she misbehaves, she is locked up in a cell and left there, until her behaviour changes. And it does not.

Prison Strikes

Three strikes have occurred at Mulawa. All have arisen from the inadequacy of medical facilities. In two cases they have occurred because of the treatment of psychiatrically disturbed women. The first strike was held to call attention of Head Office to the plight of a woman kept confined because the staff were unable to cope. The aim of the strike was to have her sent to a psychiatric hospital, although in my personal experience one is not better off there at all — with regard to medical treatment, physical treatment, or emotional treatment. The second strike concerned the totally inept male nurse. In those days, women almost died as a result of his disastrous inability to diagnose ailments — an ectopic pregnancy was simply 'constipation'. In both cases, we had staff support for the action, even though going out on strike was highly illegal and open to disciplinary action. Prisoners do not have the right to dissent.

The third strike involved the support by one prisoner of another woman who was restrained by handcuffs in the security block. The restrained woman had threatened to commit suicide but this was the first time handcuffs had ever been used in Mulawa. Understandably the other prisoners were upset. The strike action again led to the woman being transferred to a psychiatric hospital where she could be kept confined in a room, kept handcuffed and given no treatment.

Medical Attention for Prisoners

However if prisoners are not transferred to another hospital, they are kept in Mulawa where they take up beds in the hospital block. This means that women who are genuinely ill do not have beds. Otherwise, they are confined in the maximum security block with security risk prisoners; this is not the best solution to either prisoner. This happened when I was in prison and being held in security upon transfer from hospital — the place was bedlam —

and yet I was supposed to be free and released from the psychiatric centre. No way. I was right back there!

The principal problem in the gaol is the division of power between the Department of Health and the custodial staff. A prisoner cannot be admitted to the hospital except by the nurse; certainly not by the custodial staff. If a prisoner has to be sent to an outside hospital, custodial staff must supply an escort. Otherwise the prisoner does not attend. If there are staff available but no car, the prisoner cannot go. This has happened.

The under-staffing of Mulawa has reached the stage where prisoners have been released from cells and allowed to walk about the gaol when the staff is called out on strike. There are insufficient numbers to fill the skeleton-staff posting required by law in order for them to go out on strike.

A final problem is faced by both the medical staff and the custodial staff, that of what to do with the increasing numbers of drug offenders coming in as prisoners. The whole 'face' of gaol has changed since I was there, for the 'respectable crim' is no longer the average inmate. This is especially so since the prostitutes, vagrants and drunks are no longer being committed. When a drug offender comes in, if she has been a registered addict she will be given methadone. Otherwise there are haeminurine pills to help a woman going through withdrawal. On release, a block aid level of methadone can be induced, but only if the prisoner requested it. Because there are great quantities of drugs floating about the gaol, a number of women are released when they are 'stoned out'. They are not caught within the gaol, for staff are not trained in drug detection techniques and thus may pass off the woman as being 'suspicious' only. Without proof, the medical staff are unable to include drug-takers in their statistics and therefore will deny drug-taking within the gaol. Yet women inside know who is using what and in what quantities. Despite searches of women who may have access to drugs, no drugs are found. Thus according to the custodial staff also, there are no drugs in gaol.

Staff-Inmate Relationships

The program 'Prisoner' does not, of course, cover every area, but I believe it does truthfully depict what occurs. Consider for example the prisoner-staff relationship. Vera yells and is tight lipped; Meg talks and is friendly. Both individuals exist in the gaol. Both are usually hated by the prisoners because both wear blue uniforms, carry keys, and have power to lock a prisoner in punishment cells. Both are feared, distrusted and pushed together for their own common good. Thus good staff are forced into the arms of bad, closing a circle around bad staff to protect them. The prisoners do not improve the situation for, where a good staff member helps one of them, the prisoner will 'lag her in' with a clear conscience and potential for good within the staff can be easily destroyed. Most good staff quit the job, leaving only those who can stomach the conditions, being those whom I call 'bad', like Vera.

Add to this the homosexual officer (of whom there are many) who occasionally 'makes eyes' at inmates. Homosexuality cannot be condemned, but the prisoner thinks not about the relationship but how she may use that relationship to get 'contraband' — blackmailing an officer-mother for cigarettes, lipstick, perfume and drugs. Such relationships may lead to jealousy among the other prisoners who are unable to obtain contraband. This leads to fights, abusive language and someone being locked in punishment cells. Obviously, it's not an ideal situation. Homosexual staff may be attracted to an all-female environment such as gaols and psychiatric hospitals, and will figure largely on the staff.

Women treat each other better than male warders treat male prisoners. However, there are the Beas, who stand over other prisoners, threatening them. In the television program even Bea was stabbed. The reality is that these incidents are fairly rare, although I consider violence in a women's gaol is increasing as the number of drug offenders increases. It is also true that certain screws, like Vera, would watch and not interfere in a fight within the gaol. In many ways, I agree with this approach. Certain people should have a belting if they interfere with the smooth running of prison — and I would say that prisons are run by the inmates and not the staff. Otherwise, there is a ridiculous situation where a few staff members can tell a huge number of prisoners what to do, and those prisoners obey them. Prisoners have the numbers to refuse to obey orders. So when I say the 'smooth running of the prison', I mean as it is run by the inmates themselves. Anyone stepping out of line will receive a belt in the chops. In the men's prisons, they will get a knife in the back.

Fights and assaults are reasonably rare in the women's prison. Naturally, cases exist where both prisoners and staff members have gone to extremes. Since staff are supposed by law not to lay a hand on prisoners, it is done in secret. Women being bashed in isolation cells, women being bashed and kicked where particularly pregnancy may be adversely affected is certainly unacceptable. No amount of abusive language warrants this bashing. Usually, it is the mentally disturbed who receive bashings and this raises the question — how much force is necessary to restrain such women? Where does the rule book end and human frustration take over? There are always a few who bash for sheer pleasure and power. Those particular staff members have come to the attention of the media and the Royal Commission into New South Wales Prisons.

Women usually resort to psychological tactics rather than to violence. They wear each others nerves down until someone explodes. This can lead to riots and senseless destruction of property. The result can be that women fold up and crack, becoming depressed and even committing suicide. The large amounts of tranquillizers swallowed by women day after day in New South Wales gaols has been well documented in the Royal Commission's report. The women themselves support this policy, preferring to walk around in a dazed condition during their sentence than be awake and alive to the tensions and pressures of being in gaol. What is worse is that ordinary day-to-day tensions that the average person outside can healthily release is not allowed to be released in the prison system. If I get angry, rightfully angry, outside, I can shout, swear, and people listening will approve. But in gaol, I can be locked up for swearing and locked up for yelling. I am creating a distrubance, upsetting other women and not showing respect for authority. And, goddammit, there are some things that one needs to yell about; some things that require good, strong, well phrased expressions. But not in gaol! Quite often, many of the women are walking fuse-boxes who need the merest excuse to explode.

Release from Prison

Eventually, every woman in Mulawa is released. What are her chances of beating the institutionalising effects of imprisonment and readjusting to outside society? I can say they are not great. Most women in gaol have no family to return to. Their friends are usually inside or going back inside. So what happens? Everyone congregates back inside the prison, to be with their mates. I have known women being released on the Friday, to say they will be back on the Monday. Sure enough, they are. These women cannot find jobs outside and so commit a crime and land back inside. Or they are harassed by the police, picked up and charged with an offence and sent back to Mulawa. Added to that, they are released with only a few dollars in their pockets, not enough to find a room, pay the rent, feed themselves — especially if they are released on the Saturday when the dole office is not open. These women tend to commit a crime, are invariably caught and returned to gaol.

What preparation does the Department of Corrective Services make for women to be reabsorbed into society? None! The department has formally considered it was responsible only for 'holding' women in safe custody. More than that was not their concern. Far worse, the department held all women in maximum security type establishments (which it called a 'variable' prison) and only a few years back bothered to open a medium security prison for women. This was soon closed. It then opened a minimum security gaol at Tomago holding only approximately 35 women, as well as the first weekend detention centre for women — years after men had been enjoying these privileges. Women cannot move as freely as men from maximum security to minimum security, or do trade courses, attend university or study at technical colleges. The department has not provided the facilities for women it has provided for men. The Department of Corrective Services has a ridiculous criteria for those wanting to improve themselves or learn to adjust to the changing world — the criteria of the seriousness of the offence committed. Prisoners who have committed a serious offence spend longer in gaol and walk out of the gates of a maximum security prison totally unprepared for what they face, whereas other prisoners who are in for a minor offence and doing a 'sleep' (short sentence) receive all the opportunities for advancing themselves and cope with the transition of release.

What happens when the ill prepared prisoner is released is that she reoffends and returns to gaol. Society says they should never be released in the first place, and the gaol says it is not their fault — they did everything they could. Bunk!

A Half-way House for Women Prisoners

Returning to the program 'Prisoner', there is an episode in which Karen Travers opens a half-way house for women who come out of gaol and who would otherwise reoffend. They have no money, no lodgings or prospects of employment. This half-way house is my concept, since nothing has been done for women prisoners. Male prisoners have half-way houses and only one male half-way house will take women in — but those numbers are limited and it is safe to say there is **nothing** for women in New South Wales. To provide for this house I must squeeze money from the government which reflects the community's attitude that ex-prisoners are not a number one priority. So what does the community want? For these women to reoffend, someone in the community has their house robbed or is assaulted or loses a pension cheque! It is not enough to punish the first offence, but to try to ensure that future offences will not be forced upon women who, as soon as they are released, are rejected by employers, landlords and the general community.

The community does not give a damn! As soon as an offence is committed it says 'put them in gaol'. If prisoners are bashed, the community says they deserve it. When the Department of Corrective Services tries to improve conditions, the community calls the gaol 'hotel resorts'. The community has been talking about reintroducing hanging as a punishment. But I can only say that until the community wants to punish **all** offences, irrespective of status of an offender, then the community should keep its mouth shut. The screw bashers receive promotion, the prisoner receives a gaol sentence. Police take bribes, the con woman goes to gaol. Unless the law becomes impartial to the rank of the offender, the community will suffer when prisoners, male or female, are released. Sending people back to gaol is no answer.

Can the community become involved with half-way houses so to ease this situation of retribution and revenge? Usually, the average community welfare worker who helps to deal with ex-prisoners is a do-gooder menace, hopelessly out of touch with realities of the ex-prisoners' problems. They could do better by talking to a neighbour, talking to the local newspaper, trying to drum up community interest and support for ex-prisoners. Only in their numbers can they force the media to listen and to report unemotively about the prisoners' lot. Then, perhaps, community attitudes may change, and senseless and unnecessary crime will be checked. The ex-prisoner will find a job, associate with friends, not be isolated from society and so need not return to gaol.

Many of the women in gaol need not be there. Nor do they need to be held in maximum security gaols. They do not need to return to gaol. One advance has been made in decriminalising certain social offences; why not decriminalise the prisoners?

---

1. Mulawa Training and Detention Centre for women is located in the Silverwater Complex in New South Wales. This centre also has a separate psychiatric unit.

Index

Aboriginal women
  crime statistics, W.A., 169
  drunkenness, W.A., 178
  imprisonment rate, W.A., 172-174
  victims, 25
  Western Australia, 171
Adultery
  provocation in spouse murder, 11
Assault
  self-defence, 12
Atavism, 40-41

Background reports
  juvenile offenders, 108-109, 119-120
Bandyup Training Centre, W.A., 174-177
Biological determinism, 40-41

Capitalism, 32
Children's courts, Victoria
  Legislation, 106-107
Child care applications, 59, 98, 105-106, 116
Child welfare, Victoria
  Legislation, 101-103
Common law
  coverture, 2-4
Correctional philosophy
  juvenile offenders, 114, 115
Coverture, 2-4
Crime opportunities, 32
Crime rates, 140-158, 167
  comparison of male and female, 146, 158-160, 168
  female-male ratio, W.A., 168

offences against property, 151-155
offences against the person, 146-151
New South Wales, 142
Queensland, 143
South Australia, 144
Western Australia, 145
See also Criminal statistics, Female crime, Imprisonment rates, Prison statistics
Criminal behaviour
  changes, 176-179
Criminal law
  inequalities, 1
  sexism, 1-21
  social control agent, 32
  socialisation roles, 17
Criminal responsibility
  women, 2-4
Criminal statistics
  changing economic and social conditions, 163-164
  interpretation, 163-164, 178-179
  Magistrates' courts, 136-166
  official, 136
Criminological theories
  female criminality, 31-48, 55-58
  social determinism, 34, 37-40, 47

Deterrence, 31
Domestic violence, 9-13
Double standards, 32-33
  prostitution laws, 5
Drunkenness
  Aboriginal women, W.A., 178

Evangelicalism, 33-34, 47

Female crime
  comparison to male, 131, 136, 146, 158-160
  crime rates, 136, 140-158, 168
  economic causes, 130
  impact of Women's Liberation Movement, 171-172
  longitudinal studies, 128
  percentage change, 134
  statistical interpretation, 130-131, 169-180
  Australian statistics, 136
  New South Wales, Magistrates' Court statistics, 136-166
  Queensland, Magistrates' Court statistics, 136-166
  South Australia, Magistrates' Court statistics, 136-166
  Western Australia, Magistrates' Court statistics, 136-166
  See also Juvenile offenders, Women prisoners
Female criminality, 31
  etiology, 31
  history, 31-48
  role theories, 71-91
  sexuality, 56-58, 128
  theories, 31-48, 70-91, 128
Female offenders, 31-49
  femininity stereotype, 54-65
  imprisonment rate, W.A., 172-174, 176-178
  mental hospitalisation, 187-190
  rehabilitation, 34-35
  self image, 85-89
  as sexual delinquents, 54-58, 67
  symbolic interactionism, 85
  treatment, history, 93
  prison sentences, W.A., 176-179
  Queensland, statistics, 59
  Western Australia, 169-170

Half-way house
  women prisoners, 203-204
Homosexuality
  women prison officers, 200

Human behaviour
  role theory, 74
  sex roles, 83-85
  social interaction, 82
Human development, 83
  symbolic interactionism, 85

Imprisonment rate
  female, W.A., 172-174, 176-178
  interrelationship with mental hospitalisation, 186-187
Infanticide, 7-9
Institutionalisation for non-criminal offences, 65-67

Juvenile court
  history, 92-97
  U.S., history, 91-97
  Victoria, 106-107
Juvenile institutions
  history, 92-97
Juvenile justice system
  factor in female delinquency, 62, 64, 65
  South Australia, 60-61
  Victoria, 116
Juvenile non-offenders, 66, 98, 117
  See also Child care applications, Neglect, Status offenders
Juvenile offenders
  background reports, 108-109, 119-120
  female, care and control, 59-61
  care applications
    sentencing, 98
    treatment, 105-106
    Victoria, 116
  correctional philosophy, 114, 115
  female
    protectionist philosophy, 99
    sexual offences, 99-101
    sentencing, 98-99
    Scotland and England, 63-64
  indeterminate sentences, 113
  individualised treatment, 108
  protectionist philosophy, 109
  rehabilitation philosophy, 93-95, 110-115

sentence disparity, 98-99
sentencing, 98, 104-105, 113
sexual discrimination, 100-101, 111-113, 116-121
status offences, 94, 97, 98, 111
therapeutic treatment, 96, 115
treatment, 91-126
treatment theories, 93-97
treatment oriented approach, 110, 114, 115
Queensland, statistics, 59, 99
South Australia, statistics, 61
Victoria
  Legislation, 100-107
  sentencing, 118
  statistics, 99

Indeterminate sentences
  juvenile offenders, 113

Labelling theory, 114, 167
  mental illness, 182-183, 190-191
Liberalism, 32

Marital coercion, 3-4
Mental hospitalisation
  formal admission, 187
  interpreting statistics, W.A., 180-186
  interrelationship with imprisonment, 186-187
Mental illness
  labelling, 182-183
  not guilty on grounds of unsound mind, 189
  prison transfers, 189
  rates, 167
  sex role, 182-183
  social attitudes, 183-185
  statistics, data collection, 180-182
  unfit to stand trial, 188-189
Model prisons, 36
Mulawa Training and Detention Centre, 197-202

Neglect
Victoria, Legislation, 102-104

Offences against good order
  crime rate, 155-158
  female-male ratio, 160
Offences against property
  crime rate, 151-155, 162-163
  female-male ratio, 160
Offences against the person
  crime rate, 146-151, 162
  female-male ratio, 158-159

Police statistics
  inadequacies, 137-138
Prison statistics
  Aboriginal women, W.A., 169-170
  female, W.A., 169-170
Prison strikes
  Mulawa, 198
Prison violence
  women prisoners, 201
Prostitution, 4-7, 31
  Great Britain, law, 39
Protectionist philosophy
  juvenile offenders, 99, 109
Provocation, 9-13

Racial discrimination
  crime statistics interpretation, 180
  sentencing, W.A., 174-176
Rape
  court procedures, 30
  law, 13-17
  victim provocation, 14-15
  victim responsibility, 15
Recidivism
  women, 40
Rehabilitation philosophy
  juvenile offenders, 93-95, 110-115,
Role theory, 71-82, 89

Self-defence, 9-13
  spouse assault, 12-13
Self image, 83
  female offenders, 85-89
  women, 87
Sentencing
  Aborigines, 174
  female offenders, W.A., 174-179
  sex discrimination, W.A., 174-176

juvenile offenders, 98-99, 104-105, 113
racial discrimination, W.A., 174-176
Sex roles, 33, 72, 83-85, 167, 169-171
  crime statistics, 171
    interpretation, 180
Sexism
  criminal law, 1-21
Sexual discrimination
  juvenile offenders, 100-101, 111-113, 116-121
Sexual offences
  juvenile females, 99-101
Social control, 32, 115
  incarceration, 167-168, 186
Social Darwinism, 40-41
Social determinism, 34, 37-40, 47
Social interaction, 167
  human behaviour, 83
Social roles
  See Sex roles
Solitary confinement, 32
Spouse assault, 9
  defence, 11
  self-defence, 12-13
Spouse murder
  mitigating circumstances, 11
Staff-inmate relations
  women's prisons, 196, 199-201
Status offenders, 94, 97, 98, 111, 118
Stereotyping, 1, 54-65, 83-85
  See also Role theory, Sex roles
Symbolic interactionism, 81-83
  female offender, 85

Therapeutic treatment
  juvenile offenders, 96, 115

Women
  criminal responsibility, 3-4
  dependency enforced by law, 1, 11
  law of coverture, 2-4
  myths, 51-54
  penal reformers, 33-37
  self image, 87

  stereotype, 1, 52
    See also Role theory, Sex roles
  victimisation, 25-29
  victims of crime, 23
    Aborigines, 25
Women convicts, 23-25, 43-44
Women ex-prisoners, 197, 203
  community attitudes, 197, 203
Women prison officers, 196, 197
  homosexuality, 200
Women prisoners, 196-204
  Bandyup, W.A., 174-177
  drugs, 199, 201
  half-way house, 203-204
  interpreting statistics, W.A., 169-180
  medical treatment, 198-199
  Mulawa, 197-202
  prison work, 40
  psychiatric admissions, 197
  psychiatric treatment, 197-198
  recidivism, 40, 202
  release, 201-202
Women's Liberation Movement
  impact on female crime, 171-172
  role theory, 73-79
Women's prisons, 35, 196-204
  prison work, 40, 66
  staff-inmate relations, 196, 199-201
  conditions, 196
  violence, 201